Thomas Guthrie

Man and the Gospel

Thomas Guthrie

Man and the Gospel

ISBN/EAN: 9783337281199

Printed in Europe, USA, Canada, Australia, Japan

Cover: Foto ©Thomas Meinert / pixelio.de

More available books at **www.hansebooks.com**

By THOMAS GUTHRIE, D.D.
AUTHOR OF "THE GOSPEL IN EZEKIEL," ETC.

SIXTH THOUSAND

ALEXANDER STRAHAN, PUBLISHER
LONDON AND NEW YORK
1865

CONTENTS.

	PAGE
IN TRIAL,	7
REFUGE IN TRIAL,	23
IN TEMPTATION,	46
TRUE RELIGION,	74
DOING GOOD, AND BEING GOOD,	102
PURITY,	129
RICHES,	154
THE LAW OF GOD,	181
FAITH AND WORKS,	207
THE POOR,	231
CHARITY,	254
THE SHINING LIGHT,	274
RISEN WITH CHRIST—PART I.,	295
„ PART II.,	318
EARLY PIETY—PART I.,	346
„ PART II.,	365
„ PART III.,	389
„ PART IV.,	409
RETROSPECT AND PROSPECT,	430

IN TRIAL.

> "*My brethren, count it all joy when ye fall into divers temptations.*"—
> ST JAMES i. 2.

THERE is an old story of two knights who fell into a quarrel, almost into a combat, about a shield—the one asserting, and prepared with his sword to maintain, that the shield was made of gold; the other as positively asserting that it was not gold but silver. Both were right; and there was no more occasion for quarrel between them than there has often been between good men in religious controversy. Looking at a doctrine from different points of view, not having the same *stand-point*, as it is called, they quarrelled; and the quarrel was a mistake. These two knights saw one and the same shield; but looking on it from opposite sides, each saw a different face; this was of silver, that of gold.

Like that shield, the word temptation, as used in Holy Scripture, has to be regarded under two aspects. It has two meanings; and unless care be taken to distinguish the one from the other, we may fall into a very serious mistake. Sometimes temptation is employed as another word for afflictions, trials; at other times in a sense so different, that, instead of counting it all joy, we should dread nothing more than to fall into divers temptations. Whatever is calculated to inflame our corruptions, and has a tendency, from its own nature and ours, to seduce us into sin, is temptation; and it is in this sense the word is used when it is said, "Let no man say when he is tempted, I am tempted of God: for God cannot be tempted with evil, neither tempteth he any man. But every man is tempted when he is drawn away of his lust, and is enticed. Then when lust hath conceived, it bringeth forth sin; and sin when it is finished bringeth forth death."

In this, the most common sense of the word, to

fall into temptation, is often, notwithstanding our best and strongest resolutions, to fall into sin. Such is the weakness of our nature! and how can that, which leads in so many cases to sin, ever be an occasion of joy? Who would keep his body under, as the apostle says, who would be temperate in all things, who would hold the old man nailed to the cross, who would mortify the flesh with its affections and lusts, who would keep his marriage garment unspotted of the world, will not throw himself into the arms of temptation, but rather shrink from it with fear and dread. He will go out of his way to avoid temptation, as he would the road frequented by a ravening lion, a house or street where coffins were rife, and the plague was raging. "He fell among thieves," is true of him who falls into divers temptations; and he would often die under his wounds, but for Him who drew His own portrait in the picture of the good Samaritan. Beset by robbers and assassins, he may conquer through divine strength, but he has a hard fight for it, nor comes out of the battle without some wounds to heal.

"Stand in awe, and sin not;" "Watch and

pray, that ye enter not into temptation," are warnings which no good man should disregard. Is this to be a coward? Anything else were the height of rashness. Who sleeps by a magazine of gunpowder needs to take care even of sparks; who walks on slippery ice, let him not go star-gazing, but look to his feet, and take care of falling. Whatever provokes to sin, though beautiful as Bathsheba, —what is in its nature calculated, and by the cunning fiend intended to draw us into transgression,— is a danger against which we cannot be too much upon our guard. Though in themselves innocent, pleasures are sought at too great hazard that grow on a dizzy crag, or among the grass where adders creep, or in the lofty crevice of some tottering wall, or on the brink of a swollen flood; and all the more if, such as our poet describes,—

> " Pleasures are like poppies spread,
> We nip the flower, the bloom is fled;
> Or, like the snow-flake on the river,
> A moment white, then gone for ever."

The language of joy is praise: but when a man is passing through temptation, the time is not for praise but prayer; it is for sighs, much more than songs; for strong crying, and tears, and holy fears; for deep horror, and the drawn sword that gleamed in the hand of Christian, as, amidst spectral forms, hideous sights and sounds, he trode the Valley of the Shadow of Death. Count it all joy? Who consults his soul's peace, purity, and safety, instead of counting it all joy to fall into divers temptations, will do his utmost to avoid them; his constant, daily, earnest prayer, "Lead me not into temptation;" and when he falls into it, his cry—St Peter's on the sea,—" Save me, I perish!"—that of one with the coils of a monstrous snake contracting round his form, "Make haste unto me, O God, thou art my help and my deliverer; O Lord, make no tarrying."

It is in an old, but now rather uncommon, use of the word that we are to understand temptation, as used by St James when he says, " Count it all joy when ye fall into divers temptations." It stands there for what in common language we call trials;—those troubles from which the best no more than the worst are exempt; the bitter ingredients that mingle with every man's cup; the cup that is found in every man's sack; the sufferings that, in some form or other, are ever occurring between the cradle and the grave, and that chequer a life which at birth begins with a cry, and at death ends with a groan. And what a grand faith is that which glories in these tribulations! The world, a cold philosophy tell us to bear what we cannot throw off, stoutly to face what we cannot shun, and, like one who holds his breath and sets his teeth to some painful operation, to endure what we cannot cure. How divine the faith which, thrusting these cold comforters aside, comes to the mourner weeping by the coffin, visits the captive pining in his dungeon, stands by the martyr bound to his stake to say, "Glory in tribulations"—"Blessed is the man that endureth temptation, for when he is tried he shall receive the crown of life which the Lord hath promised to them that love him!" Since trials more or less painful are the lot of all, God's people should learn how to bear them.

In Old Testament times Christianity was in the opening bud; now it is in the full-blown flower. Sustained then by types and symbols, it was the eaglet when the mother stirs her nest and bears it on her wings; now a full-feathered eagle with her foot on the rock, and her far-piercing eye on the sun, she springs upwards to cleave the parting clouds and soar high above them. Still, though without our advantages, these Old Testament saints present remarkable instances, among other graces, of resignation; and as we see the trees in early spring living, standing, though autumn blasts and winter frosts have stripped off all their leaves, we see in these patriarchs how stoutly faith in God can stand when trials have robbed life of every green joy, and the days come, of which he says, "I have no pleasure in them," the poor sufferer would be happy with his head beneath the sod, to sleep where the wicked cease from troubling, and the weary are at rest. What an illustrious example of this was Job, when deep answered unto deep at the noise of God's waterspouts! Billow after billow went over him; he goes down, never as it seemed to rise again; but faith cannot drown, and how wonderful to see his head emerge, and, as he looks around on the desolation, fortune and family ingulfed, to hear him say, "The Lord giveth, and the Lord taketh away, blessed be the name of the Lord;" or, "Though he slay me, yet will I trust in him;" He has slain mine, my sons, my daughters, my joys and hopes, all are dead and gone; now let Him slay not mine but me also, yet will I trust in Him. What faith! What sublime resignation! And would we, now suffering under trials, bear them, or, having to suffer, would we meet them with like submission, we must learn to yield to, not to resist God's will.

Strive to enter in at the strait gate,—at all cost and hazard; let sinners strive after conversion—to be in Christ; but strive not, impatient of trials, to get out of them. If, like many, you are "bound in affliction," it will do you no good to fret against it; that will but make the iron cut deeper into the flesh. The yoke sits easiest on the neck of the patient ox; and he feels his chain the lightest who does not drag but carry it. Bow before the trial, as I have read travellers do when overtaken in the desert by the dreadful simoom. The Simoom! When that cry rises, striking terror into the boldest hearts, and the purple haze sweeps on, which to breathe is death, they make no attempt to fly— the swiftest Arab scours not the desert like the wing of this scourge—but, instantly, they throw themselves on the ground; every head is muffled; and there, low in the dust, trembling, dumb, in awful silence they lie, and let the poisonous wind blow over them. "Hide thee in the dust," hide thee in the dust, is the voice of God in our calamities; and the lower we lie there before Him, passive under His mighty hand, yielding to His sovereign will, we shall suffer the less when days of darkness come.

To take an illustration from more familiar scenes, we should meet life's trials as we do the billows, to which Scripture so often compares them. When the foaming breaker comes rolling in, meet it erect, with bold front, defiant of its strength, and, sweeping you off your feet, it hurls you among the seething water. We have tried it; and, all but suffocated, have risen, lacerated and bleeding, from the flinty beach. But meet the billow bent, stoop to its foaming crest, bow before its power, and, roaring, it passes harmlessly over your head; and as the waves neither come so fast, nor stay so long, but there is time to breathe between them, by this simple art you stand like a rock, and see the proudest billows burst foaming on the beach. A blessed art this, when deep is answering unto deep, and all God's waves and billows go over us! Who, seizing every opportunity to pray, bends to trials, breaks them—and is least stunned by the rudeness of their shock. And thus it is, perhaps, that Christians of a gentle spirit, by nature as well as grace more pliant than defiant, that women, by their constitution less tough and more ready to bend, have more passive courage, often bear troubles better than stout men; they let the wave go over them, not fighting against God, but saying with Christ, "Father, not my will, but thine, be done;" or with Eli, "It is the Lord, let him do what seemeth him good."

Again, the sight of God in his trials greatly helps a good man to bear them. The nearer we get to God in times of trouble, the less their pain and the greater our profit. The son who, seeking to escape correction, stands at arm's length struggling to get away, feels the full power of the rod; but light falls the stroke on him who, confessing, "I am afflicted far less than my iniquities deserve; I will be dumb, opening not my mouth, because thou didst it," flies to his father's bosom, and falls penitent at his feet. It happens in the spiritual as in the natural world, that the farther from him who strikes the heavier, and the nearer to him who strikes, the lighter falls the blow. Consider this, besides, that God never strikes his people with both hands; for who has ever sought Him in their trouble, drawn near to him in deep affliction, but found that if He was strong to smite, He was strong also to support? Did you ever see a father beating a son who resisted? He holds the boy with one hand, and he smites him with the other. It is not so God corrects a penitent, loving child. While one hand is employed to strike, what does He with the other? They who draw near to Him crying, "Though he slay me, yet will I trust in him," ever find the other employed not to hold, but to uphold them. Wiping away the tears the rod starts in their eyes, pouring balm into the wounds His hand inflicts, sustaining while He smites, kissing while He corrects, He teaches His people that trials are the badge of sonship. "Whom he loveth he chasteneth, and scourgeth every son whom he receiveth."

But submission is not the highest lesson taught in the school of trial. That school has higher instruction and nobler prizes. It is a great thing to learn submission; but it is a grand thing to rejoice in, and rejoice over our afflictions, as St Paul did; and St James says we are to "count it all joy when we fall into divers trials." Why not? why should that language surprise us? why should we start at it? why hear it with an incredulous ear, if seasons of trial are the occasions of drawing out the tenderest love of God? Why not, if they correspond to the sick-bed and sick-chamber, where we get into the innermost circle of domestic affections? By the anxiety all show for our recovery; by the midnight watching at our bed; by no trouble grudged, but sleep, and rest, and pleasure, and everything sacrificed for us; by the noiseless step and gentle whispers; by the cloud that darkens every brow when physicians look grave, and our case looks worse; by the joy that sits on every face when we are better; by a thousand little kind attentions that, never thought of in the day of health, come out shining like stars at night, we now know how precious we are to others, how much we are valued, how tenderly loved. It is almost worth being ill to know this, and receive the kindnesses that our illness calls out. Is that a set-off to thy pains of sickness? How many of the Lord's people have had this to set against their sorest trials, that they never felt nearer to God, and God never drew nearer, nor dealt so kindly with them, as when they were cast into darkness and the deeps—their affliction abounded, but then their consolations much more abounded. It was on the mount where it lightened and thundered that God showed them His glory. It was in the wilderness that water gushed from the smitten rock and they ate of angels' food; that the pillared cloud was seen by day, the pillared fire by night. It was when their bark was tempest-tossed, and the sky was dark, and the sea was rough, that Christ came walking on the billows to still the tempest, to subdue their fears. Can they ever forget how then and there He fulfilled these gracious promises—" When thou passest through the waters, I will be with thee, and through the rivers, they shall not overflow thee; thou shalt walk through the fire, and not be burned; neither shall the flame kindle upon thee. Fear not, for I am with thee. For I am the Lord thy God, the Holy One of Israel, thy Saviour."

But, as I have said, the child of God has joy not only in trials, but through them; and for this, among other reasons, because they prove the genuineness of his faith—they are the trying of your faith, as an apostle calls them.

There was a British regiment once ordered to charge a body of French cuirassiers. The trumpets sounded, and away they went boldly at them; but not to victory. They broke like a wave that launches itself against a rock. They were sacrificed to traders' fraud. Forged not of truest steel, but worthless metal, their swords bent double at the first stroke. What could human strength, or the most gallant bravery, do against such odds? They were slaughtered, like sheep on the field. And ever since I read that tragedy, I have thought I would not go to battle unless my sword were proved. I would not go to sea with anchors that had never been tried. But of all things for a man's comfort and peace, what needs so much to be proved as his faith—its truth and genuineness?

Any way, it is a serious thing to face death, and meet the King of Terrors on his own ground; but were our faith never tried till we stood face to face in the valley with our last enemy, face to face with our God at the bar of judgment, it were still more serious. With our powers of self-deception—with Satan sitting at the sinner's ear, saying, Peace, peace, when there is none to be found—with so many who have the form of godliness, but are strangers to its power—the stoutest heart might tremble for the issues. Before I go down to battle, I want to know if my sword is forged of trusty steel; before I go to sea, I want to know if my anchor is hammered out of the toughest iron; before I set out on my journey, I want to know if this is sterling money—is it genuine? has it the ring of true metal? will it stand the test? So long as it is fair weather, I want to know if my hopes rest on sand or on solid stone; when rains descend, and waters rise, and winds blow, and beat on my house, it may be too late to know the truth. I want to know it now;—now, when, if I should have been building on the sand, there is time to seek in Christ the Rock of Ages, a foundation that cannot be moved. It is of the utmost importance to have our faith tested; and God's people, therefore, have cause to bless Him, and do bless Him, for the trials that have put it to the test, and proved it true.

If like the treading of camomile, or the crushing of a sweet-scented plant, that bathes in odours the hand that bruises it, or the burning of incense that draws out its latent perfumes, your trials have called forth heavenliness of mind, child-like submission to God's sovereign will, strong trust in His providence, a ready willingness to bear your cross for the honour of Him that bore His cross for you, count it all joy when ye fall into divers trials. They have equipped you for future battles, and furnished you with recollections and experiences to disarm the greatest evils. His presence with you in the past is a pledge of His presence in the future; that He will be with you through whatever troubles, great or small, you have to go—with you always—with you even unto the end. Not one that has never been tried when days of darkness come, you can "remember the years of the right hand of the Most High." Why should you be dismayed? You stand on the vantage-ground of David, when, the host reeling back with terror, and Saul attempting to dissuade him from meeting the Philistine, he stood calm, collected, and, eyeing the giant, said, " He that delivered me from the paw of the lion and the paw of the bear, shall he not also deliver me from the hand of this Philistine?" Let the past throw its shadow, or its light rather, on the future. " That which is to be hath already been;" for " our God is the Father of lights, with whom is no variableness nor shadow of turning." Courage, then! go forward! and as in days gone by, the favour of God shall be your shield, and the joy of the Lord your strength.

Some bear their sufferings as, if we are to believe the stories we have read, the Indian bears his tortures. Tied to the stake, abandoned of hope, looking on his last sun, a crowd of enemies dance round him with frantic gestures and brandished knives; and as they go round and round in the horrid dance, though avoiding to wound, they strike at his throat and face; but the red man stands motionless, erect; nor shrinks, nor winks, nor gives sign of terror. Ingeniously cruel, they search out the most delicate seats of feeling, and

B

thrust the burning match up to the quick. Inch by inch they cut his living form to pieces; but, with blood, they wring out no groan from that defiant man. Naming their braves he has slain and scalped in battle, this hero of the forest sings his bold death-song, scorning their powers of torture. How different from the central object in this savage scene the form of Christian patience, her head meekly bowing to the hand of God; heaven in her eye; resignation in her face; and on her pale lips the seal of silence! It is pride, not patience, that sustains yonder haughty savage —stubborn endurance, the power of an iron will. And in some who, uncomplaining, suffer pain, or loss, or wrong, or calumny, their silence, though they get credit for patience, may be but pride. It is a well-known fact, that a man who stands erect can carry a heavier burden on his head than he ever can on his back; and, raising itself to the occasion, pride has stood erect under crushing burdens, confronted misfortune, and, while smarting under insult and injuries, has scorned to gratify its enemies by betraying a sign of pain. This is but the counterfeit of patience.

Nor are we to take for this Christian grace the callousness or hardening effect which sometimes follows trials of great severity. They say that the wretch condemned to the Russian knout feels only the few first blows. After these have cut to the bone, and brought away long strips of flesh from his quivering back, the power to feel is gone. The nerves are crushed, their life destroyed; his head droops, and the lash falls on the dying man as if he were already dead. And some such callousness has come over hearts that have suffered many and severe afflictions; future trials giving them no more pain than the hot iron gives the blacksmith's horny hand. I once knew one, a Christian widow, who had early lost the husband of her youth. Other losses succeeded. The pledges of their love, a son and daughter, were snatched from her arms; her house was left unto her desolate. But these blows did not, as many feared, break that bruised reed. A pious woman, she was patient, resigned to the will of the widow's Husband; still it was not patience that replied to my sympathy, when, alluding to her first great trial, she said, "My first grief made so large a hole in my heart, that now it can hold no common sorrow."

Patience is not pride; and is not insensibility. Acutely sensitive, she may feel all the pain of the rod, while kissing the hand that uses it. She bears, not because she can do no otherwise, but would no otherwise; not because she cannot help it, but would not alter it. Leaving God to choose for her as well as chastise, to select her cross as well as her crown, she meekly says, "It is the Lord, let him do what seemeth him good,"—not me, but Him, good. How noble is this grace! It makes the greatest of all sacrifices, yielding up our fondest wishes, our dearest hopes, our strongest will to the sovereignty of God. Offering the greatest of all sacrifices, it achieves the greatest of all victories; here man makes a conquest of himself: and, in the judgment of Solomon, "he that ruleth his own spirit is greater than he that taketh a city."

Let a good man, then, count it all joy when he falls into divers trials, for—God's Spirit brooding in the stormy waters—patience is born of trials. If not their child, she is their nursling; it is their storms that rock her cradle. I say not that we are to pray for trials, though, all unexpected, they may come in answer to our prayers. We seek that patience may have her perfect work, and God sends trials in answer. It is rough work that polishes. Look at the pebbles on the shore! Far inland, where some arm of the sea thrusts itself deep into the bosom of the land, and expanding into a salt loch, lies girdled by the mountains, sheltered from the storms that agitate the deep, the pebbles on the beach are rough, not beautiful; angular, not rounded. It is where long white lines of breakers roar, and the rattling shingle is rolled about on the strand, that its pebbles are rounded and polished. As in nature, as in the arts, so in grace; it is rough treatment that gives souls as well as stones their lustre; the more the diamond is cut the brighter it sparkles; and in what seems hard dealing, their God has no end in view but to perfect His people's graces. Our Father, and kindest of fathers, He afflicts not willingly; He sends tribulations, but hear St Paul tell their purpose,—"Tribulation worketh patience, patience experience, experience hope." Therefore, as he said, we glory in tribulation, therefore we should count it all joy when we fall into divers trials. Let patience have her perfect work; wait patiently for God to explain His own providences; wait patiently for the hour of deliverance,—Woman, He says, my time is not yet come; wait patiently for the hour of death, for the heavenly rest, for the blood-bought crown. A little more patience, and you shall need patience no more. One of the multitude whom no man can number, who stand before the throne, and before the Lamb, clothed with white robes, and palms in their hands,—the days of your mourning are ended.

REFUGE IN TRIAL.

> "*If any of you lack wisdom, let him ask of God, that giveth to all men liberally, and upbraideth not; and it shall be given him. But let him ask in faith, nothing wavering. For he that wavereth is like a wave of the sea driven with the wind and tossed.*" — ST JAMES i. 5, 6.

IT was a common thing for men in old times to provide themselves with a refuge against the hour when the worst came to the worst. You may see it in the crumbling ruins of our old castles, where, once carefully concealed behind the arras, it now stands exposed in the narrow stair within the thick and massive walls. By this, when the gates were forced, and the defenders, a bleeding band, were driven back from room to room, they, suddenly pushing aside a panel, descended into the dungeons;

and issuing out by some secret port, escaped with their lives. And to this day the shepherds show the hiding-places among their green hills, the "holes and caves of the earth" to which our forefathers betook themselves when persecution waxed hot, and bloodhounds bayed at their heels. A midnight march brought the ruthless soldiery in the gray of the morning to the cottage of a lone upland, where some man of God was in hiding. They surrounded the house—but missed their prey. Warned by trusty watchers, who often concealed bold daring and deep cunning under the garb of homely simplicity, he was off. Near by rose a dizzy crag, roared a foaming waterfall; and ere his enemies arrived, the fugitive had leaped the chasm, and scaled the rock, and swinging himself up by the arms of a friendly mountain-ash, whose scarlet foliage screened the mouth of a dark cavern, he was safe within, singing to the music of the cataract these appropriate words: "In the time of trouble he shall hide me in his pavilion, in the secret of his tabernacle shall he hide me, he shall set me up upon a rock; and now shall mine head be lifted up above mine enemies round about me."

The "Chronicles of Froissart" relate the strange issue of a siege which took place in the days of chivalry—and somewhere, I think, in France. Though gallantly defended, the out-works of the citadel had been carried; the breach was practicable; to-morrow was fixed for the assault. That none, alarmed at the desperate state of their fortunes, might escape under the cloud of night, the besiegers guarded every sally-port, and indeed the whole sweep of wall. They had the garrison in a net; and only waited for the morrow to secure, or to slaughter them. The night wore heavily on; no sortie was attempted; no sound came from the beleaguered citadel; its brave, but ill-starred defenders seemed to wait their doom in silence. The morning came; with its dawn the stormers rushed at the breach; sword in hand they poured in to find—the nest empty, cold. The bird was flown; the prey escaped. But how? That was a mystery; it seemed a miracle, till an opening was discovered that led by a flight of steps down into the bowels of the rock. They descended, and explored their way with cautious steps and lighted torches, until this subterranean passage led them out a long way off from the citadel, among quiet, green fields, and the light of day. It was plain that by this passage, the doors of which stood open, their prey had escaped under cover of the night. A clever device—a wise precaution. It was the refuge of the besieged, provided against such a crisis. And when affairs seem desperate, and the worst has come to the worst, how should it encourage God's people to remember that He has promised them as safe a retreat! What says an apostle? "God is faithful, who will not suffer you to be tempted above that ye are able to bear; but will with the temptation also make a way of escape." Our extremity is His opportunity.

These words of Scripture, and a whole cloud of corresponding passages—"a cloud of witnesses," indicate that God's people always have a refuge in their days of trial. According to David, "God is known in her palaces for a refuge;" and in what glowing language is that truth sung out by Moses in his parting words to the tribes of Israel: "There is none like unto the God of Jeshurun, who rideth upon the heaven in thy help. The eternal God is thy refuge, and underneath are the everlasting arms. Happy art thou, O Israel! who is like unto thee, O people saved by the Lord, the shield of thy help, and who is the sword of thy excellency!"

Now let us turn our attention to one of the many refuges and sources of support which a pious man has amid the trials of life. "Is any among you afflicted? let him pray." So says the apostle St James; and referring to the trials of the first Christians, he says: "If any of you lack wisdom, let him ask of God, that giveth to all men liberally, and upbraideth not; and it shall be given him. But let him ask in faith, nothing wavering. For he that wavereth is like a wave of the sea driven with the wind and tossed." I would ask attention to the following points:—

What we are to ask.

Wisdom! As used in Scripture, that word has a wide meaning; and here, as elsewhere, it may stand for all the graces and virtues that constitute true religion. And what of these we lack, whatever indeed we lack—not this or that man lacks, but any man, every man lacks, God promises a liberal supply of it. There is no restriction, no exclusion here. He would have all men to pray. It is their own blame if people are not saved. As a mother would do to her fallen and guilty child, God opens His arms wide to the world; and would press it to His bosom. With the offer of Christ to all, and virtue in His blood to cleanse all, who is lost is his own murderer. Who goes to hell is not excluded, but excludes himself from heaven. As the God and Father of our Lord Jesus Christ, whom He sent to seek and save the lost, God, if they will but ask it, giveth liberally to *all* men.

But though I do not understand the word *wisdom*, as employed by St James in the passage quoted, in a strictly literal sense, there is much need of wisdom, of a sound, right, practical judgment, in times of trial. That will save us much suffering, if not much sin.

It is not wise to fret under our trials; the high-mettled horse that is restive in the yoke but galls his shoulder — the poor bird that dashes herself against the bars of the cage but ruffles her feathers and aggravates the sufferings of captivity. It is not wise, overlooking the sovereign will of God, and that presiding Providence which numbers the hairs of our head as well as the stars of heaven, and without which neither a sparrow nor an angel can fall, to trace our calamities only to ourselves—that breeds but unavailing regrets; or to others—that only kindles bad and angry passions. It is not wise to look on our trials as heavier than those of others, and as warranting us to cry, in the language of Jerusalem, "Behold, and see if there be any sorrow like unto my sorrow, which is done unto me, wherewith the Lord hath afflicted me!"—that can only foster a rebellious spirit. It is not wise to forget that our blessings are loans from God; and that when we lose them, whether husband, wife, or child, health or wealth, fame or fortune, their owner but resumes His own,—otherwise we shall be ready to regard God as a robber, rather than to render Him the gratitude due to a most bountiful benefactor. It is not wise to cling too closely to the living,—else we shall some day be found embracing the dead. We are to inquire whether God has any controversy with us, whether He is not rebuking idolatry by destroying our idols, still it is not wise to regard our trials as being certainly expressions of His wrath: it were a great mistake to fancy that the goldsmith is dissatisfied with the gold he burns or the lapidary with the diamond he grinds, or the gardener with the tree he prunes. On the contrary, the metal is cast into the furnace, and the gem is ground on the wheel, and the tree bleeds beneath the knife, not because they are little, but because they are much esteemed. It is not wise to meet trials in our own strength; on the contrary, when they advance with threatening front let us run to God, and lay hold on Him; as, at the cry "Hold on," sailors seize rope, mast, shrouds, or bulwark, when the curling wave rises at their bows, and, bursting, sweeps the deck; and but for their hold would sweep them overboard, into a watery grave. I need not say that it is not wise—it is madness, it is misery in this world, and damnation in the next, to fly from grief to the intoxicating bowl. I don't say that it is unnatural. Tell the drowning man it is but a floating straw, a poor rotten twig he seizes, yet he clutches at it, grasps it; and when all God's billows are going over men's heads, those who have not comfort in God will seek it elsewhere, anywhere. Men have fled to the wine-cup to drown reflection; and I have heard a poor, wretched mother, the slave of drinking, trace her habits to domestic trials, to the desolation death had made in her home and heart. Miserable refuge! Job's friends, indeed, are these stimulants—beer, wine, spirits: "Miserable comforters are ye all!" Yet, as the wise man says, "They drink to forget their poverty, and remember their misery no more." By all means fly from sorrow to the bosom of God: but to fly from sorrow into the arms of sin is an awful illustration of the common adage, "An unsanctified affliction is the worst of all afflictions"—and also of the prophet's question: "Why should ye be stricken any more? ye will revolt more and more."

There is great need of wisdom under trials; to be enlightened as well as supported by the grace of God, and in the Holy Ghost to have a Counsellor as well as Comforter. With all thy getting get wisdom—wisdom to trace your trials to the Hand above; to bear them so that you may glorify God in the fires; to improve them, so that you may get the good intended, and be more than indemnified for their heaviest sufferings. The honey of the bee is an excellent antidote to its sting; and what comfort under trials like feeling that we are the better of them? Has not many a dark cloud, that in the distance lightened and thundered, and filled us with alarm, broke in blessings on our head—leaving us, as, passing away, it showed the bright bow of the covenant on its back, to say, "It is good for me that I was afflicted: before I was afflicted I went astray, but now have I kept thy word." "Right are thy judgments, O Lord; in faithfulness thou hast afflicted me!" "Our light afflictions, which are but for a moment, shall work out for us a far more exceeding, even an eternal weight of glory."

Next, *Of whom we are to ask wisdom.*

Of God, who giveth liberally and upbraideth not! If we want money, we go to the bank; water, we go to the well; medicine, we go to the physician; and who wants divine blessings, mercy to pardon, or grace to help, is to go to God—" He giveth liberally."

Did you ever stand in a bright summer day by the black swirling pool at the foot of a waterfall, and look up to the top of the cascade, where, scattering its liquid beads, like sparkling diamonds, it sprang boldly out from the rock into the air? How ceaseless the flow! and with its snowy foam ever flashing in the light of day, and its deep, solemn voice, in that lone glen, ever praising God through the hours of night—what an image does it offer of the stream of mercies that are continually falling on us from the bountiful hand of God!

The Scriptures employ other, and indeed many images of God's affluent bounty. God himself says, " I will be as the dew unto Israel"—but there are cloudy skies and breezy nights when no dew falls, emblem of divine bounty, to hang gems on every bush, and sow the fields with " orient pearls." Again it is said: " He shall come down like rain upon the mown grass, as showers that water the earth"—but there are days and weeks without a drop of rain. Again it is said, " I will pour water upon him that is thirsty, and floods upon the dry ground"—but it is only on rare occasions that the river, swollen by many a tributary, comes down red and roaring, and, overflowing all its banks, turns every wooded knoll into an island, and green valleys into inland seas. But, is there ever a month, a week, a day, an hour, a moment, a single moment, when from thy blessed and bountiful hand, O God! mercies are not falling in showers—thick as the rain-drops that shimmer in sunlight on the water, or as the snow-flakes that fill the wintry air!

He giveth liberally, and He giveth constantly; and, if He pours such affluence of blessings on all men, even on His enemies, even on those that trample the mercies, as they trample the snows, of heaven under their foul, guilty feet, what may not His own, His chosen people, expect? Will He deny His fathership when they, His children, His own loving children, repair to Him with wounds to stanch, with cheeks to dry, with bruised or broken hearts to bind, with cries like these—Father, help me, I am weak! Lift me up, I have fallen! Forgive me, I have sinned! Save, oh, save me, I perish! How have I seen a poor wandering vagrant, when her child, footsore and weary, had sunk, crying, on the road, true to a mother's love, take up the creature in her arms, and, shifting its burden to her own back, trudge on her weary way? And what may not you, groaning under your burdens, hope for from Him, who is as much greater than we in love, as in the wisdom that planned, and the power that built this glorious universe? You know what are your thoughts and ways to a darling child that is withering away like a delicate flower, over whose couch you hang in anxious solicitude, for whom you have prayed in agony, and whose young life you would purchase at the price of all your fortune! Hear, then, what God says: "My ways and my thoughts to you, are as far above your ways and thoughts to it, as the heavens are above the earth." I have known a mother who trod the great city's streets, with weary steps and broken heart, the long night through, searching every house and den of infamy to find her lost one. She found her. Clasping the unholy thing to her virtuous bosom, locking her in close embraces, to win the wanderer back, how did she promise her every pleasure of home, with these hands to toil and work for her, never to cast up her sins, nor speak an upbraiding word? and these yearnings of a mother's heart, what were they, but, if I might say so, a spark struck from divinity—a drop out of the ocean of love that fills the bosom of an infinite God!

"He upbraideth not." You are unworthy; you have abused my kindness; charity is wasted on you; I am tired of helping you; patience is exhausted; you come too often; you ask too much —such language never fell from the lips of God. I have often seen a shivering, ragged child, or a widow, in brown and rusty weeds, with an emaciated infant in her bosom, timidly knocking at a rich man's door, to have it, as soon as it was opened and they were seen, shut rudely in their face. And while I thought how ill it would be for them were God, in their hour of need—on a bed of death, or at a bar of judgment—to deal with them as they deal with others, it was blessed to think that the door of mercy is shut in no man's face; that God's heart is shut against no man's misery; that God's hand is shut against no man's need; that God's eye is shut to no man's danger; that God's ear is shut to no man's prayer. "He giveth liberally, and upbraideth not." Appearing in human form, and speaking through the voice of

His beloved Son, He stands up there at the wide-open door of heaven, crying, "Come unto Me, all ye that labour, and are heavy laden;" be your burden sins or sorrows, be your load grief or guilt, Come unto me, and I will give you rest; Cast thy burden on the Lord and He will sustain it; Open thy mouth wide and He will fill it.

Again, *How we are to ask.*

With faith, nothing wavering!

The pendulum of a time-piece is in constant motion, yet it makes no progress, because it has no sooner swung a certain way to one side, than it swings as far to the other. In like manner, as you may know by watching the floating weed, or the foam-bells that whiten it, or the boat that rides on its back—the mass of water that forms a wave makes no progress. Impelled by the wind, the wave advances, but not the water of which it is formed. If the water did, it would bear yonder drowning wretch to the shore; nor merely leave the wave, passing under, to raise his head to catch a sight of the blessed land, and then, rolling away to break on the beach, leave him to perish. And so, alas! will it be with many, who are not altogether insensible to religious impressions, who may even be easily affected by such influences as a sermon, the solemnities of a death-bed, the heaving swell of a revival; and being so, imagine themselves on the way to heaven, just as many careless observers imagine because the wave goes shoreward, the water also does.

As employed by St James to describe certain characters, the wave is a most felicitous figure. Look at a boat floating on the sea, at high or low water, when the tide, out or in, and on the turn, has ceased to run; or watch a boat away amid the swell of a mountain lake when the wind, retiring to its caves among the hills, has roared itself to rest! It is in constant motion between earth and heaven—now mounting to the top of the billow, and now sinking out of sight in the trough of the sea; yet with all this violent action, heaving, tossing, rolling, the skiff does not make an inch of way, but continues to ride over the self-same spot. Too true a figure of many professing Christians! Vacillating—not hypocrites, but through the influence of opposing motives—double-minded, and therefore unstable, heaven now seems to draw them upward, and then again earth draws them down—now, following Christ, they cry, with the young ruler, "Master, what shall I do to inherit eternal life?" and then, with their backs turned on Him, they are leaving Him; sorrowful, perhaps, but still leaving Him—now they are casting sin away from them, and by and by they are locked in her foul embraces—now they are fighting the Philistines, and ere long you find them sound asleep in Delilah's lap—now full of alarm, in fear of hell, pricked to the heart, their conscience awake, bent on being saved, they make a rush for heaven, and their foot is on the door-step—" they are not far from the kingdom of heaven;" but a cross lies on the threshold, and stumbling on that they fall—fall back into sin; and the last state of that man is perhaps worse than the first. One day they seem to serve Christ, and certainly serve their lusts the next. They don't want to lose heaven, yet they cannot part with earth. Often starting up in their sleep, like one disturbed by horrid dreams, they are ever falling back again into slumber; and thus, equally affected by opposite influences, they are like a wave of the sea, rising and falling, now moving heavenward, now earthward—driven with the wind and tossed. Well, of a life spent in such unsteady efforts after what is good—in sinning to-day, and repenting to-morrow—what is to be the issue? It comes to nothing; like a door moving on its hinges, they make no progress; and the fate of their hopes, when death throws them on another world, is foreshadowed by the wave, that, launched on an iron-bound shore, bursts into froth and foam· The end of these things is death.

Who, dying, would go to glory, who would be redeemed from sin and hell, who would secure a saving interest in Christ, who would have strength to endure trial, and stand its buffetings, as a rock stands the blows of waves, must have his heart steadily, resolutely, firmly fixed on divine things. "No man having put his hand to the plough, and looking back, is fit for the kingdom of heaven." Pray for unwavering faith, a strong—as Jabez Bunting, when dying, said, an *obstinate* faith in God. Seek such faith as not only lays hold of Him, but holds Him and won't let Him go; that has the grasp of a drowning man. Seek a faith greater than Joshua's, when, laying its hand on the sun, he held it back from going on; a faith like Jacob's, who, strange as it seems, held God from going away, as, endowed with superhuman energy, he wrestled the night through with an angel, and, the stronger of the two, prevailed—replying to the prayer, Let me go, for the day breaketh, I will not let thee go, unless thou bless me.

Were this too bold a freedom to take with God? No! We have "boldness to enter into the holiest by the blood of Jesus." It is the boldness of the little child that, unabashed by any one's presence, climbs his father's knee, and throws his arms around his neck—or, bursting into his room, breaks in on his busiest hours, to have a bleeding finger bound, or some childish tears kissed away; that says if any threaten or hurt him, I will tell my father; and, however he might tremble to sleep alone, fears neither ghosts, nor man, nor darkness, nor devils, if he lies couched at his father's side. Such confidence, bold as it seems, springs from trust in a father's love; and pleases rather than offends us. Well, then, if you that are evil have such hearts, and know how to give good gifts to your children, how much more will our heavenly

Father give the Holy Spirit, all, everything they need, to them who ask—asking with faith, nothing wavering!

Hope, as well as prayer, opens a welcome refuge to the good man in times of trial. "Blessed is he that endureth temptation, for when he is tried he shall receive the crown of life which the Lord hath promised to them that love him." Here, how true is the common proverb: "All is well that ends well." It is not, Blessed is he that hath no trials, whose heart they never wrung; whose tears never flowed; whose brightest prospects were never clouded; whose dearest hopes never lay withered and scattered like autumn leaves, on life's rough and rugged path; who never entered the fiery furnace, nor trod the swelling flood. He is blessed who endureth temptation; stands the test; bears his burden well; glorifies God in the fires, and comes forth shining like gold from a refiner's furnace. Every wave of trouble lifts him but higher on the Rock of Ages—wafts him nearer to the heavenly shore.

Let the downcast lift their heads, and look upward and forward! For the joy set before Him,

Jesus endured the cross and despised the shame. And He says, Learn of me; overleap the narrow bounds of a few short years, and what shall your present sorrow be but the morning's recollection of a disagreeable dream! The days of your mourning shall be ended—your cross exchanged for a shining crown. I have heard one say, as he bent over a friend who was groaning under the surgeon's knife, It will soon be over! and so Jesus, with tender fellow-feeling for their infirmities, consoles His suffering people. Amid your trials, think of that—they will soon be over; sooner, perhaps, than you fancy. Your salvation, not only nearer than when you believed, may be nearer than you suppose; even now the cry may be sounding in heaven—Room for another saint! a crown for another head! and the next turn of the road may bring you in front of the gates of glory.

Whatever be your cross, don't keep, with downcast head, looking at it; but raise your eyes to the crown that hangs yonder in heaven—beyond the grave. When grim death comes, see it glittering bright behind his awful form; nor fear the King of Terrors. Constructed of bands of metal and bits of stone, and doomed to perish in the wreck of all things, other crowns grace the brows of dying men; they are borne in the procession that carries a king to his grave—and, in mockery of the royal pageant, the heads that wore them are laid, low as a beggar's, in the dusty tomb. But this is a crown of life. Immortals wear it, and it is itself immortal—" a crown of glory that fadeth not away." And how will that moment swallow up all memory of the sorrows of earth, when, led by angels, or a father or mother, within the brilliant circle where you recognise the glorified forms of long-lost friends, you stand before the throne; and, bending low your head, receive, amid the plaudits of the sky, this crown at the hand of Jesus.

And what shall heaven see there and then? Life crowning love! not Merit, that stands proud and panting at the goal; not Success, that has filled the world with famous deeds; not Learning, that has explored all the mysteries of knowledge, human and divine; not Prophecy, with her many tongues; not even Faith, grasping the cross; nor clear-eyed Hope, with her hand on the anchor, and her gaze on heaven; but Love, the true queen of graces. She who, when Faith seemed to lose hold of Christ, and Hope to lose sight of heaven, still clung to Jesus; and, refusing to part with Him, said, Entreat me not to leave thee, nor to return from following after thee; where thou goest I will go, and where thou lodgest I will lodge. Thanks be to God who giveth us the victory, through our Lord Jesus Christ, says St Paul; and I say, thanks be to God, who bestows the crown of life on those that love Him; and can say, Though I have not honoured thee, nor served thee, nor followed thee, nor fought for thee, nor wrought for thee, nor suffered nor sacrificed for thee, as I should have done, yet, "Lord, thou that knowest all things, knowest that I love thee."

IN TEMPTATION.

"Let no man say when he is tempted, I am tempted of God: for God can not be tempted with evil, neither tempteth he any man: but every man is tempted, when he is drawn away of his own lust, and enticed. Then when lust hath conceived, it bringeth forth sin: and sin, when it is finished, bringeth forth death."—St James i. 13-15.

ONE of the highest flights of Milton's poetry is his story of the encounter between Satan and the porters of the gate of hell:

" Before the gates there sat
On either side a formidable shape;
The one seem'd woman to the waist, and fair;
But ended foul in many a scaly fold,
Voluminous and vast; a serpent arm'd
With mortal sting;—the other shape,
If shape it might be call'd, that shape had none,

> Distinguishable in member, joint, or limb;
> Or substance might be call'd that shadow seem'd,
> For each seem'd either; black it stood as night,
> Fierce as ten Furies, terrible as hell,
> And shook a dreadful dart; what seem'd his head,
> The likeness of a kingly crown had on."

The monster, thus graphically described, advances with horrid strides to bar Satan's passage. Incensed at its presumption, and fearing no created thing, he prepares, with arms, to force his way. Like two dark clouds charged with thunders, they approach each other—Satan resolved to be out, this grizzly terror resolved to keep him in:—

> "And now great deeds
> Had been achieved, whereof all hell had rung,
> Had not the snaky sorceress, that sat
> Fast by hell-gate, and kept the fatal key,
> Risen, and, with hideous outcry rush'd between.
> 'O father, what intends thy hand,' she cried,
> 'Against thy only son? What fury, O son,
> Possesses thee to bend that mortal dart
> Against thy father's head?'"

Having thrown herself between the combatants, and stayed their fury, in a tale which the poet's fancy has woven out of a passage in the Epistle of St James, this creature, half fair woman, half scaly serpent, proceeds to explain herself. Addressing her words to Satan, she tells him how her name is Sin—and how, at the time of the great revolt in heaven, she sprung, a goddess armed, from his pain-split head—and how, pregnant by him, when cast out of the celestial spheres, and sent to keep watch at the gates of hell, amid parturient pangs she gave birth to a son, who

> " Forth issued, brandishing his fatal dart,
> Made to destroy. I fled, and cried out, Death !
> Hell trembled at the hideous name, and sigh'd
> From all her caves, and back resounded, Death ! "

In this grand fashion John Milton illustrates these weighty sayings, "Let no man say when he is tempted, I am tempted of God: for God cannot be tempted with evil, neither tempteth he any man: but every man is tempted, when he is drawn away of his own lust, and enticed. Then when lust hath conceived, it bringeth forth sin: and sin, when it is finished, bringeth forth death."

Now, leaving the poet to soar away, singing on wings sublime, let us descend, and take a practical view of the temptations with which every good man has to contend.

Reflect on *the importance of this subject.*

An example of "much in little," the Ten Commandments embrace the whole duty of man. An example also of "much in little," the Lord's Prayer, in a few heads, sums up all that we should pray for. It contains but seven petitions; and how large the subject of temptation bulked in our Lord's eye, and how important therefore it should seem in ours, is to be gathered from the circumstance, that it forms the subject of one of these seven. You may guess the rank and consequence of a man by the society that he moves in, and here the subject of temptation appears in the highest company. It is classed with subjects that engage the intellects of angels, that concern God's glory, and that are identified both with our present, and with our eternal welfare. If it occupied the same proportion of man's life, a seventh part of all our thoughts, our cares, and our time, would be given to it—to resisting temptation; avoiding it; fighting it; guarding against the sins it may lead to, as well as mourning and seeking the forgiveness of those it has led to.

If the temptations that beset and assail us do not occupy such a place in our thoughts and lives —for they give some men no trouble—that admits of an obvious but melancholy explanation. It is not, that the man who is without regrets, anxieties, daily and hourly struggles, is a better man than he who has "fightings without and fears within." It is not that he is holy; never tempted; or that he never yields to temptation. On the contrary, it is because he, unresisting, yields to it. What more pleasant and easy than the motion of a vessel that, gliding down the stream, is borne onwards to the cataract that shall hurl it to destruction? But bring the boat's head round, and a struggle begins; peace is gone now; she trembles from stem to stern; and by her violent plunges, the waves that break over her bows, and, shaking every timber, threaten to ingulf her, you know the power and presence of a current that had been quietly wafting her on to ruin.

Thus it is with man and temptation, so soon as he is converted. No sooner is peace with God, through Christ, settled, than war is proclaimed;

and the man involved in its arduous and life-long struggles. I have seen one that had grown gray in the army, and yet had never been under fire; or seen the serried bayonets glance, but on parade. The Captain of our salvation has no such soldiers; His have given and suffered many wounds; and have all a sore fight of it. This conflict begins with conversion, and if I might borrow an illustration from heathen fables, the infant Hercules has to strangle serpents in his cradle. So soon as a man is new-born, and turns his face heavenward, he has hell to confront and fight with. And, besides the devil and his angels, besides the world and its seductive influences, in passions that he has lodged in his breast, and fed by long indulgence into strength, it may be said that "his enemies are the men of his own house." And such in number and in power are the temptations with which a good man has to contend, that no Christian will think the language of David extravagant: "They compassed me about; they compassed me about like bees. My soul is among lions; and I lie even among them that are set on fire." Nay, there are times, and terrible temptations, when, in the language of a psalm, part, and some suppose all, of which our Lord repeated on His cross, he may be ready to cry, "Many bulls have compassed me: strong bulls of Bashan have beset me round. They gaped upon me with their mouths, as a ravening and a roaring lion. I am poured out like water, and all my bones are out of joint, my heart is like wax. My strength is dried up like a potsherd: thou hast brought me into the dust of death; for dogs have compassed me. O Lord, my strength, haste thee to help me. Deliver my soul from the sword; my darling from the power of the dog. Save me from the lion's mouth; hear me from the horns of the unicorns."

If these figures are appropriate, how formidable are our temptations! It might seem impossible that victory could crown our arms in a war waged against enemies that swarm thick as bees; that are strong as bulls, and fierce as ravening lions. Yet, hear what God says: "Thou shalt tread on the lion and adder, the young lion and the dragon shalt thou trample under foot;" and hear Paul, as, calmly descending into the vale of death, he goes, singing, like a brave old warrior — "I have fought the good fight, I have finished my course, I have kept the faith. Hereafter there is laid up for me a crown of righteousness, which the Lord, the righteous Judge, shall give me at that day." Nor is that all — proclaiming equal triumphs through the same grace to others, he adds, "and not to me only, but to all who love his appearing." Let the good man be assured that his victory over temptation is certain, if he goes about it aright. It turns much on prayer. Thrown into the scale, that decides the battle; drawing on divine strength, that makes little Davids more than a match for giant sins. What devil is there but may be cast out by prayer and fasting?

Yet, prayer is not enough. Like our fathers when they conquered the English at Bannockburn, or the English when they conquered the French at Cressy, we are to rise from our knees; to stand up and fight; to quit us like men; "having done all," to stand. We are to put on the whole armour of God; and, since we know neither when nor where the adversary may assault us, we are never to put it off. Live and die in harness — using such precautions, as some say Cromwell did against the assassin's dagger —his dress concealed a shirt of mail: and in the council-chamber, at the banquet, in courts as in camps, he wore that always. To his workshop, the counting-room, the social circle, the market, the place of business, the scenes of his most innocent enjoyments, let a good man go, as the peasant of the East goes to his plough. With larks singing in blue skies above his head, and daisies, bathed in dew springing at his feet, and feathered flocks from sounding shore and noisy woods wheeling round, and feeding in the furrows behind him, our ploughman, void of care, and fearless of danger, whistles at his work; but yonder, where fiery Bedouins scour the land, and bullets whistling from the bush may suddenly call the peasant to drop the ox-goad and fly to arms, the sun glances on other iron than the ploughshare—a sword hangs at his thigh, and a gun is slung at his back.

To pray, to fight, are important; but not less important if we would have no man take our crown, and, resisting, overcome temptation, is a right understanding of its springs and sources. The physician is most likely to cure disease who has discovered its seat and nature; while the patient dies in the hands of him who prescribes for the head, when it is the heart that is diseased. To save a ship from sinking, we must find the leak. Temptations, like noxious weeds, are best killed by putting the knife to their root; nor will the stream of our thoughts, and wishes, and desires ever be sanctified till the salt, as at Jericho, is cast in at the spring. Let us see, therefore, where the springs and sources of sin lie.

The *source* of temptation *is not in God.*

The apostle St James is clear on this point. He says, "Let no man say, when he is tempted, I am tempted of God; for God cannot be tempted with evil, neither tempteth he any man."

In the mountains of the Black Forest an extraordinary appearance is occasionally seen. With the sun just rising at your back, you look across the valley on the curtain of mist that, hung from the skies, falls in rolling folds on the opposite hill;

and there, wearing a faint halo round his head, stands the giant spectre of the mountains—a colossal form of vast proportions, looking as if, at one bound, he could leap from hill to hill, and tearing up oaks and rocks, hurl them at the head of his enemies. The terror of superstitious peasants, the origin of many a wild, unearthly legend, this is a mere vision—a shadow without substance. It has no reality. Observed to bend or stand erect, to move a limb or arm after him, to repeat every motion of the spectator, it is nothing more than his own form, immensely magnified; and projected on the cloud, like the pictures of a magic lantern on its screen. Such pictures on the mind's fancy were the pagan deities; the object of the heathen's worship, whether Baal, or Jupiter, or Venus, or Mars, or Bacchus, being but a projection of the man himself on the field of fancy, with the faculties and passions of humanity all immensely magnified. A strange mixture, like himself, of vices and of virtues, they illustrate the words of God, Thou thoughtest that I was altogether such an one as thou art; and thus formed, these gods were tempted with evil, and with evil tempted men.

Importing this idea of heathenism, or perhaps misunderstanding the Scriptures, where God, according to an Eastern idiom, is said to do what in fact He but permits to be done—as when it is said that He "hardened Pharaoh's heart," it appears that in the days of the apostle St James, some accused God of sin; alleging, in excuse of their sins, that they were tempted of Him. We shrink with horror from such an idea. "Their rock is not as our Rock." Time casts its stains on the purest snow, and the sun shines not undimmed by spots; but we bow in the dust before God, as a being of ineffable purity and infinite holiness. More shocked than if we heard some foul crime imputed to parents we venerate and love, we recoil from the thought that He before whom angels stand veiled and in whose eyes even the heavens are not clean, could either be Himself tempted to commit sin, or could tempt any to commit it.

Yet what many would not directly, they indirectly lay at God's door—in the attempt to excuse themselves, accusing Him. Look, for example, at Adam's answer to the question, Hast thou eaten of the tree? Summoned from his hiding-place, standing beside the blushing partner of his guilt, overwhelmed by strange terrors, trembling in every limb, the prey of anguish and remorse, had his tongue, cleaving to the roof of his mouth, refused to do its office, we should not have been astonished. But he replies; and his answer betrays cunning rather than confusion. How mean and dastardly, how base and selfish and hateful, has sin made this once noble creature! How are the mighty fallen! See him trying to turn over on his poor wife the whole vengeance of an angry God! He attempts to save himself, and leave her to bear the brunt of it; hers is the guilt; she is the temptress. Hear him: "The woman, she gave me and I did eat." Nor is that all; nor "the front of his offending." More, and worse still, he divides the blame between her and God. It is not simply, "the woman gave me and I did eat," but "the woman *that thou gavest me*, she gave me, and I did eat;" a serpent in my bosom, I got her from thee; the circumstances in which thou didst place me, more than my own fault, are answerable for my sin. "The woman that *thou* gavest me!" What was this but a covert way of accusing God; a bold insinuation that God, not he, was to blame for the Fall; an excuse, that, like all our apologies for sin, adds insult to injury; and but aggravates the offence?

I do not fancy any are so bold and bad as of deliberate intent to lay the guilt of their crimes on God. Yet what else, in fact, do they, who make a scapegoat of their circumstances—attributing their sins to constitutional temperament, or to the headlong power of their passions, or to the difficulties of their position, or to the suddenness or the strength of their trials? These apologies, whether offered to men, or used to allay guilty fears, and quiet an uneasy conscience, throw the blame of sin on Providence; and to throw the blame of it on Providence, is to throw it upon God. Excuses such as these but add to our guilt. They may now satisfy, or rather stupify our conscience, but they shall stand us in no stead at the bar of Him who neither tempts nor is tempted. He has left us without excuse. Assured that God will not suffer any, that seek Him, to be tempted above that they are able to bear, but will with the temptation also make a way of escape, we are without excuse; but not without a remedy. Blessed be God! the blood of Jesus Christ cleanseth from all sin.

The *source* of temptation *is in ourselves.*

" Every man is tempted when he is drawn away of his own lust, and enticed."

If you apply a magnet to the end of a needle that courses freely on its pivot, the needle, affected by a strange attraction, approaches as if it loved it. Reverse the order, apply the magnet now to the opposite end — to the other pole, and the needle shrinks away, trembling, as if it did not love, but hated it. So it is with temptation. One man rushes into the arms of vice; another recoils from them with horror. Joseph starts back, saying, How can I do this great wickedness, and sin against God? What is loved by one, is loathsome in another's eyes; and according as the nature it addresses is holy or unholy, temptation attracts or repels; gives pain or pleasure; is loved or hated. It is our corrupt and evil passions that give its power to temptation. These are the combustibles it fires; the quick and fiery powder, that a spark which a dewdrop had quenched, flashes into an explosion.

In their visits to our world, the angels were exposed to temptation; but what harm did they suffer? None. Amidst widespread contagion, they never were infected; nor, as people import the plague from other countries, did they take sin away with them on their return to heaven, and spread the deadly pestilence in that sinless land. Can a man take fire in his bosom, and his clothes not be burned? True; yet angels suffered nothing from coming in contact with sinners; but passed among them as unstained as the sunbeam of their heavens through the murky air of our smoky cities. Like a flower that, brought from breezy hill or open moor, pines away amid the pent-up and poisoned atmosphere of our towns, Lot's graces were blighted by his residence in Sodom; it corrupted him, but not his heavenly visitors. True, it may be said that, since our unhappy fall, the stay of angels in our world has been brief, and that sin had no time to affect their constitution—that the leaven had no time to work. But time is of no account in their case; nor would it be in ours if the Fall had not furnished occasion to cry, How is the gold become dim; how is the most fine gold changed? Pure gold may remain in the fire a thousand years without loss of substance; without contracting a single stain, or losing an atom of its weight. The fire that turns the oak into ashes, marble into dust, iron into rust, has no power to destroy, or even injure, a metal that shines but the brighter for the glowing flames. Gold is therefore called, in the language of metallurgy, a *perfect* metal; and were we perfect — perfect in holiness—the only effect of life's fiery trials would be, not to burn up, but to brighten the features of God's image. Thus I believe no angel ever descended on our world, but he returned to his native heavens to abhor sin more; to hate it with a more perfect hatred; and with deeper, holier feelings to sing, as he resumed his place in the shining ranks, and joined his fellows in their song—Holy, holy, holy, art thou, Lord God Almighty, who was, and is, and art to come!

Look at our Lord's case! How clearly it shows that temptation, however much to be dreaded by us, is harmless, unless where it finds corruption—

that the seed dies, unless it falls on a congenial soil! He lived among temptations for more than thirty successive years. For more than thirty years His holy manhood was in the fire; and He came out of it without stain or sin. The Lamb of God, without spot or blemish, holy, harmless, undefiled, He was among, and yet separate from, sinners. A remarkable phenomenon this! one sinless among the sinful; pure amid pollution; a faultless man, in whose chaste and placid bosom temptation never kindled a wish, a thought, a fancy that might not be exposed to the eyes both of God and man. He himself explains the wonder—" The prince of this world cometh, and hath nothing in me."

Who, therefore, would keep out of sin, should give his chief attention to the state of his heart; ever praying with David—Create in me, O God, a clean heart, and renew a right spirit within me! Not that a good man will overlook the influence of external circumstances, the temptations of his position, or the character of his companions; not that we are ever to rush into temptation—naked into the battle; or enter it without fear and trembling till we are perfect in holiness. Stand in awe, and sin not. We cannot be too careful to keep out of the reach of sin; not to stand in the way of sinners; not to breathe pestilential air. Bathe not in the brightest waters where sharks are playing! By prayer, by self-denial, by, as St Paul did, keeping the body under, give sin no hold of you. Imitate yon ancient wrestler, who, laying aside his robes and ornaments, and all the bravery of his attire, steps naked into the arena—limbs and body shining with slippery oil; closing with an antagonist, whose hands, slipping on the unctuous limbs, catch no firm hold, he heaves him up to hurl him in the dust, and bear off the palm—honour won, less by his power than by his wise precaution. If prevention is better than cure, precaution is better than power; therefore ought a good man ever to watch and pray that he enter not into temptation; his prayer, that which our Lord has taught us, Lead us not into temptation but deliver us from evil.

Our *corrupt nature*, acted on by temptation, *is the source of sin.*

"Lust, when it hath conceived, bringeth forth sin."

The woman died because she ate of the tree: and she ate of the tree because she lusted after its fruit. In doing so, in the first instance, she toyed with temptation—a thing more dangerous than to play with fire-arms. With an overweening confidence in herself, she thought, perhaps, as many do, that she might venture a certain way; and, stopping at her own pleasure, draw up—though in circumstances where poor reason is like the driver pulling at the reins, when the coach, at the heels of maddened and mastersome horses, is whirling to an upset half-way down hill. Confidence in one's self, giving presence of mind, is sometimes of advantage; but never in those spiritual conflicts where strength is weakness; and, as leading us to fly from danger to the arms of God, weakness is found to be strength.

The fatal mistake, which our mother committed, lay in not taking alarm at the first sign of evil, and in the first bad, wrong thought, the nascent desire for a forbidden pleasure, crushing sin in the egg—putting her foot on the spark; like Job, who made a covenant with his eyes, shutting hers to the tempting colour of the fruit; stopping her

E

ears to the talk of the cunning devil; flying, as if she had seen the serpent in its own proper shape, with crest erect, and burning eyes, and form coiled to spring—flying with terror from the scene, calling her husband Adam, calling God himself from heaven to her help.

Beware, therefore, of evil in the buddings of desire! Whoever allow themselves to indulge in evil imaginations or thoughts, are preparing themselves to commit the crimes they fancy. Desires are the seed of deeds. Working in the dark, and all the more dangerous that their progress, like a miner's, is silent and unseen, they sap the walls of virtue; and thus the man of God is overthrown by temptations that otherwise had broken on him, as breaks the mountain billow on a front of rock. May not the bad thoughts and fancies, that do their work secretly and unsuspected within the recesses of the heart, account for those sudden falls and sins on the part of such good men as David, that neither they, nor others, would have ever dreamt of? The mischief is due less to the temptation than to what preceded it—and prepared for it. You are walking, for example, through a forest. Across your path, and on the ground lies, stretched out in death, a mighty tree, tall and strong—fit mast to carry a cloud of canvas, and bear unbent the strain of tempests. You put your foot lightly on it; and how great your surprise when, breaking through the bark, it sinks deep into the body of the tree—a result much less owing to the pressure of your foot, than to the poisonous fungi and foul, crawling insects that had attacked its core. They have left the outer rind uninjured—but hollowed out its heart. Take care your heart is not hollowed out; and nothing left you but the crust and shell of an empty profession.

Keep thy heart, therefore, with all diligence. Give it your chief and most anxious attention. Guard most sedulously, and cultivate most prayerfully that part of you where the true man lives; and which, unseen by any but God, neither incurs the blame, nor wins the applauses of men. It is in its inner chamber—remote from the public eye, that sins, and also noble deeds, are born: there, the play of life is rehearsed; and that performed in fancy which is afterwards acted before a thousand eyes; there, God or Satan sits enthroned; there, lie the deep, hidden fountains of good or evil; there, visited by angels, or haunted by demons, is a little heaven or a little hell. Be sure you keep it for God. Be thy body His temple, and thy heart the secret shrine, where the light of the Shechinah burns, and the holy law is preserved, and good angels spread their wings over the blood-besprinkled seat of mercy, and the spirit of man, all alone, like the solitary High Priest within the veil, holds closest intercourse with God. Holiest of temples! see that nothing enter or find lodgment there that can hurt or defile.

The fruit of sin is death.

What man is he that desireth life, and loveth many days? The Psalmist answers his own question, and in the ordinary course of Providence what rule so good as his to attain longevity, and fall at mellow autumn like a shock of corn in its season? There is more truth in his answer, though it be summed up in a single sentence, than in whole volumes on medicine and the art of preserving, or restoring health. What man, desiring life, and loving many days, would, where rosy infants play with hoary locks, see his children, and his children's children? Let him, says David, depart from evil and do good. In the ruddy cheek, and robust form, and elastic step, and bounding health, and iron frame, and the long, light-hearted, laughing, singing, happy years—the green old age which the early and continued practice of Christian virtues so often insures—we have still some links, some lingering vestiges of the old marriage tie between a sinless and an endless life.

Death has passed on all men, because all have sinned. And looking only at temporal death, see how vice hurries multitudes into the grave—shortening their days, and rudely shaking out the sands of life. Some four or five years, on an average, darkly closes the life of such as seduced become seducers; and prowl our streets, like night wolves, ravening for their prey. So perishes many a sweet flower that a villain's hand did pluck; and, when it had lost its blooming attractions, flung on the street to be trodden under foot as the veriest, vilest weed. Is not the cup where the wine conceals a serpent, and the vile dregs are shame, and sorrow, and disease, offered to the drunkard's lips by a grisly hand? Immorality wrecks more fortunes than adversity; and bad habits make more bankrupts than bad trade. Vice supplies the greedy grave with more victims than war—more of our countrymen, directly or indirectly, year by year, perish by the bottle than fell in Britain's greatest and bloodiest battle; more cruel than old Time, she plucks the scythe from his hands, and, with rapid step and long sweep, mowing down the fairest flowers of the grass, she cuts short the life of thousands he had spared for years. Time "slays his thousands," but Vice her "tens of thousands." Many do not live out half their days. Even when their sun does not go down at noon, and life's lamp, not blown, is left to burn out, how true of many are the words of the Naamathite—"His bones are full of the sin of his youth, which shall be down with him in the dust." While godliness is profitable for all things, having the promise of the life that now is, as well as of that which is to come, in the horrid diseases, and in the many grim shapes of death which follow the steps of vice, and form the train both of Bacchus and of the Paphian queen, God brands sin with the stamp of His high displeasure.

But here death does not carry our thoughts only to the grave, but beyond the grave—into eternity—down into the pit. It is a sad and awful thing to see one struggling in the arms of death; to watch the light of life sinking in its socket, till, sometimes with a dying flash, it expires; to gaze on the pale, silent, solemn, lifeless corpse; to hear the mould, from sexton's shovel, rattle hollow on the coffin; and when his spade has smoothed the grassy turf, and uncovered mourners have paid farewell honours to the dead, to leave a loved one to moulder away into the dust of death. Yet faith in Jesus can stand these trials. Soaring to the heavens where the spirit has fled, anticipating the hour when graves shall heave, and rending tombs shall open for mortal to spring into immortality, faith can go through the last parting as friends, standing on the shore, wave hands and handkerchiefs to the emigrants they are to follow in the next ship; and rejoin ere long in a better land. But where there is no true faith in Christ, and peace has never been made with God through the blood of His cross, sins are finished in a more dreadful death—the second death—eternal death

—in those doleful regions where the dying never die. " Rest for the weary;" "There is no sorrow there;" these revival hymns are sung of another land. Here is no rest for the weary; the eye never closes; no sleep brings sweet forgetfulness; no hope ever whispers, It will soon be over; but despair, with stony horror in her face, shakes her snaky locks, and, gnashing her teeth, mutters, It will never be over—never!

Looking at death under this aspect, on the brink of the "horrible pit," I almost cease to wonder that God gave up His Son to save us—there is something so dreadful in that doom. The reasonableness, as well as love of the Cross, is nowhere seen so well as by the light of these lurid gleams; and where are seen so well the unreasonableness, the folly, the mad insanity of all who put away God's mercy, and day by day neglect this great salvation? Strong in the goodness of his cause, with his back to the throne of God, and his foot planted on the rock of truth, a man can stand against the world; who is supported by a Father's hand, can stand erect beneath any load of sorrow; who has made his calling and election sure, can stand unmoved by the approach of death, and even urge him to hasten his tardy steps—with the eager voice and outstretched arms of a lover, crying, Come, Lord Jesus, come quickly! But who shall be able to stand, and hear this doom pronounced on his downcast head, Depart from me, ye cursed, into everlasting fire, prepared for the devil and his angels? From that fate, Jesus died. and is now willing—now waits to save you. Haste to the refuge! Flee to His arms from the wrath to come!

TRUE RELIGION.

> *"Pure religion and undefiled before God and the Father is this, To visit the fatherless and widows in their affliction, and to keep himself unspotted from the world."* — St James i. 27.

THE sky which, whether studded with stars or hung in gold and purple, or one azure field over which the sun wheels his glowing course, presents always a glorious, occasionally a very extraordinary appearance. Not one but two suns are there; and in the Arctic regions, as if to compensate the long periods when their skies are left to perpetual night, there are sometimes three— blazing away in brilliant rivalry, and shedding increase of light on sparkling icebergs and the dreary wastes of snow. Yet, though there were not three but three hundred suns, only one of them could be a true sun. The others, which are produced by a peculiar state of the atmosphere, being, though bright, yet mere images, are analogous, to borrow a familiar illustration, to the multiplied candles that shine on the silvered facets of a reflector. As with these suns, so is it with the various religious systems of the world. They are many; numbered not by units, but hundreds. Almost every new country that voyagers have discovered has, with new trees and new flowers and new animals, presented a new form of faith. The world has no building big enough to hold all the gods that men do worship. Yet, though greater in number, and much greater in essential differences, than the races of mankind—for, differing in colour and contour as the negro and the white man do, they meet in Adam, God having made of one blood all the families of the earth—among these many religions there is but one true ; the rest are false—false as the mock suns of an Arctic sky. For as God is one, truth is one; and though the true may be separated from the false by a line as sharp as the edge of a razor, still they stand as irreconcilable as if they were parted by the whole distance of the poles. There are "lords many, and gods many," yet but one true God; even so there are many faiths and forms of religion, and yet but one "pure and undefiled before God."

It has been said there are many ways of going out of the world, and but one of coming into it; and it may be said there are many roads to hell, and but one to heaven. No doubt, in St John's vision, where the final state and place of the blessed was represented as a glorious city, with streets of pure gold, and walls built of precious gems, all shining in light, that fell neither from sun nor moon, but streamed out in dazzling effulgence from the throne of God, he saw not one gate, but twelve. These gates, each a pearl, and opening on streets of gold, had a meaning. Standing open, and never shut by day or night, they betoken the security enjoyed by the blessed inhabitants; and also how open heaven has been made to every sinner who seeks it through the blood of Christ. Approach it in the right way, and whatever may have been your character, and is your age, country, or condition, you are free to enter unchallenged—without let or hindrance. No armed sentinels, as at earthly palaces, guard the gates that invite alike the feet of prince and beggar —Whosoever believeth in the Lord Jesus Christ shall not perish, but have everlasting life. But by these twelve gates St John never meant that there are as many different ways of getting into heaven. This portion of sacred Scripture is a figure. It is to be understood within limits; and is no more to be pushed too far than many of our Lord's parables. There is but one way to the kingdom of God—to a state of grace in this world, and a state of glory in the next. I, says Jesus, am the way, the truth, the life; not one of many ways, but the one way. Come unto *me*, he also says, all ye that labour and are heavy laden, and *I* will give you rest; and in perfect harmony with these declarations is that of an apostle, " There is no name given under heaven whereby man can be saved but the name of Jesus." There is but one true religion " pure and undefiled before God."

We have this religion in our Bible. There it flows unadulterated and undefiled, fresh and pure as it came from the upper spring. Let us draw it at this well—not taking our faith from man or minister, but directly from the word of God; lest it should be like water that acquires a poisonous quality from the leaden pipes it flows through. Yet though we have the true religion here, how many mistake what religion is; its real character; and in what its true life consists! They fancy themselves to be religious; and that all is right when all is wrong with them. There is a sense in which he that doubteth is damned; but are not many damned just because they never doubt? They go on, satisfied with themselves; not doubting but that they are on the right course, when every step they take leads them further and further astray. Sincere they may be, but it is not enough to be sincere. Sincerity and zeal, as well as ease of mind, and peace of conscience, may but more surely seal their fatal, utter ruin. For it stands to reason that the faster and further a man goes, if he take the wrong direction at starting, he goes but the further wrong: the more sail she carries, the more steam she puts on, the greater the impetus with which she takes the reef, the ship is sooner and more surely wrecked. What need, therefore, since there is but one safe course to heaven, that we should often take soundings! Why was that noble steamer which was wrecked some time ago on the coast of England lost? not simply because she was caught in the sea mist, nor because she was often thrown out of her course by porting her helm to avoid collisions, but from false security—for want of soundings! They had no doubt they were right, till the dreadful cry of breakers and a sudden crash too late revealed their danger. And if we would not make shipwreck of the faith, nor run the risk of never discovering our mistake till we find ourselves at the door of hell, or stand at the bar of judgment, to hear with black amazement the unexpected sentence, "Depart from me, for I have never known you, ye workers of iniquity," we will try our religion —put it to the test—see whether it is true religion, that which, to use the words of St James, is "pure and undefiled before God and the Father."

What, then, is the character of this religion? There are two ways of describing a thing—first, showing what it is not; and second, what it is.

Now, to follow, meanwhile, the first of these methods, I purpose showing that

True religion does not lie *in talking about it.*

In our Church and country the pulpit has all the speaking. In Jewish synagogues, as appears from our Lord's history, it was not so. Any person in the assembly who had got anything good to say, might say it. It appears from the Epistles that this custom was engrafted on the Christian Church, and flourished in its early days; and some who abused this privilege, and, being talkative and conceited, were, perhaps, ever thrusting themselves on the public notice, may have been in his eye, when St James, laying down a rule valuable at all ages, and at all times, said, Be swift to hear, and slow to speak. Though the customs of the Church have changed with time, and speaking in public is now commonly confined to the pulpit, there is still danger—and especially in these times of religious excitement—of fancying, because we can and do talk about religion, that we are religious.

There are individual as well as national peculiarities; and, in this country, the common error certainly is not to talk too much, but too little, about religion; or, at least, too little religiously. In Scotland, at least, we are taciturn; and carry our proverbial *canniness* to a fault. How little do those of us who are undoubtedly on the way to heaven resemble a body of emigrants on shipboard—on their way across the ocean to America! Listen to that group of men, women, and children that have seen their native hills sink below the wave, and, now leaning over the bows, are looking a-head! Compared with theirs, how little does our conversation turn on the land in prospect; its employments; its enjoyments; the friends that wait our coming? Throwing off false shame, let us be more faithful to the souls of men, and to a world that lieth in wickedness; and much more free in converse with each other about the Prince and the things of the heavenly kingdom—after the manner of the men of old, of whom it is said, They that feared the Lord spake often one to another.

Still, it should not be forgotten, lest any deceive themselves, that to talk about religion, ministers and sermons, missions and missionaries, religious schemes and books, revivalists and revivals, is not religion. Some have been the most fluent talkers about these things who felt them least. Shallow rivers are commonly noisy rivers; and the drum is loud because it is hollow. Fluency and feeling don't always go together. On the contrary, some men are most sparing of speech when their feelings are most deeply engaged. I have been told that there is an awful silence in the ranks before the first gun is fired, and little talking heard during the dreadful progress of the battle, or sound, save the roar of cannon, the cries of wounded, the shouts of attack, the bursts of musketry, and bugles sounding the charge. And I have also heard men say, that when the ship is labouring for her life, and every moment may decide her fate, and whether she shall clear reef or headland hangs in anxious suspense, there is no talking, nothing heard amid the roaring of the storm but the voice of officers, as they shout forth their orders—to cut away the mast—let go the sails—or put the helm hard a-port. Deep passions, like deep waters, often run silent; and men in earnest are more given to act than to talk. True, Out of the fulness of the heart the mouth speaketh; still, the fuller the heart is, the less fluent sometimes is the speech. There are things too deep for utterance. Strong gratitude, deep love, are not fluent; nor is intense anxiety. The sight of her child wrapped in flames, or tottering on the edge of a precipice, has paralysed its mother; rooted to the ground—she has gazed in speechless horror, unable to raise a shriek, or move a foot to save it.

Besides, owing, perhaps, to constitutional peculiarities, the religion of some has its most perfect emblem in Christ's own words, Ye are the light of the world. It is a thing seen, not heard; it shines, but it makes no sound; not often found on their lips, but always in their lives. Who, that ever heard, has forgotten a story told by Dr Chalmers when he pleaded for the right of Christian congregations to reject a minister against whom they felt, but could not state, objections? A woman sought admission to the Lord's table. At her examination she broke down; unable to give her pastor any satisfactory answers, she was dumb, or her replies were such as made her appear stupid and ignorant. He did not feel that he could admit her to the table of the Lord; and told her so. Cut to the heart she rose; she reached the door; but, ere she left, with the tear shining in her eye, and in tones that went to the good man's heart, she said, referring to our Lord, "Sir, though I cannot speak for Him, I could die for Him!" Blessed speech! and blessed woman! the gate of heaven was opening to her advancing steps!

Such love to Jesus Christ is the soul of true religion. And without their becoming loud talkers, or making a parade of piety, it will lead those that feel its power to "exhort one another daily;" to try to bring sinners to the Saviour; and—as many who have overcome a false modesty are now doing—to seize all opportunities of dealing faithfully with other men about their souls. Why should not we tell others the way to heaven if we ourselves have found it? Why should not we warn a man who, unconscious of his danger, is approaching the brink of ruin? Why should not we snatch the poisoned chalice from a brother's lips? Why should not we reach a hand down to the drowning, and pluck him from the jaws of death, and seat him beside us on the rock where there is room for both? If people are loud in the praises of the physician who has cured them of some deadly malady—recommending others to trust and seek his skill, why should not Christ's people crown Him with equal honours, commend Him to a dying world, and proclaim what He has done for them? Let them say with David, Come, all ye that fear the Lord, and I will tell what He hath done for my soul; and tread in the steps of the Samaritan who threw away her pitcher, and, running to the city, brought them all out—crying, Come see a man who hath told me all things that I have ever done.

It is a bad thing ostentatiously to parade religion; but it is a base thing for a Christian man to be ashamed of it; not to stand by his colours; by his silence, if not his speech, to deny his Master; to sneak away, like a coward, out of the fight. Stand up for Christ everywhere; speak for Him; suffer the scorn of the world for Him; and, among the ungodliest crew, quit you like men, saying,

"I'm not ashamed to own my Lord,
Or to defend His cause,

> Maintain the glory of His cross,
> And honour all His laws.

> "Jesus, my Lord! I know His name,
> His name is all my boast;
> Nor will He put my soul to shame,
> Nor let my hope be lost."

Religion does not lie *in cherishing bitter feelings towards those who differ from us.*

"Be slow to wrath," says St James, "for the wrath of man worketh not the righteousness of God. If any man among you seem to be religious and bridleth not his tongue, but deceiveth his own heart, this man's religion is vain." From a small town that lay in the bosom of gently swelling hills, rose, some with spires and some without them, three or four churches, belonging to the chief denominations of our country—the sign at once of our religious liberties and religious earnestness. On a sweet summer evening a traveller looked along the valley on this peaceful scene, when a shower of rain was falling. Suddenly the sun broke out, and flung a bright bow on the cloud, that, like that of mercy, discharged its showers on all. The rainbow encircled within its arms suburb and city, lofty church and humble meeting-house.

And was it not a true and happy fancy that saw in this heavenly bow an emblem of that covenant which, irrespective of minor differences, embraces all believers within the same arms of mercy?

How different from this genial spirit that of gloomy bigotry! Scowling on charity, it would probably pronounce that thought about the rainbow to have more poetry than piety in it. I would not be uncharitable even to uncharitableness; but it is very unlovely. It holds the truth; but it is in unrighteousness. It contends for the truth; but it is with unholy passions—often persuading itself that it is religious when it is but rancorous. Some appear to think that to be narrow-minded is to be heavenly-minded. A great mistake! The black, bitter sloe of the hedges appears in the garden with the fair hues and sweet juices of the plum; and it is certainly no proof that a man's temper is sanctified that it is sour. Christians never should forget the meaning hidden in the very form which the Holy Spirit assumed when He dropped from the skies on our Saviour's head. The rapacious eagle, grasping thunderbolts in his talons, and sacred to

Jove among the heathens, or rushing down from the rock on his quarry, has been the favourite ensign of bloody conquerors, and ambitious kings; now, not it, but that gentle bird which, they say, has no gall, and is sacred to love, and whose snowy plumage was never dyed with a victim's blood, descends yonder by the quiet banks of Jordan on the head of Jesus. I do not say that religious men have never cherished an exclusive and narrow spirit. I admit that some excellent men have done so.

Still, it is not religion to speak bitterly of those who differ from us; it is not religion to minister at the altar with "strange fire;" it is not religion to serve the cause of a loving God with unlovely passions; it is not religion to defend Christ's crown with other weapons than His own sword; it is not religion to be serious on light, and great on little things; it is not religion to exalt points to the place of principles; it is not religion to contend as earnestly for forms of worship as for the faith of the gospel; it is anything but religion to dip our pens in gall, to give the tongue unbridled licence, and so to speak of others as to recall these words of Scripture—Their teeth are spears and arrows, and their tongue a sharp sword. There is no religion in the narrow, sectarian, exclusive prejudices which say, Can any good thing come out of Nazareth?

In this imperfect state, it is perhaps as impossible for two parties, as it is for flint and steel, to come into collision without eliciting some sparks of fire. It were foolish to expect that there should be nothing said or done in a time of religious controversy, which good men will see no reason afterwards to regret and to recall; for that were to expect lesser men to be greater than apostles—holier than St Paul and Barnabas, between whom, as we are told, there rose a "sharp contention." Nor even after the controversies have ceased, need we wonder that their unhappy influences do not always, and all at once, cease with them. That were such a miracle as was only seen in Galilee, when at Christ's voice the winds and waves went down at once, and together. It is with human passion as with the sea, when violently agitated, stirred by some storm to its briny depths; it continues, hours after the wind has ceased, to swell, and heave, and roll its foaming breakers on the beach. We are not to wonder that wounds received in controversy, like those received in battle, take some time to heal. It is reasonable to expect that; though, as it were a bad sign of a man's constitution, if his wounds, however deep, turned into running sores, there is something wrong, unhallowed, and unchristian in our spirit, if grace does not soften the asperities, and time close the wounds of controversy.

There is a time of peace, says Solomon, as well as a time of war; and when fields, white for the harvest, call Christians to sheath their swords and put in their sickles, he must be a stranger to the spirit of the gospel whose cry is, My voice is still for war. War? "They are for war, I am for peace," said David. And they who have inbibed most of the spirit of their Master, even when contending for the faith, will engage in quarrels with reluctance, and end them with pleasure. The Christian graces, like spice-bearing trees, grow best under serene and sunny skies. Nor should Christian men ever enter keenly into any controversy that is not vital, unless it involve matters of paramount importance. The theology of our life should be the theology of the death-bed, amid whose solemn, deepening shadows small points and matters of form dwindle out of sight; or rather are lost in the blaze of coming glory. The loftiest piety ever attaches the lowest importance to party badges and ecclesiastical distinctions; and the holier the Christian grows, he will more and more resemble the holly tree, which, as it rises, and gets away from the ground, and shoots its top up to heaven, loses the thorny prickles from its leaves. Be assured that tenderness of heart, and gentleness of spirit, mark the highest form of Christianity; and that the true fire of the Spirit, the celestial flame—like that which fell at Pentecost, blazes, but never burns. Let the same mind be in you, therefore, that was in Jesus Christ; otherwise, whatever be our creed, we are none of His.

Religion does not lie *in knowledge*, or *the observance of religious forms.*

A man who rose on the wings of genius from obscurity to the highest fame, was, on an occasion of a visit to Edinburgh, walking with one who plumed himself on his wealth, and rank, and ancient family. As they strolled along the street, Burns—for of him I speak—encountered a country acquaintance, attired in rustic dress; he seized him by the hand; and leaving his companion offended and astonished, he linked his arm in the rustic's. With a manner that bespoke esteem and admiration of his humble friend, the poet made his way through the brilliant crowd that worshipped his genius, and ruined his morals. On returning, he was met with expressions of surprise that he could so demean himself, and stoop to walk the streets among his fashionable admirers with one in such a vulgar garb. "Fool," said Burns, his dark eye flashing, and his soul rising above the base pleasures and pursuits he had sunk to in high society, and returning to its own native region of noble sentiments; "Fool," he said, "it was not the dress, the peasant's bonnet and the hodden gray, I spoke to, but to the man within; the man who beneath that bonnet has a head, and under that hodden gray a heart better than yours, or a thousand such as yours." Nobly said! A true distinction —too often forgotten, between the man and his externals! Nor is this distinction anywhere more true, important, vital, than in the Church of God. Be it gorgeous like that of Rome in her stately temples, or simple like that of our fathers, with the blue heavens for a canopy, a lone glen for their church, the gray stones of the moor for communion tables, and, for music to the wild strain of their psalms, the dash of a waterfall or the roar of breakers—the ritual of a church is but her dress. And what more than his dress is a man's profession of piety, his religious forms and observances—those peculiar to the Sabbath, or common to every day? They may be worn by the dead as well as the living. While St Paul exhorts us to " hold fast the form of sound words," he speaks of some as " lovers of pleasure more than lovers of God;" as " having the form of godliness, but denying the power thereof;" and there may be much of that in these days when, in contrast to the profane swearing, and deep drinking, and loose morals, and open neglect of worship both in the family and in the church, of the last century, religion is rather fashionable than otherwise. She now walks, to use John Bunyan's figure, in golden slippers on the sunny side of the street.

Let us beware! Form, dress, and paint are not life. In the studio of the artist, and, in the shape of man or woman, there stands a figure, the first sudden sight of which strikes most with surprise, and makes some start with fear. Is it dead or alive? Supplied with joints that admit of motion, attired in the common garb of men or women, seated in a chair, or standing in easy attitude on the floor, it might pass for life, but for that still and changeless posture, those speechless lips, and fixed staring eyes. It is a man of wood. Cold paint, not warm blood, gives the colour to its cheek; no busy brain thinks within that skull; no kind heart loves, or fervid passions burn within that breast. The *lay figure* that the artist dresses up to help him to represent the folds, the lights and shadows of the drapery, it is but death attired in the clothes of life; and, like a hypocrite or formalist in the sight of God, is offensive rather than otherwise. And, as the dress there, however rich and costly, true and skilfully arranged, does not make a living man, no more do the observance of religion, attendance at church, going to the communion, closet prayer, family worship, the daily reading of God's Word, make a religious man—a living Christian.

Be ye doers of the word, and not hearers only, deceiving your own selves, says St James; and, to take that example, though some may think they are religious because they read the Scriptures daily, religion does not consist in reading God's Word, nor in going to church to hear it preached, Sabbath by Sabbath. I say nothing against hearing; God forbid. We are not to neglect the assembling of ourselves together. It is well to hear; to pitch our tent where manna falls; to sit by the pool where an angel stirs the waters, and descends to heal; to go up to the mountain of the Lord, that, surmounted by the cross, and trodden by the feet of saints, has conducted many to the skies; and on which, like mountain ranges that attract the clouds, and are watered by many showers that never fall in the valleys, the blessing most frequently and fully descends—God loveth the gates of Sion more than all the tabernacles of Jacob. But will hearing a discourse on fire warm a man? on meat, feed him? on medicine, cure him? If not, no more will it save us to know all about the Saviour. It will no more take a man to heaven than it will take him to France, or Rome, or Jerusalem, that he knows the way. We must go, as well as know—travel, as well as be able to trace out the route. We get Christ presented to our acceptance every day; but what of that? What will that avail us, unless we accept of Him? Have we done that? It is not an offered but an accepted Saviour—nor is it the word heard, but the word done—diligently, habitually, prayerfully done, that will bring us to the kingdom of heaven.

Otherwise, hearing, according to St James, is like merely looking into a glass, which never yet arranged woman's hair, or washed man's dirty face. We see the faces of others, not our own—not our own otherwise than by reflection. The wild beauty of the forest bends over some placid pool to feed her vanity, and admire charms that unadorned are adorned the most; and before an artificial mirror her refined and polished sisters, with ornaments borrowed from birds, and beasts, and worms, the mines of earth and depths of ocean, may stand bedecked, and armed for conquests over fools. To such a looking-glass, but cast for another purpose, the apostle St James compares God's Word. It is given of God that we may see ourselves spotted and stained with sin; and seeing that, may go to wash away the foul pollution in the blood of Christ. And the mere hearers of the word, before whom I would hold up this heavenly glass to show the dark stains that lie not on their faces, but on their souls, what are they? They are like one that having seen his foul face reflected in a faithful mirror, goes away, not to wash it, but to forget all about it. Their religion lies all in hearing—not at all in doing. It is therefore vain.

To know the way to heaven, sometimes to cast a longing eye in that direction, and by fit and start to make a feeble effort heavenwards, can end in nothing. Man must get the Spirit of God. Thus only can we be freed of the shackles that bind the soul to earth, the flesh, and sin. I have seen a captive eagle, caged far from its distant home, as he sat mournful-like on his perch, turn his eye sometimes heavenwards; there he would sit in silence, like one wrapt in thought, gazing through the bars of his cage up into the blue sky; and, after a while, as if noble but sleeping instincts had suddenly awoke, he would start and spread out his broad sails, and leap upward, revealing an iron chain that, usually covered by his plumage, drew him back again to his place. But though this bird of heaven knew the way to soar aloft, and sometimes, under the influence of old instincts, decayed but not altogether dead, felt the thirst for freedom, freedom was not for him, till a power greater than his own proclaimed liberty to the captive, and shattered the shackle that bound him to his perch. Nor is there freedom for us till the Holy Spirit set us free, and, by the lightning force of truth, breaks the chains that bind us to sin,—till, with the way laid open by the blood of His covenant, Jesus says to the Spirit,—Loose him, and let him go; let him fly; let him spurn the earth, and, on the wings of faith and prayer, soar away upward to the gates of glory. For that end, come Lord Jesus, come quickly!

Belonging to a church, or sect, said Baron Bunsen on his deathbed, is nothing. The direction which the mind of that great and good man took on some theological subjects is much to be regretted—very much to be deplored. We have no sympathy with it. Yet, in those solemn hours when the shadow of death falls on the bed, and the depths of the soul rise to the surface, few have borne themselves more Christianly than Bunsen, or in their dying utterances, with failing, faltering breath, brought out more clearly, more beautifully, more attractively, the spirit of pure, undefiled, living, loving, true religion. I have spoken of it; he speaks it. Let us, for an example of the religion that lies not dead in forms, but lives in faith and love, turn our steps to the chamber where Bunsen is dying, amid the glories of a brilliant sunset—emblem of his own—the tears of his family, and the regrets of the world: " My best experience," he said, " is that of having known Jesus Christ. I leave this world without hating any one. No, no hatred : hatred is an accursed thing. Oh ! how good it is to look upon life from this elevation. One then perceives what an obscure existence we have led upon earth. Upward! upward! It becomes not darker; but always brighter, brighter. I am now in the kingdom. O my God, how beautiful are thy tabernacles! Let us part in Jesus Christ. God is life, love,—love that wills; will that loves. I see Christ, and I see God through Christ. I am dying, and I wish to die; I offer my blessing, the blessing of an old man, to all who desire it; I die in peace with all the world. Those who live in Christ, in loving Him, those are His. Those who do not live by His life do not belong to Him, by whatever name they may call themselves, and whatever confession of faith they may sign. Belonging to a church or sect is nothing. I see clearly that we are all sinners; we have only Christ in God; all else is nothing. Christ is the Son of God, and we are His children only when the spirit of love which was in Christ is in us."

This is a voice from the grave; or rather from those heavens to which, notwithstanding their mistakes and errors, true believers in Christ go to join their Lord. How grand these last utterances of a long, honoured, brilliant, and useful life! One among the greatest of his age in learning, and science, and humanity, and statesmanship, Bunsen left the world with this sentence ringing in its ears,—To love God in Christ is all: to belong to a church or sect is nothing—all else is nothing.

DOING GOOD, AND BEING GOOD.

> "*Pure religion and undefiled before God and the Father is this, To visit the fatherless and widows in their affliction, and to keep himself unspotted from the world.*"
> —St James i. 27.

WITH a natural sagacity that has been mistaken for prophecy, some men have seen far ahead of them. It is related of John Knox, for example, that he sent a message from his deathbed to Kirkcaldy of Grange, who then held Edinburgh Castle, warning him to repent and turn from his evil ways, else he should be hanged up by the neck before the sun. He did not repent; and he was hanged, exactly as Knox predicted. This was not prophecy. The Reformer's vision had not become clearer as he drew near eternity; for there, as on other shores, the fog lies thickest. It grows darker rather than clearer as we are leaving the world; and the change at death is perhaps as sudden as at birth—in a moment out of the profoundest darkness into a blaze of light. The prediction was due to the sagacity by which Knox was able to anticipate the probable issue of the circumstances in which Kirkcaldy had placed himself; of the dangerous game he was playing. With such sagacity, though otherwise applied, Captain Cook, the great navigator, when engaged in the survey of New Zealand, before the foot of a white man was ever planted on its shores, predicted the day when these remote islands, lying on the other side of the globe, almost beneath our feet, would become a valuable British colony. Nearly a century before the tide of emigration set that way, he saw our flag flying in its harbours, our shepherds feeding their flocks on its fern-covered hills, and perchance the unhappy wars which now rage there—to our shame, I fear—certainly to the sorrow of its stout and gallant natives. Curiously enough, his foreknowledge grew like their fruit on the New Zealand trees. Sailing along, he saw these unknown shores covered, not with low scrub or brushwood, but with gigantic timber; and—a sagacious man—he concluded that the soil must be deep, and rich, and strong, since none other could rear such forest giants.

Now, what is true of the nature of the soil is equally true of the religion of the soul. You can always judge of it by what it yields. In both cases the crop is the test of character. By their fruits, says our Lord, ye shall know them. The soil is known by its trees; and the trees are known by their fruit. True of the vineyard of the husbandman, this is true also of the Church— the vineyard of the Lord. It is not, therefore, what we profess, but practise; it is not what a man says with his tongue, or signs with his hand, but what he does with his heart, that settles his religion in the sight of God, and on the great day of judgment shall settle his fate. Heaven is allotted to well-doers — the holy, loving, kind, gentle, merciful; but ill-doers—the impious, the unholy, the greedy, the grasping, the cruel, the pitiless, shall have their portion in hell. Hear our Lord! To those on His right hand He says, Well done; not well said, or well believed, or well professed, or even well designed, but, Well done, good and faithful servants, enter ye into the joy of your Lord; to those on the left again, Depart from me, for I have never known you, ye workers of iniquity.

The great Stagyrite thus opens one of his immortal works, This book is written not for knowledge but for action. And for what other end was the Bible written—written by men, and inspired of Heaven? Not that we might know the truth, but do it; not that we might know the way to heaven, but travel it; not that we might know, but accept of an offered Saviour. Religion does not consist in doctrinal or prophetical speculations; nor lie like a corpse entombed in old dusty confessions. She lives in action, and walks abroad among mankind—calling us to leave our books, to shut our Bibles, to rise from our knees, and go forth with hearts full of love and hands full of charities. According to St James, Pure and undefiled religion before God and the Father is this, To visit the fatherless and widows in their affliction, and to keep himself unspotted from the world.

Such is true religion *in the judgment of " God and the Father."*

God and the Father! what a blessed conjunction! God and the Father! that might breed hope in the darkest bosom; for who, though lying in deepest dungeon, despairs of mercy that knows he is to be tried by his own father? To be tried by our Father! Is not that to be assured of pity and tenderness, of great allowance for our infirmities, and of a kinder consideration both of our difficulties and defects than angels or men would give? This goes far to divest a judgment-day of its terrors. Our Father is to try us; then may we sing—

> " Such pity as a father hath
> Unto his children dear;
> Like pity shows the Lord to such
> As worship Him in fear."

Looking with fond and partial eyes on his children, how slow is a father to discover their faults, and how ready to cover them! He approves and applauds their feeblest efforts to please him. See, though her song may violate the rules both of time and tune, how the father smiles on the fairy form that, with laughing eye, and golden locks, and blushing cheek, warbles out an infant's song to please him. But what father is like our Father that is in Heaven! How easily is He pleased, and how largely He rewards! Why, He promises even a crown of glory for a cup of water given to a disciple, and raises to a throne all that have learned lessons of love, and kindness, and humility—sitting at Jesus's feet. He raiseth the poor out of the dust, and lifteth the needy out of the dunghill, that He may set him with princes—for Christ's sake forgiving our greatest faults, and rewarding our smallest works.

Still, though God will not look for perfection in our works as if they were to save those that are saved only by the righteousness of Christ, the final judgment is to turn on works. Look at the picture of that last judgment, as it was drawn by Christ's own hand! The trumpet has sounded; and at its long, loud, and solemn summons, the graves have given up their dead. Coming from their sepulchres, whether in the tombs of earth or the caves of ocean, the whole family of man is met for the first time, and met for the last—an innumerable multitude, above whose heads, in high and solitary majesty, rises the great white throne. The Son of Man, attended by all the holy angels, descends. Now the work begins. Some men of science suppose that the gold we dig out of its veins was originally diffused through the rock; and that at some remote period, and by a power unknown to us, its atoms, separated from the earthy mass, and made to pass through it, were deposited in the veins where they now lie. By a power as mighty and mysterious, that, breaking up families which had slept and rose together, sunders for ever the tenderest relationships, the mingled mass of men is separated. Even as a shepherd, says our Lord, divideth the sheep from the goats, the crowd is divided—these move to the right, those to the left. And now, amid an awful silence, and in a voice distinctly heard at the farthest bounds of the mighty crowd, the Judge pronounces sentence; and gives reasons for it. And what turns the balance in His hand?

Not the churches men belonged to; nor the creeds they signed; nor the doctrines they espoused, believed, defended, even died for. No, it turns upon works. Listen—He says, I was an hungered and ye gave me meat; or, I was an hungered and ye gave me no meat. Visitors of prisons, clothers of the naked, feeders of the hungry, advocates of the wronged, husbands of widows, fathers of orphans, bearing names unknown in courts or camps, or in the seats of learning and of science, but household words in the homes of sorrow—rising from graves you were borne to amid the griefs of the poor and needy, the crowns are for you. But for you, whether high or low, that wrapped yourselves up in narrow selfishness, the curse. No religion shall be owned then, but what now sheds blessings on misery, and lights up with rainbow hues the cloud of human sorrow.

Do not suppose because I speak thus of works, that I substitute them for Christ; or that I hold evangelical doctrine and sound views of divine truth, as is the fashion now, at a discount—as of small consequence. No—I say, Hold fast the form of sound words—Contend earnestly for the faith which was once delivered to the saints—Try the spirits whether they be of God. Right views of divine truth are of the highest importance; for how can a vessel reach her harbour if her compass and charts be wrong? Doctrines are the seeds of duties; and it proves nothing to the contrary that some good men have held grave errors. They were good, and got to heaven, not in consequence of their errors, but in spite of them; for as many men are worse, some men are better than their creeds. With gold, silver, precious stones, wood, hay, stubble, and a vast quantity of rubbish, they rest on the Rock; and shall be saved so as by fire. Under the influences of the Spirit, endowed with the grace of God and love of Christ, the rightness of their hearts overcomes the wrongness of their heads, and so they get to heaven: as I have seen a ship, under a power generated from water by fires that glowed within her hold, cross the roaring bar, and in the face of adverse wind and tide, plough her way safe into harbour.

It has not been worldlings that have done most for the world. Your creatures of fashion and lovers of pleasure, who has met them where misery dwells? If they repair to the haunts of crime, it is not to cure it. Nor is it those who talk lightly of doctrines, and profess to have neither taste nor time for religious questions, but men like Luther, that were strong in doctrine, and sound in faith, and ready to contend for it—men of ardent piety, men great in prayer, that have done most to mend the miseries of the world; and, leaving their footprints on the sands of time, have been most blessed while they lived, and most missed when they died. It cannot be otherwise; it is not in the nature of things that it should be otherwise. A belief in our lost state, in the sacrifice of a divine Redeemer, in the free gifts and grace of God, is intimately connected with the whole circle of Christian charities —is the centre from which they radiate. How can he in whose eyes all out of Christ are perishing, hanging over hell, dream away life in idle pleasures? In the light of redemption, the outcast, the vile thing many would not touch, shines like a diamond on a dust heap. The condescension of the Son of God teaches me to stoop—not to the great, but to the ground, to pluck the foulest from the gutter. Feeling that I am forgiven much, I am ready to forgive; and that I have gotten much, I am ready to give. God's costly gift to me, the free gift of His dear Son, both opens my hand, and warms my heart. Melted by His love and mercy, my icy selfishness gives way; and like a lake loosened from its wintry chains, my bounty flows freely out to others. His generosity begets my own. As in His light I see light, in His love I feel love. It is the sight of Jesus stepping from His throne to lie in a manger, and to die on a cross, that most of all inclines me to forget myself—like Him, to deny myself, that I may live and labour for the good of others. Thus, as St Paul says, the love of Christ constraineth us, because we thus judge, that if one died for all, then were all dead, and that He died for all, that they who live should not henceforth live unto themselves, but unto Him who died for them and rose again.

True religion consists "*in visiting the fatherless and widows in their affliction, and in keeping ourselves unspotted from the world.*"

To visit the fatherless and widows in their affliction, from natural pity, is beautiful; and may be called virtuous. We commend, and admire it. Still, though it cannot be true that there are people who are very religious, and yet not kind, people may be kind who are not religious. Visits and deeds of charity, to become religious, pious actions, besides springing from natural compassion, must be done in obedience to the will, and out of regard to the glory of God. The most common action, such as sweeping a floor or kindling a fire, when done because God has bidden it, and done well that He may be glorified, and religion not despised but honoured, rises into piety; and thus a humble servant cleaning shoes may be doing a thing as truly religious as a divine preaching from a pulpit, or an angel singing in the skies. Great and lofty deeds, on the other hand, that, though crowning their authors with honour, and filling the mouths of men, are done without any regard to God, have not an atom of religion. Therefore it has been said, that the virtues of an unconverted, ungodly man, are but splendid vices. They are without value in the judgment and sight of God.

But to visit the fatherless and widows in their affliction, and keep one's garments unspotted from the world, under the influence of the holiest motives, and with a view to the highest ends, though here called pure and undefiled religion before God and the Father, is not the sum-total of true religion. These are but samples of the stock—the small segments of a large circle. Here, as elsewhere in Scripture, a part, or parts, is put for the whole; and these two are selected for this among other reasons, that they are characteristic and most important; not secondary but primary; not accidental, but essential features of all true religion. To make this plainer, it is as if I described a living man by saying he breathes. But he does many things else. He sees and hears; he walks and talks; he thirsts and hungers—and a hundred things besides. Still, unless he breathes, he is not alive, but dead; and dead is the religion which does not aim at these two things, personal purity and active charity; in other words, doing good and being good.

It is interesting to discover this truth enshrined within the name we apply to the Divine Being. God! where got we that word, God? It is not Hebrew; nor Greek; nor Latin. It was invented by our forefathers. Though rude and ignorant, and little acquainted with the arts and sciences, these half-savage men seem to have penetrated the mysteries of true religion, and caught its lovely spirit. Having dismissed Woden, and Thor, and Tuesco, their stern and wild and bloody gods, to embrace the Christian faith, they had to invent a name for the new object of their worship. Leaving Rome to borrow her forms and garments from heathen temples, and dress up the new faith in the cast-off clothes of the old, our ancestors neither chose Jove from the heathens, nor even Jehovah from the Jews; nor, selecting the power, or knowledge, or justice, or offices of the Divine Being, called him the Almighty, or the Omniscient, or the Wise, or the Just, or the King. Regarding goodness as the most prominent, and to sinners as the most engaging and winning feature of His character, because He was good, and ever doing good, because He was in His nature perfectly holy, and to all His creatures infinitely kind, they called Him Good, abbreviating it into God. God and Good are certainly the self-same words; and nobody, therefore, can be God's that is not good;

who does not seek to do good, as well as to be good.

That any calling themselves Christians should believe or act otherwise, is shocking; is a scandal to religion, and enough to make it stink, like a dead carcass, in the nostrils of sceptics and scoffers. Yet read this passage of a letter from a lady, who, touched with divine compassion for a class of wretched outcasts, is appealing for help. "I suppose you are aware," she writes, "that the Christianity of the —— (I shall not say what part of our country) is not aggressive; they have a prejudice against working Christians as superficial ones; and if we are therefore to attempt to strike at the root of the degradation of this class, we must ask help from your quarter." Alas for religion! thus caricatured and misrepresented; held up to the pity of good men, and the scorn of bad, as a lifeless system of effete doctrines and beliefs— deaf, dumb, and dead to the miseries of mankind! That true religion? No; and no more like it than a dry skeleton, hung by the neck from the ceiling of an anatomical theatre, and grinning grimly down on the students' faces, is like yon man bending to the helm, and steering the life-boat ashore; or yon man, sword in hand, fighting freedom's battle; or yon man, with fire in his eye and pathos on his tongue, pleading amid plaudits or hisses the cause of the slave; or yon good Samaritan stooping over a suffering brother, and binding up his gaping wounds; or yon gentlewoman, whom we meet on foul, dank stair, concealing bread for the hungry beneath her cloak, or find on her knees at the bed of dying penitence, wiping off the clammy death-sweat, and smoothing a thorny pillow with the consolations of religion.

Working Christians, superficial Christians! Christianity not aggressive! Hear, O heavens! and be astonished, O earth, that bore on thy dusty roads and Galilee's sandy shores, the prints of Jesus's feet; and saw Him going about continually doing good! From that deformity, that vile abortion, let me turn your eyes away to the religion that illumines the pages of the Bible, and walked a world which crucified it, in the blessed form of our Divine Redeemer.

Let us successively study the two features of pure and undefiled religion of St James's picture.

It appears *in acts of charity.*

The widow and orphan are selected as the representatives of all human sorrow—their case needing our help most, and appealing loudest to our pity. It even touches us to see widowhood symbolised, there, where a tree, around which some beautiful creeper had wound its arms, spangling its robust form with flowers, lies on the ground, felled by the axe, its head prostrate in the dust; while that tender plant, crushed and bleeding but still alive, clings with fond embraces to the dead. More touching still, when the mother bird has been struck down by the hawk, to look into the bush of golden gorse where her orphan brood sit pining in their cold nest, with no mother now to sing to them; to feed them; to cover them with her warm wings — left to die unless they move the pity of some sweet child or tender woman.

Sin has not so utterly blotted out the beautiful lineaments of God, but that helplessness goes to our hearts; this, as well as some other lovely flowers, continue to grow on the ruins of our fallen greatness. In busiest hours, when other intrusion would be resented, let any one enter in the garb of a widow, pale and sad, her eyes consumed with grief, she commands our attention and respect; and on these streets where the hearse, parting the tide of business, comes with its nodding plumes, how touching it is to see two or three little boys following a father to the grave; only more touching, where poverty's one room holds the dead and living, to see an infant, attracted by the glitter, break away from kind friends to rattle the handles of a mother's coffin, and smile—pleased with the sound. I have seen that sight raise roughest hands to wipe tears from eyes unused to weep.

Widow and orphan! there is something sacred to our ears in these names. Over widows and orphans, as well as over weeping penitents, the Man of sorrows casts His shield. Their wrongs stirred His placid spirit to its deepest depths. He made no complaint of wrongs inflicted on Himself; He bore His own sufferings with divine meekness; reviled, maligned, spit upon, crowned with thorns, nailed to the tree, He was dumb, nor opened His mouth—save to pray for His enemies. But He could not stand by and see the widow and orphan wronged. See how He steps up to yonder sleek and oily Pharisee praying on the widow's floor, that he might prey on the widow's substance, and strikes the mask from his face, saying, Woe to you, scribes and Pharisees! hypocrites, for ye devour widows' houses, and for a pretence make long prayers—ye serpents and generation of vipers, how can ye escape the damnation of hell? Harlots can; publicans can; and thieves can; the Canaanite and Samaritan can; but robbers of the widow, how can ye? There you have a commentary, by way of contrast, on the words—"Pure and undefiled religion before God and the Father is to visit the widow and fatherless in their affliction." I do not believe in the Christianity that is not Christ-like: and I no more believe in a profession of piety which is not associated with His pity than in a sun that sheds no light—in a fire that gives out no heat—in a rose that breathes no perfume; they are mere painting: life-like, but dead; clever, but cold. People may talk of such and such a man being godly; but none are godly but the godlike. God is the "Judge of the widow, and the Father of the fatherless in his holy habitation;" and he only is godlike who stands to widows in the room of the dead, and in whom orphans find both a father and a friend.

True religion will express itself *in personal, actual visits to widows and fatherless in their affliction.*

The circumstances of some are such, that they can bequeath at death what they could not afford to part with in their lifetime; but there is no charity in leaving money, which we could now spare, to do good when we are dead. There is no self-denial—no cross-bearing in that. If we could carry the money along with us to another world, there might be virtue in leaving it behind; but since we cannot, and have to leave the world as naked as we entered it, there is none. In fact, we are giving away what is not ours,—what ceases to be ours the moment of our death,—what our right to expires with life. Men are called by the apostle to mortify the flesh with its affections and lusts; but by such *mortifications*, as they are called in Scotland, men do not mortify themselves, but their heirs—whom they cheat of their expectations, to purchase a worthless name. The fortunes that rear such falsely splendid charities prove nothing in favour of the donors; but rather the reverse. They only show how hard, and cold, and grasping, and avaricious these men and women were; and that only death could compel the miser to relax his iron gripe of the widow's and orphan's bread. Whatsoever thy hand, therefore, findeth to do, do it with thy might; for there is no work, nor device, nor knowledge, nor wisdom, to be found in the grave whither thou goest.

Now, in regard to the works of charity which religion requires, it is a pity that some, willing and anxious to do them, should miss the way of doing them well. They overlook the importance of giving a literal obedience to the words of St James. They help, but they do not *visit*, personally visit the widows and fatherless in their affliction. Such direct intercourse is of as great advantage to those that give as to those that get; softening, if not sanctifying, the hearts of both. Many do not seem to know how much charity resembles a delicate perfume that, by being poured from one vessel into another, loses the finest part of its aroma: and that to awaken gratitude, it is not sufficient that the giver dole out his bounty through a middle party—by the hands of a hired, and it may be a hard, official. Let thirsty lips drink, not at the pipe, but where the grateful spring bubbles up fresh and cold from its native fountain. Wherever possible, therefore, distribute your charities with your own hand; for there is much the same difference between sending your servant, or the agent of a society, and carrying the gifts yourselves, that there was between Gehazi with his master's staff, and the living prophet—the first may fill the hand, but, as when Elisha took the dead boy in his arms, it is the last that sets the heart a-beating. The kindly visit, the look, the tone, the starting tear of sympathy, the patient attention to the tale of suffering, these make our gold or silver shine with double brightness, and impart a double sweetness to the bread we give. By this, without lowering yourself, you will lift up the poor; and win them, perhaps, to God and goodness. A hand laid kindly on a child's head has been laid on a mother's heart; and with hold of that, God helping you, you may save the perishing, and steer a whole household right to heaven. See, whether you eat or drink, or give meat and drink, you do all to the glory of God.

Some think that they have no leisure or means to undertake such missions. Roman Catholics leave them to Sisters of Charity; and we, in these Protestant lands, too much to hired agents, benevolent societies, and kind Christian women. Now, though not able personally to do all that we wish, we should do all that we can; for I am sure that to be brought into personal contact with the poor is good both for us and them. How much is in our power "the day will reveal," when, called by name, some of once straitened circumstances and humble life shall step out from the crowd to hear the Judge say, "I was an hungered, and ye gave me meat: I was thirsty, and ye gave me drink: I was a stranger, and ye took me in: I was sick and in prison, and ye visited me; for inasmuch as ye did it unto one of the least of these, ye did it unto me." Woe that day to them who find time to visit the great, and rich, and noble, but the poor never; time to spend on luxurious banquets, and at theatres and balls, where delicate feet thread the gay dance, that never stood on the bare floors of poverty; who regale with music ears that never listened to the wail of widows, or the moaning child that cried for bread and its mother has none to give it; who stoop to worship wealth and rank, but never to raise the fallen, or bend, with words of comfort, over the bed of some poor, trembling, dying sinner!. "Go to now, ye rich men, weep and howl for your miseries that shall come upon you; your gold and silver is cankered, the rust of them shall be a witness against you, and shall eat your flesh as it were fire."

None are without time and means for such missions of mercy. To convince you, let me guide you to a scene where pure and undefiled religion stands before us in those who had little time to spare, and less money to spend. Enter this foul close with me; bend your head to this low-browed door; climb one dark stair, another, and still another. Now, you are in a cold, empty garret; and there, beneath a patched and dusky skylight, lies a dying woman, a stranger in a strange land; beside whose lowly pallet stands a pale, gentle, weeping child. Called to many a dying bed, I have seen death in all shapes and forms—some despairing; some rejoicing; many afraid to let go, and clinging to the earth; others eager to be gone; but that garret, where I knelt on the bare floor, seemed nearer than any to heaven. It seemed as if the angels that carried the beggar to Abraham's bosom were there—waiting the last sinking breath to bear that saintly spirit to the skies. I saw not them; but in the room where the orphan stood by her mother's corpse, seemingly without a friend in all the world, I met two God-sent angel-women. They took the child to their own home. Bereft of one mother, in them she found two. They shared their scanty meals with her; and when the world was sleeping, plied their needles to earn her bread, to send her to school, to rear her in comely virtues, and shield her young head and heart in an evil world. What inspired this noble generosity? They had come from the country, and were themselves poor; but touched with the sight of much poverty greater than their own, they resolved that though they could not do much, they would do what they could. If many around them must perish, they could, at least, save one; and so, each taking this sinking child by the hand, with the other free, these sisters buffeted the billows of adverse fortune, and, unknown to the world, but amid the applause of Jesus, and of angels that watched their progress from the skies, they brought the orphan in safety to the shore. There was pure and undefiled religion before God and the Father.

May the Spirit of God inspire you to go and do likewise. Better walk in the steps of these lowly women than in the dazzling train of queens. Better have our names written on the hearts of widows and the fatherless, than on the pages of immortal history. Let crawling worms creep upwards, and leave behind them the slime of their meanness, and base methods of reaching heights, from which death's rude hand shall cast them down into the grave. Be it ours rather, like God's heavenly creatures—the sun, the rain, the dew—to descend in blessings on those beneath us. How many fruits that sun ripens, how many cold things he warms, how many flowers he paints and opens, how many birds he sets a-singing before he sinks in night! I would be the rain-drop that, ere it returns to its parent sea, leaves a blessing at some lowly root. Nay, I would be the tiny dew-drop that, glistening in the morning sunbeams, refreshes the lips of some thirsty flower ere, exhaled by the sun, it ascends to heaven! Do, at least, some, and try to do much good ere you die. Seek to live loved, and to die lamented; to be blessed in life, and to be missed at death. Live so that over your grave, however lowly, they may raise a tombstone, inscribed with the words, "Blessed are the dead that die in the Lord; they rest from their labours, and their works do follow them."

PURITY.

> "*Pure religion and undefiled before God and the Father is this, To visit the fatherless and widows in their affliction, and to keep himself unspotted from the world.*"
> —St James i. 27.

DISTINGUISHED from other jewels that have but one colour, such as the fiery ruby, the milk-white pearl, the sapphire that borrows its tint from the sky, and the emerald from the sea, diamonds owe their beauty, brilliancy, and costly value to this, that they burn with many hues. Turned round, they sparkle with shifting colours, as the light flashes from their different faces. Still, though it appears in this variety of aspects, the diamond is one gem—"pure and undefiled," as a dew-drop distilled from the skies.

And why should not Christians believe that the Church of the living God is also one, though in forms of worship, ecclesiastical constitutions, and somewhat even in doctrines, it presents various aspects—as St Paul says, "There are differences of administration, but the same Lord."

Like the costliest and most brilliant of gems, pure and undefiled religion before God and the Father presents itself under various aspects. Every one is beautiful, heavenly in its source—like the rays of the diamond caught from the sun; yet each differs from another, as much as do the properties which St James assigns to divine wisdom. In this passage, "the wisdom that is from above is first pure, then peaceable, gentle, easy to be entreated, full of mercy and good fruits, without partiality and without hypocrisy," we have something like a full description; but in saying that "pure and undefiled religion is to visit the widow and fatherless in their affliction, and keep himself unspotted from the world," the apostle does not attempt to give a full-length portrait. Out of many he mentions but two features; but these, though highly characteristic, neither embrace all the duties of a Christian's life, nor exhaust the graces of his character. On the contrary, as the sun in his annual course passes through all the signs of the zodiac, pure and undefiled religion, overlooking no commandment, but endeavouring to keep the entire law of God, walks the whole circle of Christian duties. Then, though some may be more prominent and more fully developed than others, the believer, "complete in Christ," is bedecked with every Christian grace. None are wanting; all are there, like the precious stones of the high priest's breastplate, when, with a blood-filled bowl of purest gold, wearing his crown, and robed in white, he drew aside the veil; and vanishing, entered into the Holy of Holies to commune alone with God. With this explanation, let us now study the second phase of true and undefiled religion.

It requires us *to keep ourselves unspotted from the world.*

An obstruction to our prayers, efforts, and progress meets us here, *in limine,* — on the very threshold, which it is necessary to take out of the way. It lies in a feeling, or fancy, that it is impossible to keep ourselves unspotted from the world, or even to come within sight of such a high attainment. To live in this world, and yet keep ourselves uncontaminated by its influence, pure in heart and life, seems as impossible as to be immersed in water, and yet keep dry; or to walk a muddy road, and keep our garments clean; or to take fire into our bosom, and not be burned. Well, if not more impossible than these, it can be done. It has been done—to some extent, at least, by help of Him who says, " My grace is sufficient for thee."

To be plunged overhead in water, and yet keep dry, is not impossible. From rocking boat, or sandy shore, observe yon sea-fowl poised on white wing above the deep. Catching sight of her prey, see! she descends like a flash of light, diving into the belly of the wave; ere long she emerges, and bearing no touch of damp on her snowy plumage, rises into the air with feathers dry as the eagle's, that springs from the rock to soar in sunny skies. With feet webbed to swim, and broad sails to fly, and warm downs to preserve her heat, God has furnished this bird with an oil, that, coating her feathers, protects them from the touch of water.

Nor is it impossible to crawl undefiled in mire. How often have I seen a creeping thing come wriggling out of the foulest mud, pure; clean; without a speck on its ringed and slimy form. And if God enables it, by a fluid secreted from its lubricious skin, to pass through defilement undefiled, may not the Christian say, Shall He take such care of the poor worm that we tread upon, and not preserve from worse pollution those whom He has called to heaven, and redeemed with the blood of His beloved Son?

> "He who His Son, most dear and loved,
>   Gave up for us to die,
> Shall He not all things freely give
>   That goodness can supply?"

Grant that contact with a sinful world is like taking fire into our bosom;—it does not follow that we shall certainly be burned. With the troubled king, his nobles, and the eager multitude that crowd round the fiery furnace, look at these three Hebrews! Their naked feet are on glowing coals! they breathe the burning flame! and yet they come forth, no hair singed on beard or eyelash, nor smell of fire upon their clothes.

We might meet this difficulty with such answer as the holy Leighton once gave to such another plea. Grieved with the unhappy state of his country, and the failure of his own well-meant attempts to reconcile his countrymen to prelacy, and stop the bloody cruelties of the time, he had retired into England to pass the clouded evening of his life in the house of a married sister. Having a family, she had many domestic cares; and cumbered by them, she came far short of his close and devout walk with God. One day, addressing her brother, who had never married, she said, "It is easy for you to live a holy life; it is otherwise with me; with children and many household cares to occupy my thoughts and engross my attention, such a life as yours is to me impossible." With one blow of his gentle hand, Leighton demolished her plea. He engaged in no argument, nor set himself to prove her wrong; but kindly turning to her, and quoting God's own word, he said, "Enoch walked with God, and begat sons and daughters." Like her, many deem high degrees of grace beyond their reach; therefore they aim low, and in consequence of that their attainments are low; for few are so fortunate as the son of Kish, who, leaving home to seek his father's asses, found a crown on the way. We expect too little; and to those who would dismiss this subject, abandoning all efforts after a purity which they deem as impossible in this world, as to live in water, or breathe unhurt in fire, I have an answer, drawn also from the Word of God—an arrow taken from the quiver where the good Archbishop found his shaft. What saith the Lord? He puts the case in your own form, and taking your very figures of fire and water, says, "When thou passest through the waters I will be with thee, and through the rivers they shall not overflow thee; thou shalt walk through the fire, and not be burned, neither shall the flame kindle upon thee."

To keep themselves unspotted from the world,
God's people are *carefully to avoid its vices.*

There is much vice in the world. Thousands make no profession of religion; having broken loose from their anchors, and drifted into practical infidelity, they have no connexion with any church, and seek none. Thousands besides are to be found within the Church who are dead — dead as the bodies that rot and moulder outside its walls! They have the form of godliness, but are strangers to its power. It requires neither an intimate nor an extensive acquaintance with society, to discover that thousands are living in open profligacy. The vices of town and country indeed thrust themselves on our notice. Though not exactly defended, they are allowed and winked at—now excused on the plea that the young must sow their wild oats, as if it was no solemn truth that "what a man soweth that shall he also reap"—and now varnished over by giving respectable names to bad things. For example, seduction is called an affair of gallantry; murder by duel, an affair of honour; drunkenness, intemperance; the debauchee who ruins his health, is a fast liver; and he who cheats another, is a sharp man of business. Licentiousness, with brazen front and painted face, openly walks our streets—pushing virtue aside, and putting modesty to the blush; while immoral and impure habits, though discreetly veiled, like an internal cancer, are destroying the health, the fortunes, the happiness, the bodies and souls of thousands. With idiot look, drunkenness reels abroad in the face of day; and events ever and anon are coming to light that show how many of both sexes, and of all ranks, are the secret slaves of this debasing vice. What falsehoods are told, and frauds largely practised in commerce, and in almost every kind of business! and are not the poor often defrauded of their wages, helpless widows and orphans of their substance, to maintain a splendid extravagance—a false position in society, to blow and keep up a bubble that sooner or later bursts? By how many is God's holy name profaned; and how many more—like the drunken king, who, in carousal with his wives and concubines, made winecups of the vessels of the sanctuary—profane the Sabbath by idle recreation, or feasting, or business, wasting its sacred hours on the most common purposes!

To warn religious people against such vices may seem unnecessary. I know that they will not practise them; yet they may fall into what they will not practise. Fall? alas! how have the mighty fallen! and were all our secrets revealed, how would it be seen that many who never fell, had been on the point of falling—tottering, when God's arm pulled them back, on the very edge of the precipice. What sore battles have been fought of which the world knows nothing! Examples of this, that "the righteous scarcely are saved;" wounded, and bleeding, and all but overcome, their shield and helmet battered, their crown in danger and all but taken, they have come off conquerors only by help of Him who finds his opportunity in man's extremity, and saves at the very uttermost.

It is not the practice of fathers to publish the faults of their children; they are slow to believe them; they are much more ready to conceal than to reveal their failings. And for what end were the sins of Noah, and Jacob, and St Peter, and David, written in the Bible, and proclaimed in the ears of the world, but to warn us? Their moral is this, Let him that thinketh he standeth, take heed lest he fall. Do any, astonished and indignant at the insinuation, resent it, saying, There is no fear of me? Ah! the day was when these good men would have said the same, asking with horror as great as yours, Is thy servant a dog, that he should do such a thing? Yet they did it; and, though with Noah's sons we would throw a mantle over their shame, the sound of their fall has its echo in our Saviour's words, Watch! Watch and pray, that ye enter not into temptation.

We are to abstain *from all worldly pursuits and pleasures that are of a doubtful character.*

The atmosphere is sometimes in such a peculiar state that the spectator, on coast or shore, looking abroad over the sea, cannot tell where the water ends and the sky begins; and as if some magician had raised them out of their proper element, and turned their sails into wings, the ships seem floating in mid-air. But occasionally no line of separation is more difficult to draw than that which lies between what is right and what is wrong. Whether such and such a business or amusement, pursuit or pleasure, is wrong, and one, therefore, in which no Christian should engage, is a question that, so far as the thing itself is concerned, may be difficult to answer. But it is not difficult to answer, so far as you are concerned, if you doubt whether it is right. The apostolic rule is, Let every man be fully persuaded in his own mind; and unless you are so, then, "what is not of faith is sin"—sin at least to you. No man, I freely admit, has any more right to add to the duties than he has to add to the doctrines of religion; and he assumes an authority which belongs not to man, who pronounces anything to be positively sinful that is not clearly forbidden either by the letter or by the spirit of God's Word. These are the impious pretensions of the Church of Rome. Still, whatever others may feel themselves at liberty to do, if you are not satisfied in your own mind and conscience that the thing is right, that the pursuit, or pleasure, or enjoyment, is lawful, it may be right for others, but it is wrong for you to do it. Hence the Word of God says, He who doubteth is damned! not that he is damned in the common sense of that terrible expression; not that he is damned to hell; but that he is convicted, condemned of wrong-doing, in doing that which he is not sure is right.

In regard to the lawfulness of certain pursuits, pleasures, and amusements, it is impossible to lay down any fixed and general rule; but we may confidently say, that whatever is found to unfit you for religious duties, or to interfere with the performance of them; whatever dissipates your mind, or cools the fervour of your devotions; whatever indisposes you to read your Bibles, or engage in prayer; wherever the thought of a bleeding Saviour, or of a holy God, of the hour of death or of the day of judgment, falls like a cold shadow on your enjoyment; the pleasures which you cannot thank God for, on which you cannot ask His blessing, whose recollections will haunt a dying bed, and plant sharp thorns in its uneasy pillow,— these are not for you. These eschew; in these be not conformed to this world, but transformed in the renewing of your minds—" Touch not, taste not, handle not." Never go where you cannot ask God to go with you; never be found where you would not like death to find you; never indulge in any pleasure which will not bear the morning's reflection. Keep yourselves unspotted from the world! nor from its spots only, but even from its suspicions. If the virtue of Cæsar's wife, according to the Romans, was not even to be suspected, may I not say as much for the purity of the Lamb's Bride? Remember that the character of a Christian is easily blemished; that they who wear white robes need to take care where they walk; that the smallest stain is visible on snow; that polished steel takes rust from the slightest touch of damp. Keep your garments clean. Keep your conscience tender—tender as the eye that closes its lids against an atom of dust, or as that sensitive plant which I have seen shrink and shut its leaves, not merely at the rude touch of a finger, but at the breath of the mouth. Walk holily, and humbly, and circumspectly, lest your good should be evil spoken of, and you should give occasion to the enemies of the Lord to blaspheme. Mould your life on Christ's; and, in the noble words of His apostle, "Whatsoever things are true, whatsoever things are honest, whatsoever things are just, whatsoever things are pure, whatsoever things are lovely, whatsoever things are of good report; if there be any virtue, if there be any praise, think on these things."

Religion does not require us *to retire from the world.*

In the strict sense of the term, the world has nothing to defile us. It is a beautiful world—

furnished with delights, and full of loveliness. Its fields carpeted with flowers; its mountains wreathed with mists, or bathed in sunshine, or crowned with glistening snows; its bright skies and green woods ringing with merry music; its air loaded with the perfumes of ten thousand censers; its seas and lakes spread out like great mirrors of living gold or silver; its various elements teeming with happy myriads, that, gathering what God gives, are the pensioners of His bounty —the world is full of God; and converse with nature, so far from corrupting or defiling us, has a tendency to purify our thoughts and improve the mind. It was not of this world, in the ordinary sense of the term, that our Lord spake, when, seeing Satan advance to the combat, He said, " The prince of this world cometh, and he hath nothing in me." Our earth owned not Satan, but Christ, as its Prince. It felt the pressure of His foot; its waters sustained His form; its midnight sky rang with the song of His nativity; its air bore Him up as He rose to His Father; in a golden cloud it provided the Conqueror with a chariot; its waves and winds in their wildest uproar were obedient to

His command; at His bidding its water reddened into wine, its graves opened to give up their dead, its bread multiplied to feed His train; and, as if the blow that struck Him had fallen heavy on its head, it trembled with horror as it received His blood. It never gave its iron to be nails for His blessed hands; nor grew its thorns to pierce His brow. With high heaven, the earth was a mourner at Christ's death; and as if it were never to recover the shock of that day, when they hung its King and Creator on a tree, an old legend says, that the reason why the aspen leaf is ever trembling on its stalk is because the cross was made of an aspen tree.

It is not the world, but the men of it, that are corrupt and corrupting. It is from these that religion calls us to keep ourselves unspotted. Uncontaminated and unstained by their vices, we are to recoil from them, saying, My soul, come not thou into their secret; with them, mine honour, be not thou united. In Scripture, the world often stands for the ungodly; and the application of that term to them proves, alas! that the ungodly form the great mass of mankind. God's enemies are the majority; His people the minority; and in some places a very small minority. Hence they are called a *peculiar* people—a description altogether inappropriate, were the mass of society holy and leavened with divine principles; for in that case it would be the bad, not the good who were peculiar—distinguished from the multitude, like the man at the marriage feast who wore no wedding garment. An important, this is a serious and alarming consideration. It makes it all the more difficult to keep ourselves unspotted by prevailing ungodliness; just as it is more difficult to make way in the streets against a rush and press and crowd of people, than against a few individuals advancing in a direction opposite to our own. Here number is power; mass is power; as in the ball that goes crashing through walls of oak, or grinds granite stones to powder, and owes as much to its mass as to its momentum—to its weight as to its velocity.

Alarmed at this, and deeming it impossible, if exposed to it, to stem the flood of evil, and maintain a successful resistance against such odds and power of numbers, some have fled from the world.

There are good Christians now-a-days who shut themselves up as they would in a town where the plague was raging; retreating before danger, they keep aloof from society—mingling little, or not at all with the world. Under the same fears, though allowing themselves to be carried to greater lengths, men in old times withdrew to the solitude of deserts, rocks, and forests; and became hermits. Content with a bed of dry leaves for their couch, a bare cave for their home, wild fruits for their food, the crystal spring for their simple drink, they renounced the society of man for that of the more innocent beasts, that they might escape the contaminations of an evil world. It were unjust not to admire the self-denying, brave devotion of these old anchorites; yet they mistook the path of duty. While all, and especially young Christians—the raw recruits as they may be called—should carefully avoid the dangers of temptation, still, I ask, If the leaven is withdrawn from the lump, how is the meal to be leavened? If the candle is removed, how is the house to be lighted? If Christian men and women are to retire from the world,—pity the world! how is it ever to be converted? It is well to retire at times, by prayer, and meditation, and communion with God, to get our wounds healed and our strength renewed for the warfare and the work. But though our Lord, for example, did occasionally withdraw Himself to lone shores, and desert places, and mountain-tops, His common walk was among the haunts of men. Now He is at a merry marriage feast, and now in the silent house of mourning—here He dines with a pharisee, there He accepts the hospitalities of a publican—His footprints are on the sands of busy shores and the dusty streets of Bethsaida, Capernaum, and Jerusalem. He went about continually doing good.

Followers of Jesus! seek others' good as well as your own. We are to leaven the world, not to leave it; not to run away, but to stay. "The field is the world," said our Lord; our ploughshare is to gleam in its furrows, and with flashing sickles we are to go in and reap it. Though He sent them out as sheep among wolves, to be hunted, and torn, and murdered, Jesus said to His disciples, as to us also, Go ye into all the world, and preach the gospel to every creature. The part of a brave sailor is not to take to the boat, pull ashore, and leave the shrieking or sleeping passengers to perish; but to stick by the ship so long as there is a hope of saving her. And the part of a Christian is not to desert his post in the world, but to stay by it—to keep the ship afloat, the world from perishing. They fall well, and are saved who fall at the post of duty. He who gave Paul the lives of all on board, has given Christ the souls of all His people; and though the world should go down like a foundering ship, they perish not with it—sinking, it does not, whirlpool-like, suck them down into destruction. Those that Thou hast given me, says Jesus, I have kept—they shall never perish—no man shall pluck them out of my Father's hand.

Look at these two illustrations of the difference between *leaving the world*, and *remaining to leaven it*.

In a beautiful town of Switzerland, there is a large convent belonging to an order of Dominican nuns. Ill-guided, but, let us hope in charity, seeking the religion that, pure and undefiled, keeps itself unspotted, these timid women have fled from the world to devote themselves to what is called a religious life, and become candidates for the highest honours of their Church. Who visits the scene, and—having read of such convents as Le Vive Sepolte by the Tarpeian rock, where the living interred occupy themselves by incessant mortification, fast continually, never read, direct their constant meditation to death and corruption, never change their dresses, and their under garments only twice in the year, never see their connexions, nor yet hear their voices, nor even know anything about them, are not permitted to see the sacrament, but have it administered to them through a hole in the wall, through which, also, they make their confession and receive absolution—has associated such a life with severe austerities will be agreeably disappointed. Beautiful order, neatness, and a fine feminine taste, reign within the convent walls. The attire of the inmates, who occupy themselves to such an extent with works of charity as to ward off *ennui*, is no doubt odd and funereal-like, and not calculated to gratify female vanity. Still, their appearance betokens no rigid fasts, or painful mortifications. The apartments are small, but most tastefully adorned. The walls are hung with needlework and pictures; every couch is white as the snows of the neighbouring Alps; and at our visit, the summer breeze, as it whispered among the leaves of the vines, and stole in at the open window, filled the room with a sweet scent of beautiful flowers that grew on the window-sill. It was a sunny scene, where one could dream away life, remote from the battles and turmoil of the world, but remote also from its duties; and I could not but look on these fair devotees as deserters who, selfishly consulting their own safety, and distrusting the grace of God, had abandoned the post of duty. They were not keeping themselves unspotted from the world, but had fled from it.

Not in that, but in this other scene we meet the pure and undefiled religion which, while in the world, keeps itself unspotted. Go with me on a winter's night into one of the worst quarters of London. Threading streets that here blaze with the gas and glare of lowest drinking shops, and now dark and dismal, are the walk of prostitutes, and the haunts of robbers, we reach a large, dingy building. Ascending by a trap-stair to a spacious loft, we find ourselves in the strangest scene of human woe and wickedness you could look on. It is a Night Refuge for houseless women—for the friendless, those who, thrown out like faded flowers to be trodden on in the streets, had sunk into dark depths of loathsomeness and degradation. The hour is late, and though a few lingered by the stove, the most, glad to stretch their weary limbs, had lain down on the pallets that, spread on the floor, were ranged along the bare walls. Every head was raised, and all eyes turned on us as we entered. And what looks they had! Here vice stared with her unblushing front. Some had the look of fiends; treachery, brutal cruelty, falsehood, wrongs, and neglect, having turned whatever kindliness had once been in the heart into gall and wormwood; and now hatred both of God and man shot forth in their scowling looks. Others wore an expression of most touching sadness: one reclined with her back to the naked wall, gasping for breath, and dying of a raking cough; while another sat upright in a corner, a living form of death. The tide of night had floated in this *wrack* for the sake of a meal, a fire, the humblest of couches, and a roof to cover heads that otherwise had lain on the cold flags, or been pillowed on a doorstep.

In the centre of this scene, just risen from her knees, beside a table where the Bible still lay open, from whose pages, accompanied by prayer, she had been reading words of hope and peace to these wretched outcasts, stood a woman—I might say an angel. Leaving father, mother, brother, sister, pure associations, and a sweet home, to breathe this foul atmosphere, and take those forlorn creatures to her arms, she had become mother, nurse, physician, comforter, saviour, guardian of those from whom all others shrunk as the filth and offscourings of the earth. When Carey and his associates contemplated a mission to the heathen, he, on condition that they would raise the means at home, volunteered to go abroad, boldly saying, "If you will hold the rope, I will go down into the pit." Never had we seen this graphic speech so nobly illustrated. I stood rebuked in the presence of this noble woman. Pure, virtuous, and delicate, what a sacrifice had she made for Christ and perishing souls! It was one for angels to sing, and for Christ himself to reward with, Sister of mine, well done. More than any sight I ever saw, it reminded me of Him who left His Father's bosom, and the honours paid by angels, to become the associate, and be called the Friend of sinners, to save us by His blood, and teach us by His example how to labour for the world's good, and keep ourselves unspotted from its evil.

RICHES.

> "*My brethren, have not the faith of our Lord Jesus Christ, the Lord of glory, with respect of persons. For if there come unto your assembly a man with a gold ring, in goodly apparel, and there come in also a poor man in vile raiment: and ye have respect to him that weareth the gay clothing, and say unto him, Sit thou here in a good place; and say to the poor, Stand thou there, or sit here under my footstool: are ye not then partial in yourselves, and are become judges of evil thoughts? Hearken, my beloved brethren, Hath not God chosen the poor of this world rich in faith, and heirs of the kingdom which he hath promised to them that love him?*"—ST JAMES ii. 1-5.

THE same cause produces different effects under different circumstances. Look, for example, at volcanic action. As the higher we rise in the air, though we approach the sun, it grows the colder; the deeper we descend into the bowels of the earth it grows the hotter, by something like a degree for each hundred feet; every fathom down being, in fact, six feet nearer the fire —nearer to that immense, central mass of burning matter, around which this green earth, where we build our houses and reap our harvests, lies like the shell of an egg around its contents; and which, once it burst out, will remove the doubts of sceptics, and supply fire enough for the flames of the last day. To this imprisoned power, struggling to escape, we probably owe the earthquakes that make the frame of nature tremble, as well as those volcanic phenomena, which, though all arising from the same cause, present so many different appearances: as in Iceland, where, preceded by a noise like thunder rolling underground, a vast column of hot water is suddenly projected to a great height into the air, amid discharges like artillery and clouds of snowy vapour; or as in one of the beautiful islands of the Pacific, where the mud of the soil is constantly boiling over the thin crust that there separates the surface of the ground from the fires below; or, as in the lofty ranges of the Andes, where flames and smoke are ever rising from what have been called the chimneys of the world — the tops of mountains that are wrapped in a mantle of perpetual snow.

As it is with such physical forces, so it is with the passions that rage and burn in human breasts; their expression varies with circumstances. It is affected by the period and condition of life. It is modified by the influence of the gospel and of civilisation, by the customs and the laws of different countries — human passions no more than the earth's fiery contents exploding everywhere alike. The detracting word dropped of one who has injured you, the abuse bandied between two scolding women, the curse one rough and angry man hurls at another's head, the sudden blow dealt by a boy in the playground on the cheek of his companion, are ebullitions of the same passion that used to place two men on the dewy ground, amid some peaceful, rural scene, to aim their bullets at each other's hearts; and which still, in the south of Europe, steals with noiseless foot and coward steps on an unsuspecting enemy to plant the poignard in his bosom, and wipe the bloody steel with a grim smile of satisfied revenge.

Like revenge, the love of money, the thirst for gold, the inordinate desire for wealth, against which God's Word raises some of its most awful warnings, presents itself under a variety of aspects. Proteus-like, it assumes sometimes one form, sometimes another; but in whatever form it appears a base, soul-destroying passion, it is accursed of God; insidious as it is fatal; one on which our Lord pronounces this decisive sentence, "Ye cannot serve God and Mammon." In such a country as ours, which owes its greatness to its commerce, whose ships plough the waters of every sea, whose manufactures clothe the natives of every land, where millions rise every morning to the sound of the factory-bell, and trade is carried on to an extent, and with an energy unexampled in the history of the world, we especially need to guard against the worship of money, the inordinate desire for its possession, giving to mere wealth the honour that belongs to moral worth. For this end, let us look at the way in which an undue regard to wealth appeared, according to the apostle St James, among the first Christians.

The church is met for worship; or rather perhaps to sit in judgment on a dispute between two contending parties, who, according to the directions of the apostles, have referred their difference to the decision of the church rather than of heathen judges. The court is constituted; the case is called; the clients enter. One is sumptuously attired; good living in his shining face, and wealth upon his back; the gold ring that glitters on his white, soft hand bespeaking his condition; he advances with pomp and dignity. But what is this other object that the same door admits?—a moving heap of rags. Hunger in his haggard cheek, sorrow in his sunken eye, his whole mien and bearing betraying a crushed and broken spirit; it is a poor man in vile raiment, with a starving wife and children perhaps at home. The law of God, in directing judges how to act in such circumstances, utters no uncertain sound. Its noble words are, "Ye shall not respect persons in judgment: ye shall hear the small as well as the great; ye shall not be afraid of the face of man." That in one place; this in another: "Ye shall do no unrighteousness in judgment; thou shalt not respect the person of the poor, nor honour the person of the mighty; in righteousness shalt thou judge thy neighbour." Thus spake God; and in the case put by St James, a right-minded judge would lean to neither side, but with steady hand hold the balance even—neither allowing pity for the poor man on the one hand, nor respect for wealth on the other; to sway his decision, to turn the scales. These noble and divine instructions, which contrast so strikingly with the old practice of Scotland, where it used to be said, "Show me the man, and I will tell you the law," and deserve to be written in bright letters of gold on the walls of every court, were admirably embodied in the figure which the old Egyptians gave to justice. She was symbolised by a human form without hands—to indicate that judges should accept no bribe; and not without hands only, but sightless—to indicate that the judge is to know neither father nor mother, nor wife nor child, nor brother nor sister, nor slave nor sovereign, nor friend nor foe, when he occupies the seat of justice. He is not to see the client, but only to hear the cause; and, uninfluenced either by fear or favour, to decide that upon its merits.

But in the assembly of which St James gives us a picture, the hideous form of Mammon sits enthroned above Christ and the law of God. Indicating their bias, and inflating the pride of wealth, neither, on the one hand, teaching the proud man that his lofty airs go for nothing there, and that their eyes are not to be dazzled by the flash of his ring; nor, on the other hand, telling the poor client to hold up his head like a man, and be assured that his vile raiment will not tempt them by an unjust judgment to defile the purity of their ermine, they invite the first to a place of honour, and say to the other, Stand back! stand there! or if you will sit, sit on the floor under my feet!—feet, some one might whisper, that shall trample on you because you happen not to be rich, but poor. Betraying by this conduct an undue regard to wealth, let them be beacons to warn us off a shore where many have made sad and unlooked-for shipwreck. Christ was poor;

and let us not forget that poverty is the lot of many of the excellent ones of the earth; that if it comes not through our vices, it is the cup our Father has mingled for us; and that many of those on whom wealth looks down in haughty contempt, God has chosen to be rich in faith, and heirs of the kingdom which He hath promised to them that love Him.

Years ago, a trial took place in the highest judicial court of our country, which shook this kingdom to its centre, and drew on it the eyes of the world. A queen was on her trial. On that occasion, a great man, with the passions and power of the Crown arrayed against him, stood up boldly in her defence; and, confronting royalty as a rock confronts the surging sea, flung back the threats with which they attempted to deter him from his duty, saying, with defiant air and attitude, "An advocate is to know no person on earth but his client." But a judge is not even to know the clients. He is to know nothing but the cause. It appears, however, that such judges did not preside in the court that incurred the censure of St James:—" My brethren," he says, " have not the faith of our Lord Jesus Christ, the Lord of glory, with respect of persons. For if there come unto your assembly a man with a gold ring, in goodly apparel, and there come in also a poor man in vile raiment; and ye have respect to him that weareth the gay clothing, and say unto him, Sit thou here in a good place; and say to the poor, Stand thou there, or sit here under my footstool; are ye not then partial in yourselves?" In these words the apostle charges them with having respect of persons. Nor was it, strictly speaking, respect for persons these first Christians showed; it was something worse, meaner, baser still — it was respect merely for dress, attire, gay clothing, a gold ring. It was not moral worth that procured one of them a distinction which was denied to the other—it was but the wealth of which the raiment and the ring were tokens.

Here, then, in the very house of God, these Christians bowed the knee to Mammon; and, like the spaniel that licks the hand that beats it, they crouched to the power that smote, persecuted, and oppressed them. How mean that was! To what baseness will the love of money make men stoop!

The scene fires the apostle's just indignation. It bursts out in these exclamations :— " Ye have despised the poor ! Do not rich men oppress you ? Do not they blaspheme that worthy name by which ye are called ?" This injustice, viler than the poor man's raiment — this cringing, crouching, creeping baseness, shows how the love of money, the inordinate regard for wealth, demeans men, demoralises them ; and what need we, in this busy, trading, commercial country, have to guard against a passion that has enslaved the sovereign on the throne ; corrupted the judge on the bench ; seduced the priest at the altar ; and which, almost more than any other passion, is so incompatible with piety, that the apostle St John says, " If any man love the world, the love of the Father is not in him."

This passion appears among us *in the inordinate desire after riches.*

What a scene of bustle, and hurry, and trouble, and toil we live in ! It is not for bread to eat, and raiment to put on—nature's wants are few and simple. It does not accord with the unambitious prayer of our Divine Teacher, Give us day by day our daily bread. As on the turf, where, abreast each other, with foaming bits, and panting sides, and distended nostrils, high-mettled horses strive which shall first reach the winning-post, so is that race for riches in which we see the law of God, the cross of Christ, the interests of the soul, the wellbeing of the body as well as of the soul, trampled under foot by the eager competitors. Were the crown of heaven, all sparkling with the gems of redemption, hung aloft on the goal, and were there but one crown to a crowd of candidates, people could not be more earnest, eager, bent upon their object. How they run, and sweat and toil, to the whip and spur of this master-passion!—not seldom meeting the fate of the poor race-horse, that, distancing his fellows, and reaching by wide and rapid strides the goal, drops dead in the moment of triumph. How many embitter, and how many shorten their life in pursuit of a wealth they live not to enjoy—leaving people, as they carry the rich man with parade and costly pomp to his grave, to moralise on his folly, and exclaim, Vanity, vanity, all is vanity!

This desire, which is so apt to grow into an incontrollable passion, has no warrant in Scripture. The Scriptures teach us to pray, and pray earnestly, to be saved, good, wise, holy, kind, lovers of God and man; but nowhere to be rich—and a man should never try to be what he cannot pray to be. Indeed, we are taught to pray, not for, but against riches. And so men pray; but how often, like one who rows a boat, do they look one way and pull another? It is not uncommon for people to say that ministers should not be rich; and some take good care, as far as they are concerned, that they shall not—muzzling the ox that treadeth out the corn. When pleading the cause of my poorer brethren, not seeking riches for them, but only a competency, and that those that serve at the altar should live by the altar, the response I met from one who "fared sumptuously every day," was—Oh, ministers should not be rich; it is not good for them. But was Agur's prayer intended only for the lips of ministers? On the contrary, I believe that riches were less dangerous in their hands than in those of most other men. Brought more than others in contact with the poor and needy, they would be more likely to make a generous, and hedged round by the sacredness of their office, they would be less likely than many to make a vicious use of their wealth. At any rate, other men have as much need as the ministers of religion to pray with Agur, "Give me neither poverty nor riches."

But some say, the tide of fortune flows in on us—the money comes unprayed for, and unsought. If so, if it flows in on you, then let it flow out from you in as full a stream. Be like yonder lake, that, refusing to be surcharged with water when thunders are pealing and lightnings are flashing among the dark hills, and a thousand foaming torrents leaping down their sides, pour a flood into its bosom, ere long pours forth a corresponding flood at its exit; and, giving to the earth as it gets from heaven, swells the river, that, rising on its banks and rushing from the glen, winds its bright and blessed way onward to the sea.

The desire for riches, while unscriptural, is, in many instances, in the highest degree irrational. Hoarding is a strange insanity. I discover divine wisdom in the hoarding habits of some animals; in the honey the bee stores up in waxen cells, and in the wealth of nuts the brisk and merry squirrel packs up in the hollow tree. Their supply of food is uncertain; and, with more than suffices for present wants, God teaches them through their instincts not to waste the bounties of nature, but lay them up for a time of need. And though it seems foolish in the dog who has a kind master, and gets his regular meals, yet it rather amuses us than otherwise to see him, under the influence of instincts which domestication has dulled rather than destroyed, steal away into the garden, and, cautiously looking round to see that he is unnoticed, scrape up the soil with his paws to bury a bone for future use. This hoarding is the natural habit of the animal—the true instinct of his wild life—of value to the dog. But for a man with ample means, possessing already more than he can require or use, to hoard up wealth—clothes when the poor are naked, food when the poor are hungry, money when others have not wherewithal to buy a meal, and children, to use the touching words of Scripture, are crying for bread, and their mothers have none to give them, is, to say nothing of its inhumanity, a species of madness. *Cui bono?* What is gained by it? Nothing. Nothing can properly be called a man's own but what he can use. There is no profit of it under the sun. God has no respect for persons; in His eyes wealth is not worth; and you may know how little God thinks of money by observing on what bad and contemptible characters He often bestows it. Forfeiting man's respect as well as His, the greedy, griping, grasping lose the shadow as well as the substance; despised by the great and detested by the humble, they live unloved, and die unmourned. Yet to that miserable end the craving for wealth brings us, unless we are kept by the grace of God. There is a witchery about money-making, as well as gambling, against which those who make it honestly, and use it well, and save only what is wise and prudent, cannot be too much on their guard. He who is saving money should look well to the saving of his soul. He is mounted on a steed which has often run away with its rider. He is sailing on the rim of a whirlpool which is apt to draw him in; and where, though the water seems smooth as oil, and placid as a lake, he may detect this fatal tendency—ay, and catch the distant roar of its devouring vortex. He is working at a machine which, without constant care, will draw in his finger; and after that his hand; and then his arm; till by and by spectators stand aghast to see his body whirled round, a bloody, mangled, lifeless mass. Make wise and prudent provision for the future; yet let it be your daily and most earnest prayer that God would keep you from forgetting the great future of eternity, or allowing carefulness for this world to grow into carelessness of the next—into that love of money which is the ruin of so many souls, and which the word of God declares to be the " root of all evil."

This undue regard for wealth may be seen *in the conduct of parents.*

The foremost thing with them should be the spiritual and eternal interests of their children—otherwise the authors shall prove the curse of their being. Carry them in the arms of prayer to Christ. Seek not that they may be great, but good. Care not though their names are not in the temple of fame, if they are found in the Book of Life. Teach them to strive not so much for the honours of the school, or of their profession, as for the "honours that come from God only." Train the branches upward; guide their aspirations heavenward; point them to the skies. Let their ambition rise above an easy or prosperous life, to a useful one. Teach them to spurn the maxims of the world, and live for others—loving and loved. What though they have a humble home on earth if they have a mansion above the stars; though they are poor in this world's goods if they are rich in faith; though their road below be rough and flinty, if it conduct them to the cross of Calvary, and by that to the gate of heaven and the bosom of God.

Yet, alas! how often are children sacrificed to wealth? Crimes that were done at the altars of Moloch are repeated at the shrines of Mammon. To come down from generalities to matters of actual and every-day life, see in these, among many other things, the undue regard paid to wealth, and the gross neglect of higher interests.

Parents eagerly seek *rich marriages for their daughters.*

Wealth is weighed against worth; and in the estimation of many outweighs it. The happiness of children is cruelly sacrificed, or never consulted in these wretched money-matches. The only plain rule which Scripture lays down in regard to marriage is trodden in the dust. Not forbidding the bans where there are differences of rank, or fortune, or race, or colour; the apostle says, " Be not unequally yoked together with unbelievers." Yet see the court paid to a man who has neither brains in his head, nor generosity in his heart, nor piety in his soul, but only money in his purse— the money, not the man, the true attraction. With hand and heart cruelly divorced, many a poor girl is sacrificed at the marriage altar. She wears chains of slavery in the gold she wears! Not less than yon dark negress who, rudely handled, stands blushing, or with swimming eyes fixed on her lover, weeps on the auction-block, this fair creature is sold for gold; not by a master but by her parents; not by heathens but by Christians; and in a land, too, where the soil boasts such liberty, that the bondsman who touches it is free. Forced, perhaps, to part with the true gem of a kind, true, attached, and loving heart for these dead things, the diamonds that, flashing on her attire, blind others' eyes to the desolation within her soul, are the marks of her bondage. Compared with parents that sacrifice their children for money, a title, rank, estates, how noble the Hebrew chief! Jephthah sacrificed his daughter, but not for gold. He offered her up on the sacred altar of his country. Patriotism dictated, and piety demanded the sacrifice; he said, I have opened my mouth unto the Lord, and I cannot go back. Still, though animated by the purest motives, and sustained by the highest principles, it was in the bitterness of his heart, he stood over the gentle sufferer, meekly bending her head to the stroke, to cry, Alas, alas, my daughter! But the bitterness of that hour is not to be compared with the self-reproach and wretchedness of him who, sacrificing his child for money, has broken her heart; giving her to some ungodly man, has ruined her soul; and is left to cry in unavailing regrets, Alas, alas, my daughter!

The undue regard of wealth appears *in the lucrative positions parents seek for their sons.*

How and where, in what profession, business, town, country, their children will make most money, and find the surest, shortest road to fortune, is the only consideration with many—and the chief one with some whose Christian character might have warranted us to say, "We hope better things of you." In this matter how may we ask of many unquestionably devout and pious parents, What do ye more than others? How rare is it, for instance, to find Christians in affluent circumstances educating a son for the ministry; like Samuel's mother, dedicating a child to the service and house of God! Ever and anon the churches lift up a loud and urgent cry for more volunteers to storm the breaches God's providence is making in the walls of Heathendom, for more missionaries to carry the cross to pagan lands, for more candidates to supply the lack of service at home; and all this, while other professions are overstocked, and Christian parents are sending off their sons by thousands every year to seek wealth beyond the wide seas, in inhospitable climes, and on heathen shores. Why is this so? It cannot be because the office of the ministry is not respectable. In influence and dignity, the pulpit yields to no place under the sun. Others hold their commission from the Sovereign, but the minister of the gospel holds his from the King of kings and Lord of lords; and fills an office of such dignity as in the eyes even of the world to impart a measure of respectability to its holder, though he may have no claim otherwise to respect. But it is not lucrative. There is the key to the mystery. It is usually a poor office; and pity 'tis 'tis poor! and thus, though Christ was poor, and made Himself poor to make us rich, those for whom He gave His blood, refuse Him their sons. Let Christians blush to read the story of the rude clansman who, after seeing six stalwart sons fall defending his chief, called for his seventh and last boy, his Benjamin, to fight and die with him in the noble but hopeless struggle.

In the profession of the ministry, it is true men may save souls; but in others, they will save money. In this they may win jewels for Christ's crown, but in these they may hope to array wife and daughters in the glittering pride of jewellery. In training a son for this office, they will place him in circumstances the most favourable to virtue and piety; still, though removed far from a father's care, and a mother's prayers, and the means of grace, in secular occupations, in lands where he hears no Sabbath-bells, or amid the temptations of great cities, where no one cares for his soul, he may make a fortune—and so money carries it over the highest and holiest considerations. The youth is launched forth on the world. The helm is in the grasp of a feeble hand. The storm of temptation comes. His father's parting prayer, his mother's last tender look, and the holy recollections of home, still fresh in his mind, he makes an effort to hold on in his virtuous career; but by and by he gives up the unequal struggle, and with "youth at the prow and pleasure at the helm," drives on to ruin—becomes a total wreck. What a fate for a parent to weep! What a sorrow for his life! As he recalls the image of the boy whom he sacrificed to the love of gold, how will remorse wring from his heart more than the bitterness of David's cry, O my son Absalom! my son, my son Absalom! would God I had died for thee, O Absalom, my son, my son!

The undue regard to wealth appears *in the desire of parents to bequeath riches to their children.*

If parents, without any respect to the spiritual, looked only to the temporal interests of their children, they would not be so anxious to leave them wealth. Few greater misfortunes could befall a youth than to be left a fortune. How would that event increase his danger; and, filling a father's heart with new fears, cast a dark shadow over the hopes he had begun to cherish of his son! The world presents temptations enough to youth without that. It needs a steady foot and a cool head to stand on the edge of a dizzy cliff; a steadier hand than most young men possess to carry a full cup. With few, or almost no exceptions, they have a roaring sea of temptations to swim through; and to how many has their wealth proved a bag of gold, which a foolish parent's hand has tied round the neck of the unhappy youth? We have watched their course, and seen their heads, after a brief struggle, go down beneath the wave; while those who had nothing but their own exertions and God's blessing to depend on, finding in that emptiness a life-buoy, have struck out manfully for the land, and stood alive on the shore of a sea thickly strewn with the drowned bodies of others, to thank God that they had had a hard battle to fight, and the yoke to bear in their youth. Look around and see who those are that stand on the heights of their profession, or business! With few exceptions, they are those whom riches did not tempt to be idle; who wrought under the spur of a sharp necessity; whose purses were lighter than their hearts; who, receiving little else from a father but a good education and an honourable name, had no portion of goods to spend "on harlots and riotous living"—hand over hand, by their own manful exertions, they have climbed to the positions of honour, affluence, or usefulness they fill.

Now, look on the other hand to the common—not universal, but common fate of those for whom anxious parents have laid up stores of wealth! In how many instances has it proved their ruin; Well and truly does the Psalmist say, "He heapeth up riches and knoweth not who shall gather them." It is well he does not. He sleeps, but it might disturb him in his grave to see how recklessly squandered is all that he carefully gathered!

that the portions he left are spent with the prodigal's folly without being followed by the prodigal's repentance; and that no inscription so describes his life and befits his tombstone, as —Vanity, vanity, and vexation of spirit! He has enriched his children; and ruined them. He sowed the wind, and they reap the whirlwind; and may use in hell the words of one who, mourning the dissensions that a fortune they succeeded to had bred among her brothers and sisters, the deplorable wrecks which it had made of youths once full of promise, exclaimed, as she wrung her hands—Oh, that wretched money! that wretched money!

Let us not be misunderstood. It is the duty of parents to make a prudent provision for their children, and against the accidents of life. An apostle, speaking of him who provides not for those of his own house, says, that he "is worse than an infidel, and has denied the faith." That man certainly commits a crime against his children who rears them in the habits of affluent circumstances, and leaves them beggars at his death. Such conduct, however common, is inexcusable and cruel in the upper classes. And it is unwise and wrong in the humbler, not to make honey or hay when the sun shines; and stand prepared for days when the right hand has lost its cunning, and the brawny arm its strength, and the back that bore itself erect under the burden of life's daily toil, bends beneath the weight of years. Only let money be kept in its own place. Its place is in your hands, not in your affections. Lodge it in the bank; but not in your heart—keep that for God. Gold is a good servant; but a bad, base, exacting, cruel, despotic master. Be on your guard; if it is not your servant, you must be its slave. Well does the Bible pronounce the love of it to be "the root of all evil." It drew Lot into Sodom, from whose fiery ruin he escaped but by the skin of his teeth. Demas was an apostle, and it made him an apostate. It turned Judas into a traitor, and, loading his name with eternal infamy, sank his soul into eternal perdition. Money cannot be safely made, or safely saved, but by those who through grace receive and use it as a gift from God; who would not give one red drop of a Saviour's blood for all the gold of banks; who amid all other questions of profit and loss, are most impressed and most occupied with this,—What shall it profit a man though he gain the whole world, if he lose his own soul? What shall a man give in exchange for his soul?

THE LAW OF GOD.

> "*If ye fulfil the royal law according to the scripture, Thou shalt love thy neighbour as thyself, ye do well: but if ye have respect to persons, ye commit sin, and are convinced of the law as transgressors. For whosoever shall keep the whole law, and yet offend in one point, he is guilty of all. For he that said, Do not commit adultery, said also, Do not kill. Now if thou commit no adultery, yet if thou kill, thou art become a transgressor of the law. So speak ye, and so do, as they that shall be judged by the law of liberty. For he shall have judgment without mercy, that hath showed no mercy; and mercy rejoiceth against judgment.*"—St James ii. 8-13.

GOD always uses such means as are best suited to the work He has on hand—carpenters, architects, mechanics, in employing various kinds of tools, but copy the great Maker and Monarch of all. Long ages ago—ten thousand, perhaps ten hundred thousand years ago, when God was preparing this world for the abode of man, working on rough materials, He employed agents of tremendous power. What fires they were that fused the solid rocks; how they roared and flamed, when—as science teaches and the Bible tells—"the hills melted like wax at the presence of the Lord!" We talk of stormy seas and mountain billows that toss our stoutest ships like feathers on the wave, and round the rattling shingle as it is swept up and down the foaming beach; but what waves were those that, surging up the valleys, broke on the tops of our highest hills, and flinging their spray in the face of heaven, left the plains covered with immense beds of gravel, and our glens with those granite boulders, whose rounded forms speak of long ages during which they had been rolled about on the shores of tremendous seas! Who reads the pages of the book of Nature cannot doubt that, like man, our earth had been born naked—not clothed as now with soil and verdure. And what forces of ice, of iceberg, of glacier, were they that ground the surface of the rocks to dust, which, borne off by rivers, was spread out on the bottom of the ocean to form the forest lands and corn fields of future continents! And when in the course of time these were ready to be raised, how tremendous the power that heaved up, for example, the Alps, the Andes, this island, from the bed of the sea, and gave the rocks around which fish once swam and sea monsters sported, to be the home of the eagle—for clouds to girdle and snows to crown!

These forces have disappeared. They have done their work. And now God in Nature works by other and gentler agencies—soft falling dews, summer showers, the silent light, the feathery snow, the golden clouds, the ebb and flow of tides, and seas that—turned by sails and steam into the high road of distant nations—man ploughs as safely almost as he ploughs the land—"He is wonderful in counsel and excellent in working!"

In His spiritual kingdom, in the dispensation of grace, as well as in the department of Nature, we find God also selecting instruments suited to the work He has in hand—using rough or gentle means according to the subject he has to work upon. And in turning our attention to the law of God, I may remark that this accounts for the circumstances in which the moral law was delivered to the children of Israel at Mount Sinai.

These circumstances were of a kind to rouse the attention of the most stupid, and strike terror into the stoutest hearts. Two days of preparation have passed, since Jehovah announced His intention of descending on the mount; and many an eye is turned on Sinai, that, with its gray head lifted calm and peaceful against the evening sky, wears no sign of the approaching event. If any asked, Where is the promise of His coming? the third morning sealed the lips of cavillers and set all doubts at rest. A burst of thunder that shook the earth and heavens roused the sleeping camp; and brought old and young to their tent doors to gaze with pale faces on Sinai. Wrapt to its feet in a sable mantle, it stands up a mass of solid blackness. Lightnings played around it: pierced it: and streaming from it, mingled many peals into one long, continuous, stunning roar of thunder. The mountain, as if kindled by these fires, vomited forth a smoke that, spreading a lurid cloud over the sky, darkened the face of day; and the earth, as if infected with the terror of the people, began to tremble beneath their feet. The thunders cease —but to give place to sounds still more awful. Out from that terrible darkness, loud and long, louder and still louder, till it rung like the summons that shall wake the dead, pealed the notes of a heavenly trumpet. Next, as I read the story, the trumpet ceases; and the people who, struck with a panic, had fled from the borders of the mountain, and were standing afar off, heard a voice. It issued from the dark bosom of the cloud; and audible not to hundreds, nor thousands, nor tens of thousands, but to the millions of that mighty multitude, it rang out loud and clear those ten commandments which, forming the moral law, expressed the will of God, and should ever prove the rule of man. Overwhelmed, half dead with terror, ready to exclaim with Jacob, How terrible is this place! the people ran to Moses, crying, Speak thou with us, and we will hear; but let not God speak with us, lest we die.

Such were the circumstances in which the ten commandments were first spoken to man; and looking only at circumstances—in which that law appears clothed and crowned with terrors, without reflecting on the reasons for them, or considering the peculiar nature of the case, we allow ourselves to associate the law of God with His terrors, and only the Son of God with His love—as if God in the law, and God in redemption appeared in different characters. Ask a man where the love of God is to be seen, he would never dream of pointing to the table of the ten commandments. He turns his back on Sinai, and his face to Calvary, saying, There, on that bloody tree, in its blessed burden, behold the love of God! This is a mistake; a very great mistake; a pestilent heresy. No doubt it is hardly possible to imagine a greater contrast than the scenes of Sinai, and those in which the Saviour of the world was born: —shepherds watching their flocks on the quiet uplands of Bethlehem; the calm night with its sparkling stars and soft falling dews; the world around

—the babe on its mother's breast, and children locked in each other's arms, all hushed in slumber; the deep silence broken by no sound save the baying of a watch-dog, the tinkling of mountain streams, or the distant murmur of a waterfall; a beautiful light far up in the deep blue sky, descending, brightening till the stars are quenched in its glory; then a gentle voice, sounding down from above to banish the alarm of these simple shepherds, and saying, Fear not, behold, I bring you good tidings of great joy—then the whole sky suddenly bursting into light, and songs of sweetest voices singing, as they sing before the throne, Glory to God in the highest, and on earth peace, good-will toward men.

Still, in delivering the moral law amid circumstances so different from these, the God of love was only using such means as the work required. True, they were circumstances of terror; but they were needed. Slavery had been for centuries the cruel lot of the children of Israel; and that— which John Wesley rightly called "the sum of all villanies"—had sunk the Hebrews, as it does every race it curses, into the lowest depths of ignorance, stupidity, brutality, mental and moral debasement. Their history is crowded with proofs of that; they were a stiffnecked people, ever longing to return to Egypt—preferring its onions with bondage, to liberty with the bread of heaven.

In dealing with such a people God had the rudest materials to work upon. Rough work requires rough instruments: to use a figure whose appropriateness may excuse its familiarity, men don't cut blocks with razors. It is with an axe the woodman fells the forest. It is with the strongest stimulants — in a case we knew of, pouring boiling water on his naked thighs—that the physician rouses one sunk into deadly stupor. Snow melts before the soft breath of spring; but rocks are only split by the stroke of lightning or the blast of powder. Gold is beaten into shape without the aid of fire—not iron: more stubborn metal, it has to be thrust into the roaring forge.

A dull, gross, animal, apathetic congregation requires a rousing preacher—that he who occupies the pulpit be no Barnabas but a Boanerges, a son of thunder. Even so, God having in Israel to deal with a hard-hearted and obdurate people, adapted His instruments to the material He had to work upon: thundered out His law in their ears, and sought by these circumstances of terror to impress it on their hearts. These, however, being but the dress it wore, do not properly belong to the law; nor are they the true exponents of the mind of the Lawgiver. There is the same love in the law as in the gospel—the difference is only in expression, as when I warn one against venturing into the roaring flood, and when, on his leaping madly in, I follow to save him. In the law Love warns, in the Cross it redeems. Both are, as I undertake to show, the true mirror of Him who thus defines His own character, "God is love"—"Fury is not in me."

The *spring of the law is love.*

With its, Thou shalt not do this, and Thou shalt not do that, the law presents rather an ungracious aspect. We like ill to be bidden, but worse to be forbidden. But does Love never forbid? A mother, does she never forbid her child; but, on the contrary, indulge every caprice and grant all its wishes? How disastrous the fate and brief the life of a child denied nothing; indulged in everything—allowed to play with fire, or fire-arms; to devour the painted but poisonous fruit—to bathe where the tide runs like a racehorse, or the river rushes roaring into the black swirling pool. And who frets against the restraints of God's holy law because it forbids this and the other thing, is no wiser than the infant who weeps, and screams, and struggles, and perhaps beats the kind bosom that nurses it, because its mother has snatched a knife from its foolish hands.

No doubt the law restrains us; but all chains are not fetters, nor are all walls the gloomy precincts of a jail. It is a blessed chain by which the ship, now buried in the trough, and now rising on the top of the sea, rides at anchor and outlives the storm. The condemned would give worlds to break his chain, but the sailor trembles lest his should snap; and when the gray morning breaks on the wild lee-shore, all strewn with wrecks and corpses, he blesses God for the good iron that stood the strain. The pale captive eyes his high prison wall, to curse the man that built it, and envy the little bird that, perched upon its summit, sings merrily, and flies away on wings of freedom; but were you travelling some Alpine pass where the narrow road, cut out of the face of the rock, hung over a frightful gorge, it is with other eyes you would look on the wall that restrains your restive steed from backing into the gulf below. Such are the restraints God's law imposes—no other. It is a fence from evil—nothing else. I challenge the world to put its finger on any one of these ten commandments which is not meant, and calculated to keep us from harming ourselves, or hurting others. There is the same love in the law that there is in the gospel; and between them a harmony as perfect as the music of that heaven where the harps are gold, and the strings are touched by angels' fingers. The hand, indeed, that wrote these commandments is the same that was nailed to the cross; and amid Sinai's loudest thunders Faith recognises, though it speaks in other tones, the voice which prayed for mercy on murderers, and promised paradise to a dying thief.

The *spirit of the law is love.*

By her subtle arts chemistry extracts from the

crude and bulky substance its spirit, essence, essential element: offering us in a small phial of the costly attar the fragrance of a whole field of roses, and in a few drops drawn from the poppy juice, that potent element which dulls the sense of pain, and charms suffering to sleep. But no odour distilled from the blushing rose smells so sweet, no spirit drawn from the gaudy poppy soothes the smart of pain, as the spirit of love which Jesus finds in a law that so many regard with dread—fears groundless as those that saw in Himself a spectre of the deep, and which He laid, as His voice on another night did the waves, with It is I, be not afraid. With such reassuring, comforting words, God, as a God of love, comes to us in this dreaded Law. Jesus takes these ten commandments into His hands, analyses them, extracts their true essence and spirit—and what is it? It is love—love toward God, and love toward man. Whoever doubts it, let them listen to His answer, when a lawyer, tempting Him, came and said, Master, which is the great commandment? Jesus said unto him, "Thou shalt love the Lord thy God with all thy heart, and with all thy soul, and with all thy mind; this"—not, thou shalt have no other gods before me; nor, thou shalt not make unto thee any graven image; nor, thou shalt not take the name of the Lord thy God in vain; nor, thou shalt not kill, or steal, or commit adultery—"this is the first and great commandment; and the second is like unto it, Thou shalt love thy neighbour as thyself—and on these," He adds, "hang all the law and the prophets."

Take, for example, the second table of the law, those six commandments which respect our conduct not to God, but to our fellow-men. Do not these enjoin the very things which Love would prompt to; and teach us to carry into practice the golden rule, as it is called, that grandest maxim which ever fell on human ear, Do unto others as ye would have others do unto you? Who that loves his neighbour as he loves himself would steal from him, would kill him, seduce his wife, or swear away his fair name, his liberty, or life? Does not the loveliness and divine excellence of the law appear in this, that no man, however much he might wish to have liberty to break it for his own pleasure against others, would wish that any should have licence to break it against himself? What villain coolly laying, devil-like, his snares to seduce another's wife, sister, or daughter, would consent that others should have licence to seduce his own? Even thieves insist on honesty between each other. Traitors consign to death the man who turns traitor on themselves. Thus the worst of men pay homage to the law—it is sacrificed to their passions, but like the victims of old that were led to the altar crowned with garlands of flowers.

With their bad passions raging against it as the sea foams and rages against the shore that confines its waves within their bounds, men, like the fool who hath said in his heart, There is no God, have sometimes wished there were no law; and that every one was left, as in Israel when there was no king, to do what was right in his own eyes. No law! That wish were hardly granted when it would happen with them as with the man of heathen fable, who had sought and received from Jupiter the power of turning all he touched to gold. And when the bread he hungered for changed in his hand to gold, and the water he raised to his thirsty lips turned at their touch to gold, and the downy pillow on which he laid a weary head stiffened into a solid, unyielding, uneasy mass of gold, he besought the god to resume the grant, and relieve him of this fatal gift. Fancy what a world this would be, set loose from the restraints of God's holy law—no written, no inner law—no conscience—no ten commandments—the reins flung loose on the neck of passion—all men and women left to obey every impulse of appetite, and do what was right in their own eyes! What a Sodom, Gomorrah, hell! Remove these restraints, and iniquity in such deluge as would pour on a neighbouring land were its sea-dikes thrown down, would drown the earth and destroy men from off its face.

On one occasion the barons of England addressed their king, saying, We do not wish the laws of England changed; and we have only to fancy what a dreadful world this would become, without the restraining influence of these laws of God, to say, We do not wish one of them changed! Not prisons and police, not the baton of the constable or the bayonet of the soldier; but these are the bond of society; the shield of virtue; the protection of innocence; the strength of weakness; the guardian of public morals and domestic peace. And nothing but the base bad passions that spring from our corrupt nature, hinders any from saying with David, Oh how love I thy law, O Lord: it is my meditation all the day—teach me thy statutes—the law of thy mouth is better to me than thousands of gold and silver—therefore I love thy commandments above gold, yea, above fine gold: and esteem all thy precepts concerning all things to be right.

The *sacredness of this law.*

The apostle St James says, "Whosoever shall keep the whole law, and yet offend in one point, is guilty of all." This seems hard measure—to make a man offender for a word—to treat him for breaking one commandment as one that had broken all the ten. It looks at first sight as if the unprofitable servant who hid his master's talent in a napkin, had some reason for speaking of him as an "austere" man. How do we justify that? We might leave God to justify Himself. We might ask, Shall not the Judge of all the earth do right? And leaving this, with many other mysteries, to be solved at the last day, or in that world where, with eyes purified from the mists of sin, we shall see as we are seen, and know as we are known, we might answer with St Paul, "Who art thou, O man, that repliest against God? Shall the thing made say to him who made it, Why hast thou made me thus?" But the case is not without a parallel in our own judicial proceedings—and as done in our courts of law who thinks the practice wrong? A witness, for instance, sworn by Almighty God to tell the truth, the whole truth, and nothing but the truth, is giving evidence in a case where a man is on trial for his life. He states many, as lawyers say, *damning* facts, and makes out a case against the accused clear as daylight. What need of further witnesses? The jury lay down their pens, the judge throws himself back in his seat, and the spectators, turning to the poor, pale wretch at the bar, look on him as a dead man, feeling as sure that he will be hanged as that the sun shall rise to-morrow. And yet he is not hanged—the tables are turned in an instant; and like one in battle from whose head the sword has shorn his nodding plume, the man escapes—

escapes, as the Bible says, by the skin of his teeth. The witness whose evidence had brought him to the scaffold, and to the very brink of ruin, tells a lie; one clear, deliberate falsehood. It may be on a very small point; it does not matter. All his other evidence may be true as the gospel—it does not matter; that one lie nullifies all his other testimony—blotting it clean out—reducing it to nothing. Convicted of perjury on one point, his evidence is dealt with as if he had been guilty of perjury in all; and that for this good reason—that one capable of swearing to a single lie, is capable of swearing to twenty. Even so—though you may start at the bold assertion, and when you think of some gross and horrid sins may be ready to exclaim, Is thy servant a dog that he should do such a thing?—the man who is capable of breaking one of God's commandments, is capable of breaking them all; in mind and spirit, he that offendeth in one point is guilty of all.

There are degrees, no doubt, of guilt as there are degrees of glory; there is a descending as well as an ascending scale; there are higher places in heaven, and hotter places in hell. It shall be more tolerable for Sodom and Gomorrah in the day of judgment than for Jerusalem sinners: and more tolerable for Jerusalem sinners than for the sinners of our land and cities,—for us if we reject or even neglect the great salvation. Still there is no degree of guilt but is fatal; sin is a poison of which the smallest drop kills; the law is so sacred that one offence, one breach of any of its commandments, exposes us to the wrath of God as certainly as a thousand. The case finds its apt illustration in yonder arch which spans the waters that reflect its bending beautiful form—drive out not ten stones, but one, and the whole pile tumbles into a mass of ruins. Or to vary the figure, a woman's virtue is as certainly lost by one fall as by twenty; and he is as certainly a thief who steals a penny as he who steals a pound—who filches but a farthing from a ragged beggar, as he who plunders a bank of its gold, or robs a king of his crown. "He who offendeth in one point is guilty of all."

Tried in this balance, who is not wanting? Tried by this test, who can stand the ordeal? Well is it said, "If thou shouldst mark iniquity, O Lord, who shall stand?" You have not been great sinners! What of that?—he who offendeth in one point is guilty of all. I admit that there are unconverted people "lovely in their lives," in temper amiable, very likeable, kind-hearted, generous, just in their dealings, honest to a farthing, and in their friendships true as steel; such that, were Christ to walk this world now as He did eighteen hundred years ago, He would love them as He loved the young ruler who came, and, falling at His feet, cried, Master, what shall I do to inherit eternal life? Suppose you were such,—and that is not supposing little,—what of that? What man or woman can hold up their hands to say, These hands are clean; uncover their bosom, lay bare the secrets of their hearts, to say, My heart is pure—then, alas! he that offendeth in one point is guilty of all—One, but one sin! Ah! that is the dead fly in the apothecary's ointment; there stands the spot of leprosy on beauty's brow. There are none, not the loveliest of human characters, but have sinned; and he who offendeth in one point is guilty of all. This bolts the door of heaven against all self-righteous hopes. Looking down on others, shrinking from the society of the openly licentious, the ungodly or profane, and saying, as we push our way on, to this and that one, Stand aside, I am holier than thou, we may march bravely up to the gate. But to our plea, I have not been a great sinner, or I have not sinned like others, or I have been honest, and sober, and virtuous, correct in my deportment, and constant in my attendance on religious ordinances, there follows no drawing of bar and bolt—but only through the unopened door this stern reply, these words of doom, He that offendeth in one point is guilty of all.

Terrible, yet blessed words! Like the muttering of distant thunder, they warn us to haste to the refuge opened in the gospel. Like a friendly notice, they warn us in letters which he who runneth may read, No road to heaven this way. They shut us up to Christ. No misfortune that! In Him we have all fulness of mercy to pardon, and grace to help; and as men who, when they have done their utmost to stop the leak, and keep the ship afloat, find her settling down in the deep, in that terrible hour, with death staring them in the face, thank God for the life-boat that, pulled by strong hands, bears down on the sinking wreck, so we thank God for Christ; we hail the Saviour of the lost. He has hastened to our relief—He is at our side—He invites us to His arms—for in Him, though the law condemns, "mercy rejoiceth against judgment."

The gospel brings *salvation to the law-breaker.* Mercy does not rejoice against the justice of God. The claims of Justice were not ignored or repudiated; but satisfied. Jesus bore our punishment, dying, the Just for the unjust, that He might bring us to God;—and the gospel that saves does not present the sword of Justice broken, but, though red with blood, wreathed with roses. Nor does Mercy rejoice against the law of God, —Christ tells us that He came not to destroy the law and prophets, but to fulfil them;—and when the Son of God, leaving His Father's bosom, became a man to obey the precepts of the law, and pay the penalty due by us for breaking them, He crowned the law with higher honours than it had worn though Adam had never fallen, and Eden had ne'er been lost. It was great honour done to the law when God wrote it with His own finger on tables of stone; but it receives a higher honour when, dipping His finger in the blood of Christ, He writes it on the fleshly tablets of a living, loving heart. There have been great sermons preached and printed on the ten commandments, but the Cross is the greatest sermon that was ever preached on the law;—and as we have seen a lofty mountain best, not from the plain, but from the top of another, it is on the summit of Calvary that you command the grandest views of Sinai.

It is against not God's law or justice, but the devil and death, the grave and hell, that Mercy rejoiceth. Rejoiceth! grand, wonderful word, it lays open the very heart of God. Father of the prodigal, kind, loving, joyful man, running to meet thy trembling son, folding the poor wretch in thy fond embraces, lavishing tears and kisses on his haggard cheek, bestowing forgiveness before confession, and with answers anticipating prayer, thou wert but a dim, imperfect image of our Father which is in heaven. It is not only that God "has no pleasure in the death of the wicked." What father has? The more wicked the son, the calamity is the greater; the deeper goes the knife into a bleeding heart, as that greatest, blackest grief gushes forth in a cry like this, O my son Absalom! my son, my son Absalom; would God I had died for thee, O Absalom, my son, my son! Nor is it only that God is "not willing that any should perish." He is God and not man; and even we are not. I have seen the life-buoy spun out to a drowning man, and, amid the crowd on the pier that gazed in horror, there was none, as they watched its course over the roaring waves, but wished in his heart that it might reach its mark. Nor is it only that God is "willing that all should come to Him, and live." What mother but would open her door who heard the knocking, and recognised the well-known voice of some poor, fallen child, that had sunk down there amid the winter drift, and cried, with failing breath, O mother, mother dear, open and let me in. And who thinks so ill of God as to believe that when He hears such a cry at the door of mercy, He will not rise to let us and to welcome us in! More than all that, God *rejoiceth* to save, and receive back to His bosom the worst and unworthiest of His erring children—of those who, like lost sheep, have gone astray. Mercy rejoiceth against judgment. It is a blessed thing to fill a mother's heart with joy, and pour a tide of gladness into the bosom on which we hung— so deeply loved and tenderly cared for in helpless infancy. And be he poor or rich, prince or peasant, I honour the man who would do, dare, suffer anything to gild the evening of a father's life, and smooth the thorns of his dying pillow. It is a grand thing to make glad a parent's heart. But here we may do a thing grander still. Turn to the call of mercy, and you fill the great heart of God with joy, and angels' harps with praise. It may be that you do not love Jesus. Well, Jesus loves you; and pities you. You spit on Him, despise His love, repel His approaches? Well, His blessed hand arrests the gleaming axe, as He turns to His Father to say, "Father, forgive them; they know not what they do!"

Thus mercy rejoiceth against judgment. And let none stand back as if their sins were too great to be forgiven, or their case too bad to be cured. Jesus is an Advocate who never lost a cause—a Physician who never lost a patient—His blood cleanseth from all sin, and through Him the door of heaven stands open to publicans, harlots, the chief of sinners. Let all come! See there Mercy, sweet Mercy, wearing a form of celestial beauty, with a blood-bought pardon in this hand, and a sparkling crown in that, stands aloft on the summit of the Cross, ringing forth this old cry, "Sing, O daughter of Zion; be glad and rejoice, O daughter of Jerusalem.—The Lord hath taken away thy judgment; he hath cast out thine enemy.—Fear not, and let not thine hands be slack. The Lord thy God in the midst of thee is mighty; he will save."—Save? save is almost a cold and feeble word. More, much more than save; "as a bridegroom rejoiceth over his bride, so will thy God rejoice over thee."

FAITH AND WORKS.

"What doth it profit, my brethren, though a man say he hath faith, and have not works? can faith save him? If a brother or sister be naked, and destitute of daily food, and one of you say unto them, Depart in peace, be ye warmed and filled: notwithstanding ye give them not those things which are needful to the body; what doth it profit? Even so faith, if it hath not works, is dead, being alone. Yea, a man may say, Thou hast faith, and I have works: show me thy faith without thy works, and I will show thee my faith by my works. Thou believest that there is one God; thou doest well· the devils also believe, and tremble. But wilt thou know, O vain man, that faith without works is dead? Was not Abraham our father justified by works, when he had offered Isaac his son upon the altar? Seest thou how faith wrought with his works, and by works was faith made perfect?

FAITH AND WORKS.

> *And the scripture was fulfilled which saith, Abraham believed God, and it was imputed unto him for righteousness: and he was called the Friend of God. Ye see then how that by works a man is justified, and not by faith only. Likewise also was not Rahab the harlot justified by works, when she had received the messengers, and had sent them out another way? For as the body without the spirit is dead, so faith without works is dead also.*—St James ii. 14-26.

THERE is no analogy between mind and matter more remarkable than the reaction to which both are liable. Set free the pendulum which you have drawn to one side, and, obeying the law of gravitation, it returns to its centre; but in doing so, swings over to the other side. Or, twist a cord that has a weight attached to it; and set loose, whirling rapidly on its axis, it untwines itself; but does more, taking many a turn in the opposite direction. Or, follow the billow that, driven by the tempest and swelling as it advances, flings itself on the iron shore; it bursts, thundering, into snowy foam; but does more—like men from a desperate charge, it rolls back violently into the sea. Even so on a change of opinions and manners, how prone are men to pass from one to the opposite extreme, borne by the recoil beyond the line of truth—a danger this against which reformers, whether of states or churches, of public morals or private manners, need to be on their guard.

Thus we account for the extraordinary judgment that such a man as Martin Luther, that champion of the faith, pronounced on the book of St James. He denied its inspiration; and not content with robbing this book of divine authority, he scrupled not to speak of it in contemptuous terms—calling it a *chaffy* epistle. It is easy to account for his saying that, when he believed it. He was a man of dauntless courage. Remaining at Wirtemberg when all others had fled, he faced the plague, saying, It is my post; should brother Martin fail, yet the world will not fail. When Melanchthon, and every friend he had on earth, urged him not to go to Augsburg, to be given up to the machinations of the legate, They have already, he replied, torn my honour and my reputation, let them have my body if it is the will of God—my soul they shall not take. Entreated on his approach to Worms not to enter a town where his death was decided on, he pushed forwards, saying, Tell your master, that if there were as many devils at Worms as tiles on its roofs, I would enter. And there, before the world's great Emperor, face to face with a host of princely and priestly enemies, he stood a lion at bay, and to the reiterated question, Whether he would retract, with a sword suspended over him, and a grave yawning at his feet, replied, I will retract nothing; here I take my stand; I cannot do otherwise. So help me God. Amen. This was a man to speak whatever he believed!

Nor is it difficult to account for Luther's error. One day while climbing a stair at Rome on his knees, in hope of thus climbing to heaven, of meriting salvation through such pains and penances, the Spirit of God flashed this great truth into his mind, with the effulgence and force of lightning, "The just shall live by faith." He rose a new man; a second St Paul; his mission henceforth on earth, to preach life by faith—the glorious doctrine of justification by faith without works, through the blood and merits of Jesus Christ.

Well, look now at his position. There, hoar with age, strong in the personal interests of her priests and the profound prejudices of her people, resting on salvation by works, ceremonies, pay, and penance, stood the old walls of Rome; and on their ramparts the cowled Dominican, selling indulgences, and boasting—(I quote his very words)—"I would not exchange my privilege against those that St Peter has in heaven, for I have saved more souls by my indulgences than he by his sermons. Whatever crime one may have committed, let him pay well, and he will receive pardon." All that he said, and something about the Virgin more shocking—too shocking for your ears. This profanity, this daring blasphemy, and that whole Romish system which substitutes the crucifix for the Crucified, and for His merits man's wretched works of penance and pilgrimages, sackcloth for the skin, and fish on Friday, these produced on Luther's impulsive mind such a tremendous recoil, that in the rebound from error he passed the line of sober truth. Fancying something in the Epistle of St James to be at variance with the doctrine of justification by faith, as set forth in the writings of St Paul, he rejected it; rashly rejected it—scared by a phantom, the mere appearance of discrepancy. And doing so, he has furnished the Church of God with another illustration of the words, "Put not your trust in princes,"—nor in Luther, nor Calvin, nor in Cranmer, nor Knox—"nor in the son of man, in whom there is no help."

Between the sentiments of these two apostles there is no real discrepancy. Before St James had written his Epistle, the doctrine of justification by faith without works had been abused, and turned to the vilest purposes. "Wresting," to use St Peter's language, the words of St Paul from their true meaning, some made them a cover for the grossest sensuality, holding this immoral, horrible doctrine, that men could be saved by mere knowledge of the truth, mere intellectual assent to sound doctrines—miscalled faith, though they were impious in heart, and in practice impure. It was against this pestilent heresy, this poisonous weed, that, native to every soil, has sprung up in all ages, and against those who confessed Christ in words, but in works denied Him, that St James took pen in hand, saying, What doth it profit, my brethren, that a man say he hath faith and have not works? Can faith—this faith, such a faith—save him? Faith, if it hath not works, is dead, being alone.

We are *saved by faith in the merits of Jesus Christ.*

Can faith save? Certainly; if it be not that false and spurious thing which - St James pronounces dead; but true faith. Sooner than believe otherwise, even on the authority of an epistle attributed to St James, I would believe with Luther that the apostle's name was a forgery; and that the epistle which bore it, and was bound up with the Bible, had, like Satan among the sons of God, or bad money among the current coin, got into company better than its own.

And how are we saved by faith? Not by any merit in our faith, for that is the gift of God and the work of His Holy Spirit; and is, so to speak, but the rope which the drowning man clutches, and by which another pulls him living to the shore. God its author, the heart its seat, good works its fruit, Christ is its object; and it saves by bringing us to the Saviour. It weeps with the Magdalene at His feet; it prays with the thief, Lord remember me; with the blind it gropes for Christ, crying, Thou Son of David, have mercy on us! and with Simon, as he sank amid the roaring billows, seeing help in none else, it stretches out its arms to Jesus, with Lord save me, I perish! Greatest act of the soul, it lays my sins on Jesus, and so relieves my conscience of a load of guilt; and taking off my rags to put Christ's righteousness on me, it covers a poor sinner with a robe fairer than angels wear.

May any be thus saved; without works; without merit; guilty as he who said, I believe that I have committed every sin possible to man unless murder? Ay, and with murder to boot. It is the glory of Christ's blood that it cleanseth from all sin, and was poured out freely for the chief of sinners; so that if any man, troubled for his sins, in terror of divine wrath, afraid to die, afraid even to go to sleep lest he should awake in hell, is crying, Oh, sirs, what shall I do to be saved? I say with St Paul, when the jailer, at midnight, on his knees, was putting the same question, "Believe in the Lord Jesus Christ, and thou shalt be saved." I know no other way. There is none. There is no name given under heaven whereby we can be saved but the name of Jesus; and united to Him, though by the weakest, slenderest faith, you are safe.

Christ drew divine lessons from gay flowers and singing birds. And in the conservatory I have seen a plant from which such saints as Bunyan's Mr Feeble-mind might draw strength; gather something more fragrant than its odours, more beautiful than its purple flowers. Climbing the trellis, which it interwove with spreading verdure and flowery beauty, it sprang from the soil by a mere filament of a stem. Unlike the mountain pine and sturdy oak, that seem built for the heads they carry, and the storms they have to encounter, one had to trace it upwards and downwards to be convinced that this thread of a stalk was the living, nourishing, sustaining channel between these flowering branches and the hidden root. How like that seemed in its feebleness to the faith of some! But there the likeness ceased. Roughly handled, that fragile stem was broken;

and, severed from their root, branches and flowers all withered away; but thanks be to God that, united to Christ, even by the feeblest faith, we can affirm that, Neither death nor life, nor things present nor things to come, nor height, nor depth, nor any other creature, shall be able to separate us from the love of God, which is in Christ Jesus our Lord.

Good works are the certain fruit of this saving faith.

One of the greatest marshals of France had for his opponent in a civil war the Prince of Condé. In him Turenne found a foeman worthy of his steel—the only man indeed who could rival him in military genius, moving troops, the arrangement and fighting of battles, sudden surprises and successful attacks. One night, when the prince was supposed to be many leagues away, Turenne lay sleeping securely in his camp. He was suddenly roused, to hear in cries and shouts, the roar of musketry and cannon, the signs of a midnight assault. Hasting from his tent, he cast his eye around him; and at once discovering, by the glare of burning houses, the roar of the fight, the skill with which the attack had been evidently planned, and the energy with which it was being executed, the genius of his rival, he turned to his staff, and said, Condé is come! Now, in some cases especially of sudden conversion, the advent of faith may be as certainly pronounced upon. The peace of death is broken, conscience awakes, sin appears exceeding sinful, empty forms no longer yield any comfort, carelessness about divine things gives place to all absorbing and intense anxieties, Death seems crowned with terrors, Sinai clothed with thunders, and exclaiming, What shall I do to be saved, the trembling soul hies to the Cross, clasps it, clings to it, to cry, Lord, save, I perish: in such circumstances you can safely say conversion is come, salvation come, Christ come; and there is no presumption then in using, as we fall at Jesus' feet, the language of him who said, Lord, I believe; help thou mine unbelief!

But though thus saved through faith, and not of works, as St Paul says, lest any man should boast, St Paul is not less explicit about works; on that subject his trumpet has an equally certain sound; for in the very same passage he tells us that believers, they that have a true saving faith, are not only cleansed through Christ from guilt, but are created in Christ unto good works, which God, he adds, "hath foreordained that we should walk in them"—that these in fact are, in all cases, as surely as divine foreordination can make them, the fruit of living faith. How should it be otherwise? Is not faith in every other condition of its existence full of works; the world's great worker? Look abroad! In yonder husbandman who, though snow lies on hill-tops and frost bites in the air, and nights are long and days are short, and woods are bare, and birds are mute, believing that spring will come, summer come, and autumn come, gives his labour to the naked fields, Faith ploughs the soil. And in yon sailor, who though he sees the land sink beneath the wave, boldly pushes out on the pathless deep, and trusts not to sight, for he sees only a wide waste of water where other keels have left no furrow, but to his charts and trembling needle. Faith ploughs the sea. And there were men, inspired with confidence in their comrades' bravery and commander's skill, march to their positions on the battle-field as on parade, stand up facing the deadly hail, or, crouching like lions to the spring, wait the word to rise and charge, Faith fights and wins. Not cannon, nor bayonets, but mainly Wellington's faith in his men, and his men's faith in Wellington, won Waterloo; and who takes time to follow out the thought will find that faith in God's providence, in what are called the laws of Nature, in the fidelity of husbands and wives, in the affection of children and parents, in the justice of masters and honesty of servants, in man's integrity where they buy and sell, exchange or manufacture goods, in every mill and market, in every harbour and counting-room, is the working power of the world—the mighty wheel that most turns its machinery.

Well, if faith is so productive of works outside the region of religion, how much more within it? If faith in man so works, how much more faith in God? Such faith as naturally produces what are called good works, as vines produce grapes, or sorrow tears, or joy smiles; as the soil beneath us yields fruits and flowers, or the skies above us showers and sunshine. In the character of God, in the person, love, and work of His Son, in an eternal world, in the Bible, its gracious promises and its glorious prospects, it has to do with the grandest truths; and for a man whose heart is not devout, nor his life holy, to say that he has that faith, is to deceive himself—and furnish an awful illustration of the saying, "The heart is deceitful above all things, and desperately wicked." Let no man deceive you. Not I, but God says, "No whoremonger, nor unclean person, nor covetous man who is an idolater, hath any inheritance in the kingdom of God."

Therefore *the hopes of salvation that rest on a faith without works are false, and being false, are fatal.*

Last century, faith was out of fashion; the peculiar doctrines of the gospel were ignored, unless it might be at a communion time. "Christ and Him crucified" were thrust out of sight; unless in the form of some old mouldering stone, which the hammer of Reformers had missed, the cross was removed from the Church; children learned to repeat the creed, but the boasted creed of many was that sung by Pope—

> "For modes of faith let graceless bigots fight,
> His can't be wrong whose life is in the right."

Virtue and vice, the beauty of the one and the deformities of the other, were the favourite topics of the pulpit. Yet the people had so little taste, that they did not appear to fall in love with virtue; nor were even some of those much smitten by her charms to whom she sat for her portrait. Men drank deep last century; swore profanely; talked obscenely; and indulged in a very loose morality. Strange to say, good works were never so much preached, and so little practised. The more they were found in Sabbath sermons, the less they appeared in everyday life. Yet not strange! "Thou bleeding Love," as Young sings—

> "The grand morality is love of Thee,"

and Jesus, His love, His life, His death, excluded from pulpits, there was nothing to produce good works; no pith in preaching; no seed to yield a harvest; no straw to make bricks; no solid backbone, so to speak, to support the soft parts, and keep the frame erect. And the attempt at home to have a morality without religion proved as signal a failure as that abroad, in France, to have a nation without a God.

Morality without religion is a dream; but not less a dream, and wild a dream, is religion without morality—a faith that lies in an orthodox creed without a godly and honest life—that lies in the cold assent of the understanding to truths that never touch the heart or affect the conduct. This won't stand the day which shall try the tree by its fruits, and by Christ's own lips pronounce perdition on the workers of iniquity. We want a religion that walks in the path of the ten commandments—saying, Blessed is the man that walketh not in the counsel of the ungodly, nor standeth in the way of sinners. We want a religion that, not dressed for Sundays and walking on stilts, descends into common and everyday life; is friendly, not selfish; courteous, not boorish; generous, not niggard; sanctified, not sour; that loves justice more than gain; and fears God more than man; to quote another's words—"a religion that keeps husbands from being spiteful, or wives fretful; that keeps mothers patient, and children pleasant; that bears heavily not only on 'the exceeding sinfulness of sin,' but on the exceeding rascality of lying and stealing; that banishes small measures from counters, sand from sugar, and water from milk-cans"—the faith, in short, whose root is Christ, and whose fruit is works.

Any other St James pronounces dead—not like a dead stone which in flashing diamond, or sculptured marble, may be beautiful—but dead like a lifeless body; putrid, horrible, in decay. Not more loathsome to me the fetid corpse where no trace of beauty lingers, than to a holy God the man who holds good doctrines, but lives a bad life; who unites a low practice to a high profession; who, in words, exalts the Saviour's Cross, but in works—in crucifying His flesh, in living for others, in acts of self-denial, won't take up his own. Like some of old, does he say, I am for St Paul, not for St James? St Paul is not for him. I can fancy that apostle, in horror, rending the garment he wears in heaven; repudiating the connexion. One in glory before the throne, he and St James are one in sentiment in this Bible. St Paul, indeed, counted all things loss for Christ. He held the Cross aloft; and, shaking that banner from its folds in the face of friend and foe, he waved it over the scaffold where his testimony was sealed with his blood. But the faith he preached was a faith that worketh—worketh by love; crucifieth the flesh; purifieth the heart; and overcometh the world. Mark his last words to the Christians of a city in whose dungeons he had sung Christ's praises, and whose jailer he had conducted to Christ's feet. "Finally, brethren, whatsoever things are true, whatsoever things are honest, whatsoever things are just, whatsoever things are pure, whatsoever things are lovely, whatsoever things are of good report, if there be any virtue, and if there be any praise, think on these things."

Believers are called by Christ's word *to be workers*.

There are times—and such are ours—when, the inspiration of God's Word, the propitiation of the Cross, the necessity of conversion being denied, sound men are called to close their ranks, and contend together for the faith once delivered to the saints. The Captain of our salvation now seems to address His Church, as a commander the hollow square that with its front rank on the knee presenting a hedge of bayonets, and the second on their feet, with eyes glaring along the deadly barrel, is formed to receive cavalry. Their swords flashing in the sun, thundering on they come, with the impetus of a tremendous shock. The moment, how critical! Let courage fail, the line waver, offer an opening, and in sweeps the foe like a whirlwind of steel. It is the moment for their commanding officer, as he runs his eye along the grim and stern faces, and ere he gives the word that, in a burst of musketry, empties many saddles, and rolls back that array like a broken, bloody wave, to cry, Be steadfast, immovable! In regard to matters of doctrine, attacked in our day from strange quarters, so Christ speaks to us now; but He adds as when He first spake these words by the mouth of St Paul, "always abounding in the work of the Lord." Yes! Believers are now and then to be warriors; but always to be workers.

Indeed, an idle Christian is a contradiction in terms; as much so as a drunken, lying, or adulterous Christian. For is not the Church a body, that has Christ for its Head, and His people for its members? But did God ever make a body which He encumbered with idle members? Never. What part, what member of this frame, moulded of clay, yet so fearfully and wonderfully made, does not work, was not made for working? The eye is formed to see; the ear to hear; the tongue to speak; the feet to walk; the hands to grasp; the lungs to breathe; the brain to think; the busy heart—the first to live and the last to die, a clock that needs no winding—to beat—and beating, send its blood through all the throbbing arteries. Let all, or even some of these members cease to work, I die instantly. Let any work irregularly, my health suffers; the whole body, where each member has sympathy with another, suffers. Every member works. And the harbour, with its forest of tall masts, the city, with the grinding noises, and rolling carriages, and hurry of crowded streets, present no scene of activity so wonderful as that which, covered and concealed by our untransparent skin, is going on within us —innumerable organs all at work—working the livelong day—the night that stills the hum of streets, and throws the world's machinery out of gear, bringing no pause to them.

Although in communion with this or that other Church, a member of an Episcopalian, or Presbyterian, or Independent Church, who is not a working Christian, is no member of Christ's Church. Let those who are, work—do all the good, to all the persons, at all the times, in all the ways they can—abounding in good works. Every day they live, the busier—the shorter the time, the busier—the nearer the grave, the busier; as a stone, descending the hill, rolls with increasing speed, till, taking its last bound, it plunges into the lake, and sinks into its placid bosom.

So may the grave, with its "rest for the weary," close above our heads; and, as heaven opens to receive our spirits to the repose of the just, may Jesus meet us at the gate, with His "Well done, good and faithful servant, enter thou into the joy of thy Lord."

Believers are called by Christ's example *to be workers*.

It is common to speak, by way of distinction, of the *working classes*. And men of lofty social position, and loftier minds—for, after all, there is nothing great about man but mind—when they stand on the platform of a popular assembly addressing the sons of toil, to win their ears and hearts, will sometimes, referring to the labours and brain-work of office, rank themselves among the working class. But whatever be their sex, sphere, or talents, all true followers of Jesus are of the *working class.* They were otherwise no followers of Him who is not our Propitiation only, but also our Pattern; who is not our Propitiation unless He is also our Pattern; and whose life, begun in Bethlehem, and closed in Calvary, was spent in " doing good."

Bone of our bone, and flesh of our flesh, true man as well as God, He drank of our cup—enjoying as much, and more than we, the pleasures of friendship, the loveliness of nature, the feast kindness spread, the happy faces of a marriage scene, seasons of welcome rest amid mountain solitudes, by Galilee's smiling lake, in the sweet society of Bethany. But was it for these He lived? for enjoyment, or for employment? for others, or Himself? Himself! He denied Himself; forgot Himself; barely allowed Himself the rest that nature needed. His heart felt, and His eye wept, and His hand was ready for all human wretchedness. Who so patient with the bad—so gentle to the erring—so tender to the penitent? Who sought His help in vain? What poor beggar unpitied, or poor sinner unpardoned, ever left His door? What blessings fell from the hands, on what errands of mercy went the sacred feet, they nailed, O Calvary, to thy cruel, accursed tree!

In the charity that covereth a multitude of sins, that hopeth and believeth all things, I can believe much. I believe that God will have mercy on the chief of sinners. I believe there is no sin you or I have done but may be washed out in the fountain where sins are lost and souls are saved. I believe that the vilest creature who pollutes society and degrades humanity, may creep into heaven at the back of the thief, shine with the purity, and mingle her voice with the song of angels. I believe no one is to be despaired of; not even the man who is just going over into the pit. Let him turn to Christ—He saves at the uttermost. But I cannot believe that a God of truth, with reverence be it spoken, will tell a lie—and what but a lie were it to say to a man that had wasted his life in ease, and pleasure, and self-indulgence, Well done! How could He, who made it His meat and drink to do His Father's will, who lived and laboured for His Father's glory, who died for the good of men, say to one who came up with his talent in a napkin, Well done, good and faithful servant—follower of mine, Well done! Certainly not. None share in Christ's joy but those that, in a sense, have shared in His agony. They enter into His rest who, baptized with the Spirit as well as the blood of Calvary, have entered into His labours. The wages, no doubt, are of grace; yet no work, no wages! No work, no wages—as true an aphorism as the well-known saying, No cross, no crown. Crowns are for living brows, but faith without works is dead. Ours be such a life as grace forms, and the poet sings,—

> "I live for those that love me,
>   For those that know me true,
>   For the heaven that smiles above me,
>   And waits my coming too.
>   For the cause that lacks assistance,
>   For the wrongs that need resistance,
>   For the future in the distance,
>   For the good that I can do."

THE POOR.

> *" If a brother or sister be naked, and destitute of daily food, and one of you say unto them, Depart in peace, be ye warmed and filled: notwithstanding ye give them not those things which are needful to the body: what doth it profit ?"—*
> ST JAMES ii. 15, 16.

THERE are elements in nature which, though not always apparent to the senses, pervade, and, pervading, affect every substance. Heat, for instance. There is warmth even in ice, cold as it feels; heat as well in the icicles that hang from his thatch as in the glowing iron the smith, amid a shower of sparks, hammers on his ringing anvil; fire not only in the sun, in the blazing grate, there where swarthy men tap the furnace, and molten iron rolls forth like liquid gold, but fire also, though asleep, and waiting the touch of steel, in the cold and coal black flint. Never dead, nor even altogether dormant, this all-pervading element is everywhere active; the seeds and eggs which lie buried in the frozen soil owing to it their life, and the great ocean its fluidity—the waves that roar or ripple on its shores, the path it offers to our keels, and the innumerable myriads, from whales to shrimps, that people its depths and shallows.

There are also laws in nature which, though often working in secrecy and silence, are dominant in every place and acting on every substance—the law of gravitation, for instance. We may recognise it only in its more striking displays: in the spheres where planets roll; in the orbit which our earth describes around the sun; in the skies, where the eagle, pierced by feathery arrow or bullet, and leaving for ever its airy fields, drops dead, like a stone, at our feet; or on the mountain, where some rock, leaping from its lofty base, rushes down into the valley with the speed of lightning and the roar of thunder. Still, this law affects as well the mote of the sunbeam as the sun, and alike shapes the tear on an infant's cheek and the stars in heaven; it is there, running in the sands of an hour-glass; there, sounding in the tinkling of the tiniest rill; and by the same power that bends the tail of a fiery comet and its path back to the sun, it bends the neck of a snowdrop, and thereby preserves from perishing the herald and harbinger of spring.

As it is with such elements and laws in the kingdoms of nature, it is with the presence and influence of religion in a good man's life. It may not be always apparent, but it should be always present—its influence felt where it is not seen. Often, like those greatest powers of nature, heat and light, and electricity and magnetism, acting silently — sometimes, like the will when moving our lips to form words, or our limbs to produce motion, acting unconsciously—yet always acting; so that in everything we do, in every step we take, in every duty we discharge, though it cannot be said with strict propriety that all our actions are religious, yet none are contrary to religion, and all of them are done religiously. Is not this just the mark at which St Paul teaches us to aim in saying,

"Whether therefore ye eat, or drink, or whatsoever ye do, do all to the glory of God?" Doing so, human life, in its lowliest spheres, from man's cradle onward to his grave, or rather from his conversion to his death, may be made one long, continuous, noble, religious service; more sublime than any poem John Milton wrote; more instructive than any sermon of the greatest preacher; and more acceptable far to God than any services performed within dead stone walls, amid cathedral pomp, and before ten thousand spectators.

Now, in the whole range of duties there is none which, if not strictly religious, and, in the highest sense of the expression, a religious service, is more nearly allied to religion, and should be more under its presiding and holy influence, than that charity to the poor which is plainly dictated, and indeed powerfully enforced, in the question, "If a brother or sister be naked, and destitute of daily food, and one of you say unto them, Depart in peace, be ye warmed and filled; notwithstanding ye give them not those things which are needful to the body, what doth it profit?" Religion imposes this duty on us. In proof of which—

God presents Himself to us *as having a peculiar and tender care of the poor.*

It is not the robust but delicate child of the family, around whom a father's and mother's affections cluster thickest, and are most closely twined. The boy or girl whom feebleness of body or mind makes least fit to bear the world's rough usage, and most dependent on others' kindness, is like those tendrils that, winding themselves round the tree they spangle with flowers, bind it most closely in their embraces, and bury their pliant arms deepest in its bark. And what a blessed and beautiful arrangement of Providence it is, that they who cost most care, and lie with greatest weight on parents' arms and hearts, are commonly most loved! Helplessness, appealing to our pity, begets affection. Thus was the heart of the rough sailor touched, when, tossing with other castaways in an open boat on the open sea, he parted with a morsel of food, which, hidden with more care than misers hide their gold, he had reserved for his own last extremity. Around him lay men and women; some dead with glassy eyes; some dying, and these reduced to ghastly skeletons; but none of these moved him to peril his own life for theirs. The object of his noble and not unrewarded generosity—for, as if Heaven had sent it on purpose to reward the act, a sail speedily hove in sight—was a gentle boy that, with his face turned on hers, lay dying in a mother's arms, and between whose teeth the famishing man put his own last precious morsel. Of this feeling I met also a remarkable illustration in my old country parish. In one of its cottages dwelt a poor idiot child; horrible to all eyes but her parents'; and so helpless, that, though older than sisters just blooming into womanhood, she lay, unable either to walk or speak, a burden on her mother's lap, almost the whole day long,—a heavy handful to one who had the cares of a family, and was the wife of a hard-working man,—and a most painful contrast to the very roses that flung their bright clusters over the cottage window, as well as to the lark that, pleased with a grassy turf, carolled within its cage. Death, in most instances unwelcome visitor, came at length,—to her and to their relief. Relief! so I thought; and, when the father came with invitation to the funeral, so I said. Though not roughly, but inadvertently spoken, the word jarred on a tender chord; and I was more than ever taught how helplessness begets affection in the very measure and proportion of itself, when he burst into a fit of sorrow, and, speaking of his beautiful boys and blooming girls, said, If it had been God's will, I would have parted with any of them rather than her.

Now this kindness to the helpless, of which man's home, both in the humblest and highest walks of life, presents so many lovely instances, and which, you will observe, moves the roughest crowd on the street, without taking time to inquire into its merits, to throw themselves into the quarrel of a woman or weeping child, is a flower of Eden, that clings to the ruins of our nature,—one beautiful feature of God's image which has to some extent survived the Fall. "The Lord is very pitiful and of tender mercy." Well named, "Our Father who is in heaven;" he sets Himself forth in his Word as the Patron and Protector of the poor; he recommends them in many ways and by many considerations to our kindness; and teaches us that, if we would be like Himself, we must remember their miseries amid our enjoyments, and fill their empty cups with the overflowings of our own. In proof of this—

Observe the sentiments of His Word toward the poor.

It breathes the most tender regard to them: for example—Whoso reproacheth the poor, reproacheth his Maker; Blessed is he that considereth the poor, the Lord shall deliver him in the time of trouble; He shall judge the poor and needy; He shall stand at the right hand of the poor; The needy shall not alway be forgotten; the expectation of the poor shall not perish for ever. How different from the spirit of a sordid age, which, as if there were no worthiness in genius or sense, or bravery, or virtue, or grace, values man by his money; and speaking of what he is worth, takes into account nothing but his wealth! There are some, too many, in whose eyes money, like charity, covereth a multitude of sins; and who would esteem a piece of gilded fir more highly than odorous and imperishable cedar, or marble that vies with driven snow. But the poverty which incurs their contempt demeans no one in the sight of God. He is no respecter of persons. At His height, all ranks appear on a level; and if there is any advantage, the poor have it, in a better chance, if I may say so, of getting to heaven than the rich. I go, said the dying Rutherford, when summoned in the king's name to appear before an earthly tribunal, to obey a higher summons; I go to a place where there are few kings. And does not heaven open to the poor a refuge where there are few rich? St James asks—My beloved brethren, hath not God chosen the poor of this world, rich in faith and heirs of the kingdom? And what said St Paul?—" God hath chosen the weak things of the world to confound the things which are mighty; and base things of the world, and things which are despised, hath God chosen, and things which are not, to bring to nought things that are: that no flesh should glory in his presence." Let honest poverty then lift up its head; next to infants, those unblown buds which the Lord has plucked to open out their beauties on His bosom in heaven, no class is so fully represented in the general assembly of the first-born as the poor. They not only form the largest class on earth, but by much the largest in that kingdom where, before Mary's Son, and by Mary's side, they may lift up her hymn, and sing —He hath put down the mighty from their seats, and exalted them of low degree ; He hath filled the hungry with good things, and the rich He hath sent empty away.

Observe His enactments on behalf of the poor.

A legal provision for the poor is no modern invention. It is a common notion that regular poor-laws date from the days of Elizabeth of England; but it is a mistake. They are of much older date. A divine institution, they are found in that system of polity which God set up among His ancient people by the hands of His servant Moses. He did not leave His poor to depend altogether on the fits and chances of a precarious charity. One of the many provisions made to supply their wants, was lately brought to our recollection, when travelling through a valley, where embowering vines threw their clusters over the road ; and planted on rising terraces, occupied the sunny slopes of mountains that rose to skies of deepest blue—clothed with shaggy forests, and crowned with eternal snows. One of the guides, without consent asked or given, left the path, and, stepping into a vineyard by the wayside, plucked a rich bunch of grapes. The customs of that country may, perhaps, permit a freedom with property which would not be tolerated in ours. Standing on the extremest rights of *mine* and *thine*, we will send a poor vagrant child to jail for taking a turnip to satisfy his hunger; but in the Holy, might I not add, and Happy Land, where God would have no man starve, the beggar, any hungry Israelite could take such freedoms without let or challenge. His hunger was his need, and God's law was his right to do so. "When thou goest," said the Lord, "into thy neighbour's vineyard, thou mayest eat grapes thy fill; but thou shalt not put any in thy vessel;" and so long as a poor man kept within this limit, he had full liberty to satisfy the wants of nature; nor was branded as a thief for doing so.

Another provision kindly and divinely established on behalf of the poor, in these good old times, was, though in the way of contrast, also recalled to our recollection on passing, one of these autumn days, a harvest-field at home. In a teethed machine, which, raking the stubble-land, gathered up the stalks of grain that the reapers had left, we saw a custom which God forbade on the soil that was trodden by a Redeemer's feet. He, who reserved the seventh day to Himself, reserved, along with the standing corn that grew in the corners of the fields, the gleanings of the whole harvest for the exclusive use of the poor; and thus all those whom Ruth and Naomi represented — the widows of Israel, the fatherless, and the orphan—had a share of others' plenty, and their own joy in every harvest.

Nor were the corners which the husbandman was forbidden to reap, and the gleanings of harvests and vineyards which the proprietors were forbidden to gather, the only bounty which the earth poured into the lap of the poor; and to which they had a legal and unchangeable claim. By God's express appointment, the land was to enjoy a sabbath once every seven years, during which the fields were to lie untilled, the olive-trees and vines to grow unpruned. Now, the whole produce of that sabbatical year belonged to the poor; none of it to the proprietor. "Six years," said the Lord, "thou shalt sow thy land, and shalt gather in the fruits thereof: but the seventh year thou shalt let it rest and lie still; that the poor of thy people may eat; and what they leave the beasts of the field shall eat. In like manner thou shalt deal with thy vineyard and with thy oliveyard." God's care of His poor, like a mother's for her babe, extended even to what might be considered minute and trivial matters. The rich were forbidden to make any charge for money lent to a poor man; and if his necessities obliged him to pledge bed or garment, God took care that he should not suffer for it. Many a poor wretch in our cities is left with his children to shiver through cold winter nights, while their blankets are locked up in the broker's store. Better care was taken of an unfortunate Israelite. "In any case," said the Lord, "thou shalt deliver him the pledge when the sun goeth down, that he may sleep in his own raiment."

Stern and severe as were some aspects of the Mosaic law, it looked kindly upon poverty. That law treated it not as a crime, but as a misfortune deserving the tenderest compassion. And though not required to copy its details, ought we not to preserve their spirit; and in dealing with honest poverty, meet it in the benevolent spirit of the commandment, "If thy brother be waxen poor, and fallen in decay with thee, then thou shalt relieve him, though he be a stranger or a sojourner, that he may live with thee?" No man can read these old laws, so full of tender care and regard for the poor, without seeing the point and feeling the power of the apostle's question, "Whoso hath this world's good, and seeth his brother in need, and shutteth up his bowels of compassion from him, how dwelleth the love of God in him?" Let us then, as St John says, "not love in word, neither in tongue; but in deed and in truth."

Observe His judgments for the wrongs of the poor.

Thy holy cities are a wilderness, Zion is a wilderness, Jerusalem a desolation; our holy and our beautiful house, where our fathers praised thee, is burned up with fire; all our pleasant things are laid waste. So spake Isaiah, looking with prophetic eye on the future, where he saw the grass grow rank on the city's untrodden streets, and the fox looking out of the temple window, and satyrs dancing in the holy place— the shrine deserted, its lamp extinguished, and the ashes of its altar cold. And what dreadful sins were those which brought down such judgments on a guilty land — moving God to cast away His people as a loathsome thing, and make them a by-word, and a proverb, and a hissing on the earth?—Sabbath-breaking, idolatry, drunkenness, loose-living?—Yes; these, but others also; wrongs inflicted on the poor. Hear how these bold and bearded prophets speak—"The spoil of the poor is in your houses"—as it is, now, in every house where a fortune has been built on their ruins. Again, "Ye grind the faces of the poor,"—as is done still, when advantage is taken of his necessities to deny the labourer a fair day's wage for a fair day's work. Again, "They buy the poor for silver, and the needy for a pair of shoes," — crimes perpetrated, high treason against God committed, as it were but yesterday, yonder where, under the flag of liberty with its brave motto, All men are born free, the hammer of the auction-room knocked down men and women for so many hundred dollars. These old preachers, asserting the sanctity and liberty of the pulpit, deemed it their right, and used it as a privilege, to proclaim from that place of truth the wrongs of the poor, and the judgment of their oppressors. Inspired of God, they were fearless of man. Hear how they spake to the times:—"Is it," they asked, speaking in their Master's name, "such a fast that I have chosen—a day for a man to afflict his soul? to bow down his head as a bulrush; to spread sackcloth and ashes under him? Wilt thou call this a fast, and an acceptable day to the Lord? Is not this the fast that I have chosen? To loose the bands of wickedness, to undo the heavy burdens, and to let the oppressed go free, and that ye break every yoke? Is it not to deal thy bread to the hungry, and to bring the poor that are cast out into thy house? when thou seest the naked, that thou cover him, and that thou hide not thyself from thine own flesh?" This is not done. Many of our poor go hungry and houseless.

Stretching themselves upon their couches, eating the lambs out of the flock, and the calves out of the midst of the stall, chanting to the sound of the viol, drinking wine in bowls, anointing themselves with the chief ointments, and not grieved for the affliction of Joseph,—many, realising this voluptuous picture, leave the poor to herd in filthy dens; and out of houses not fit for human beings, not compatible with health, or decency, or virtue, come swarms of ragged, uncared-for, and uneducated children, to turn the tread-mill, and feed the prison. It is not for us to scan the ways of Providence, but the dying echoes of past judgments sound us a solemn, may it be a timely warning. What shall be, says the wise man, is that which hath already been. The wrongs of the poor have a way of avenging themselves. Neglected poverty may rise some day like the blind, strong man to pull down the prosperity and pillars of the land; and when no Joseph shall appear in providence to avert the impending evil, a worse future may come than was foreshadowed in royal dreams, when, in visions of the night, Pharaoh saw the seven lean kine eat up the seven fat. It is with judgments God arms Himself, when He says, "For the oppression of the poor, for the sighing of the needy, now will I arise, saith the Lord." See how, in this terrible aspect, He arose in that land from whose shores Atlantic waves lately wafted the boom of cannon to our own. Would that after the roar of that fratricidal war, America may hear the voice of rebuke, sounding down from the throne of God! Undoing the heavy burdens, and letting the oppressed go free, out of the broken fetters of emancipated slaves, let her make a lightning-conductor to turn away the bolts of a righteous, roused, and angry God! Then, in the beautiful words of the prophet, "shall her light break forth as the morning, and her health spring forth speedily, and the glory of the Lord shall be her rear-ward, and her darkness shall be as the noonday—and she shall be like a watered garden, and like a spring of water whose waters fail not."

Observe how Jesus showed His care for the poor.

The poor, He said, ye have always with you, and whensoever ye will ye may do them good—repeating in substance God's much older words,

"The poor shall never cease out of the land; therefore I command thee, saying, Thou shalt open thy hand wide unto thy brother; to thy poor; and to thy needy in the land." How beautifully this divine tenderness to the poor comes out welling and warm, in the very terms applied to them; it is not, if a man or woman—but if a *brother or sister* be naked—thou shalt open thy hand wide unto thy *brother*.

In dealing with the poor we are not, however, to put all over in the same boat—huddling together the good and bad, virtue and vice, decent age and hoary sin in our plans, as is done in our poorhouses. There is no line of separation between peer and peasant so broad as divides the two classes of the poor. There are God's poor, whose cause I chiefly plead. These, reduced to want, brought to suffering by no fault of theirs, have the strongest, at any rate the first, claim on our compassion. There are the poor of providence; and a much more numerous class, the poor of improvidence—the devil's poor, who, reaping as they have sowed, and drinking as they have brewed, are suffering under these righteous laws: "He becometh poor that dealeth with a slack hand;" "If any will not work, neither should he eat;" "He that loveth pleasure shall be a poor man." None are in some respects, I admit, greater objects of compassion than these. It is pitiable to see the wrecks of comfort, and decency, and humanity, that go drifting about our streets. How foul and forbidding with the rags that vice has hung on their back, and the wolfish look that want has given their faces! Yet many of them were once bright and sunny children; dandled on a father's knee; and sung to sleep by kind mothers, who, putting their little innocent hands together, taught their infant lips to pray. We are not to loathe them; nor will, if we remember that they cannot be so black or so bad in our eyes as we were in God's when He gave up His dear Son to save us. Yet how profoundly are they to be pitied! They have got to the dregs of their cup; and how bitter they are! They dare not look back on the past, with its recollections of early innocence, a virtuous home, and the venerable image of a mother or father, whose gray hairs they brought in sorrow to the grave; nor dare they look forward on the future; and unless religion come to their help, what will they or can they do, but "drink to forget their poverty, and remember their misery no more?" What else are you to expect of impiety under sufferings greater than wrung from God's servant the cry, "Oh, that my mother had been my grave; wherefore came I from the womb, that my days should be consumed with shame?" Theirs is not the poverty that has wealth in heaven, and, touched by lights from another and better world, is a cloud that wears silver edges; nor is theirs the cup which faith sweetens with the promise of all things working together for good. Without God or hope, they are the poorest of the poor; and claim in a sense our deepest and holiest compassions.

Still, our compassion must never take the shape of a bounty on idleness and vice. Such philanthropy is mischievous; and finds not the semblance of encouragement in our Lord's example. He went about doing good; and chiefly in the walks of the poor. But how? He restored health to sickness, vigour to the withered arm, sight to the blind, speech to the dumb, hearing to the deaf, reason to the insane; and, doing so, taught us the wise charity that helps a poor man to help himself. He did not maintain the poor in idleness, but sent them back with renovated powers to their different fields of labour. It is as instructive as it is remarkable, that on only two occasions did our Lord create food; and money only on one—leaving the law of God not only to its righteous but beneficent course, "in the sweat of thy face shalt thou eat bread." Not even in the days when He scattered miracles around Him in divine profusion, did He anything to counteract the lesson of those wondrous years when His neighbours heard the carpenter early at His bench; and honest labour sharpened His appetite and sweetened His simple fare; and at every week's end, a pattern of filial duty and model to our youths, He poured His earnings into a mother's lap.

While our Lord, employing His miraculous powers to help the poor to help themselves, showed them the wisest and truest kindness, He forgot not, even in His narrow and straitened circumstances, the claims of a helpless poverty. It is evident that the bag which Judas carried served a double purpose; the poor had their share of its scanty store. The patriarch says, I did not eat my morsel alone. No more did Jesus—with this difference, that Job was rich, but Jesus was poor. Yet what He had, He gave. Ay, His generosity but dimly shadowed forth by the widow who "of her want did cast in all she had, even all her living;" He gave not His living but His life for a greater poverty than stands in ragged beggar at our door; He made Himself poor that He might make us rich; He poured out His soul unto death—dying, the just for the unjust, that He might bring us to God

CHARITY.

> "*If a brother or sister be naked, and destitute of daily food, and one of you say unto them, Depart in peace, be ye warmed and filled: notwithstanding ye give them not those things which are needful to the body: what doth it profit?*"—ST JAMES ii. 15, 16.

AN Arab possessed a horse so famous far and near for its beauty, gentleness, and matchless speed, that he had many tempting offers to part with her. He refused them all; and, in particular, the repeated solicitations of one who offered an enormous price. One day, as, with head wrapped in mantle and lance at rest, he was pressing homewards through the burning desert, his horse suddenly started; and there, right across the path, lay a poor traveller—alive, for he groaned;

but exhausted, and apparently at the point of death. Like the good Samaritan—for, though fierce, these wild Bedouins have savage virtues, are hospitable and friendly—he dismounted, and finding the unfortunate traveller unable to walk or even to stand, set him in his own saddle. No sooner done than, as if the vigour of the steed had been imparted to its rider, the bowed and languid form became instantly erect; the horse suddenly wheeled round, sprang off to the stroke, and a laugh of triumph revealed the trick. The man who had offered him an enormous price for the horse was on her back. Assuming the guise of distress, he had taken advantage of the other's generous feelings, to steal what he could not buy. The injured man did not curse him; nor, fortified by the stoicism which the Mohammedans' belief in fate imparts, merely bow his head to the misfortune. He soared above it to a height of moral grandeur which few reach. Calling on the other to halt, he said that he had one favour to ask; it was this, that he would never tell how he had won the horse, because, were that known, it might hinder some from receiving help in circumstances of danger not feigned, but real—and so doom the unfortunate to perish. It is but justice to human nature to add—what indeed shows that fine feelings may lie dormant in the worst of men—that the other was so touched by the unselfishness and nobility of this appeal, that he relented; and, riding up to the man he had wronged, gave him back his horse.

Human nature is a plant that, unchanged by climate, colour, or circumstances, presents the same characters, and bears the same fruit, amid the smoke of crowded cities as in the lonely desert. And this appeal of the Arab, in the advantage so often taken of our kindness, in the bad persons on whom it is bestowed, and the bad uses to which it is turned, touches what forms the greatest obstruction to the flow of charity, and our ready, literal obedience to the precept—"Deal out thy bread to the hungry; if thou seest the naked, clothe him, and bring the poor that are cast out into thy house." But because others do ill, is no reason why we should cease to do well. The case is one to which the apostle's words are specially appropriate, "Be not weary in well-doing." This leads us to remark—

That the *abuse* of our *charity* should never *dry up our hearts.*

Who is David, and who is the son of Jesse? so Nabal replied to David's appeal for help, at the time he and his men were hiding in the wilderness of Paran—adding, by way of reason, this reproach to refusal, "There be many servants now-a-days that break away every man from his master." Perhaps there were. The earthquake that casts towers and castles to the ground, brings vile reptiles out of it; the storm that sinks the noblest ships, throws sea-weeds and *wrack* upon the shore; and the political convulsions of Nabal's time, producing corresponding effects, had very probably thrown the dregs of society, like scum, to the surface; and relaxing the bonds of order set loose bands of marauders on the land. These supplied the sordid churl with an excuse for refusing David; and so does the abuse of our charity those who seek to throw over their covetousness the cloak of some decent pretext. Theirs is never abused; their excuse but the sound of a hollow heart, the rattle that a withered kernel makes within its shell. I do not now address myself to these, beyond reminding them of the solemn, awful, warning words, "Your gold and silver is cankered, and the rust of them shall be a witness against you, and shall eat your flesh as it were fire."

But there are many who feel for the poor. They would gladly relieve their wants. They are pained to see these wretched mothers, and yet more wretched children; but having found their charity often misapplied and thrown away on the unworthy and ungrateful, they are afraid to give; and not seldom tempted, on discovering how they have been imposed upon, to say in their haste as David did in his, All men are liars! But if charity often fails in its object, so do other things. The sun shines on many a fair blossom that never turns into fruit, and the clouds pour their bounties on fields that yield no harvest. But to leave figures for facts. Education, as well as charity, often fails: it is but a small proportion of children that become ripe scholars. Moral training fails; how many parents, besides David, have had their hearts wounded and torn by wicked children! The labours of husbandry fail; it is but a proportion of the seed that springs; and a still less proportion that, reaching maturity, in golden sheaves rewards the farmer's toil. Physic fails; diseases rage, and patients die in spite of it. Even the pulpit fails; but what preacher thinks of abandoning it, because many of his sermons do no good; nay, like abused charity, do positive harm—hardening those they fail to soften, and making people as indifferent to the most solemn things as a hoary sexton to the mouldering remnants of mortality, the skulls he tosses out of the grave?

Man is answerable for duty; but not for results. And as with faith in a promised blessing, we are always to preach, in season and out of season, to sow beside all waters, you are never to cease your charities. Let not the cold ingratitude of other hearts freeze your own. Ingratitude! Abuse of mercies! Who met so much of these as our blessed Lord? Yet the fountains of His heart were ever full, and, till that heart was broken, never ceased to flow. His miracles yielded no adequate return; nor out of thousands to whose limbs they had given vigour, whose tongues they had loosed, on whose blind eyes they had poured light, brought one, so much as one, to cry, Crucify him not. Yet His works of beneficence were like a river that, breaking over every obstacle, and in its ample flood, burying the stones that would impede its course, widens as it runs, and is largest at the beach where it is lost in the sea. So let it be with our sympathies and charities! May our hearts, with advancing age, grow less sour and more sweet, less hard and more tender, like downy peach or golden apple that ripens to its fall.

Our charity should be discriminating.

Discriminating, first, as to its objects. The " household of the faith" have a prior claim on Christians. "If thy brother or sister be naked and destitute of daily food"—thy brother, thy sister, these tender expressions apply to them in a holy and peculiar sense. Next come others; and last, but not to be omitted, our enemies. We never rise so high above ourselves, and so near to God as in yielding obedience to these wonderful divine words — If thine enemy hunger, feed him; if he thirst, give him drink; for in so doing thou shalt heap coals of fire upon his head.

Careful discrimination is required also both in what we give, and how we give. This is implied in the words, Blessed is the man that *considereth* the poor; and is brought out fully by those who turned these psalms into rhyme—

> "Blessed is he that *wisely* doth
> The poor man's case consider."

This is true of public charity. The poor man's case has not been always wisely considered. Very much the reverse. Listen, for example, to this description of the old Poor-laws of England. "The pauper was led to think that the Government had undertaken to repeal the ordinary laws of nature; that children should not suffer for the misconduct of their parents, nor the wife for that of her husband; and that no one should lose the means of subsistence whatever might be his indolence, prodigality, or vice. They offered food to the idle, and impunity to the profligate." And out of those convents that swarm with lazy monks and idle nuns, where shall we find more questionable, and, in many of their results, more pernicious charities than the splendid hospitals that rise around our city? These, not like its old walls, a defence, are monuments of the folly, if not of the vanity of their founders. There they stand, tempting parents to cast on cold officials the loving burden which God lays on a father's back and in a mother's bosom. Moses might never have been the man he was unless he had been nursed by his own mother. How many celebrated men have owed their greatness and their goodness to a mother's training! What is the law of nature? God has committed children to the care of their parents, and the care of parents to their children; and the charity that interferes with this law of Providence is the parent of evils far greater than it cures. In Scotland, the people once were poor, but not mean; and if our countrymen were proverbial for pride and poverty, it was the pride, if such term could be applied to a feeling so noble, which made sons and daughters work late and early, walk in sober gray, and live on the hardest fare to keep a venerable and venerated parent off the poor's-roll. For the aged man or mother there was always a corner, and that the warmest in the cottage, where one whose infancy they had nursed tenderly watched their declining years. Within these homes, sacred to filial piety, I have seen a lovely counterpart to the scene without, where the ivy which once found support in old wall or hollow tree, now embracing, supports it in its turn, and covers its hoar decay with a graceful and glossy mantle. Honour to the humblest home whose thatch covers a parent's head; where daily toil is cheerfully borne to obey the precept that finds an echo in our hearts, " Honour thy father and thy mother, that thy days may be long in the land which the Lord thy God giveth thee!"

Discrimination as to whom, and what, and how we give, is also necessary in the distribution of private charity. St Giles, the patron saint of our city, in devout imitation of Him who made Himself poor to make us rich, is said to have sold all his property for the benefit of the poor,—to feed the hungry and clothe the naked. And what were the result if any of us should blindly follow his example, and pour our fortunes into the lap of the parish that bears the old saint's name? What good would it do the haggard men and women that there and elsewhere swarm so foul and thick from this rocky castle to yonder silent palace? We should make ourselves poor, but, alas! not them rich. They owe their poverty to intemperance and improvidence; and a stream of money turned on them being less like water poured on a sand-bed than oil on raging flames, would but increase their wretchedness, and feed the vices that have hung them in rags. "It came to pass that the beggar died, and was carried by the angels into Abraham's bosom;" but now-a-days rags are more frequently than otherwise the devil's livery.

The love of drink is "the root of all evil." In an obscure and wretched close you have lighted on a decent and devout widow, with no cordial by her dying bed but a cup of water. Happy to find such a person there, as a flower blooming in the desert, you hasten to minister to her necessities; these words of Jesus sounding in your ears. "Inasmuch as ye did it unto one of the least of them, ye did it unto me." But the wine given to touch dying lips a wretched daughter turns to another purpose; so one day, when engaged in prayer, the opening of a door, thick and strange mutterings, a reeling step, the noise of one falling, induce you to open your eyes—and there, before you, on the same bed, lies a dying mother and a dead-drunk child. You have often climbed the stair to read and pray by the bed of a woman who talks religiously; and whose sickly husband, and pale, ill-fed, ill-clad children, have drawn out your bounty. Circumstances occur to excite suspicion,—suspicions darken, deepen; and one day, from beneath a pillow, on which her head and God's Word lie, you drag the evil to light,—draw out the drunkard's bottle. Away, high up in a garret room, you find a young man, sinking under a slow decline, and shivering beneath a thin, threadbare coverlet, in the cold that blows keen through patched and broken window. You try to raise his thoughts to the Saviour and the house of many mansions; and leave to send warm coverings for his emaciated form. Before your return, that wretched apartment has seen a terrible struggle. Turning a deaf ear to his pitiful cries, unmoved by the tears on his hectic cheek, his father and mother have pulled the blankets from his body;

and sold them for drink. I speak what I know; what my own eyes have seen, and ears have heard. These are examples of the difficulties that beset the feet of charity, and teach the necessity of discrimination, if we would not increase the evils we attempt to alleviate.

Nor is that all. What we bestow on idleness or on vice is so much taken from the worthy poor. They have the first claim on what we can spare; and to throw away our means on others is to defraud the widow, the orphan, and poor, innocent, suffering children. It is, therefore, our duty to meet improvidence and intemperance sternly—no doubt with Christian pity, but that mingled with the indignation due to those who are not so much robbing us, or the rich, as heartlessly plundering the worthy poor. There are such—many worthy poor. We should seek them out; and it should be our happiness to contribute to theirs. Let us earn for ourselves what is better than gold that perisheth—the blessing of them that are ready to perish—a character such as His, who, at once the painter and the subject, has left us in this likeness of Himself the most beautiful portrait of man,

"When the ear heard me, then it blessed me; when the eye saw me, it gave witness of me. I was eyes to the blind, and feet to the lame. I delivered the poor that cried; the fatherless and him that had none to help him. The blessing of him that was ready to perish came upon me; and I caused the widow's heart to sing for joy."

Charity brings its reward—first in this world.

While there is no class more tender-hearted than physicians, I have observed that people who live amid their comforts, and are seldom brought into relationship with suffering, are apt to grow selfish. In such circumstances our nature, like a single tree that stands out in the open field, grows dwarfed and gnarled. Indeed, just as without sin the character of God had not been fully developed, nor shone forth full-orbed—merciful and gracious, as well as great and holy, it is difficult to see how, without the presence of suffering, helplessness, and poverty, our nature could have been brought out in some of its most attractive aspects. Sympathy with suffering, as well as our sense of what is right and wrong, separates us by an immeasurable distance from the lower animals. It presents one of the truest and noblest characteristics of humanity. The pampered dog never turns a piteous eye on some lean, and hungry, and houseless fellow; but, growling at his approach, and rushing open-mouthed to the assault, drives him from the door. It is fellow-feeling, not mere feeling that raises a man above a beast. It is that which allies us to the angels who take a lively interest in mundane affairs, and, watching the struggle between good and evil, fill heaven with joy as often as the battle goes for Christ, and a sinner is saved. And those gentle sympathies and kindly feelings which the abodes of poverty awaken, are means whereby the Spirit of God softens us—moulding the plastic heart into the likeness of that blessed Saviour who is "touched with a feeling of our infirmities," and of that blessed God who is "very pitiful and of great mercy."

The hammer and the iron are both hardened by the same stroke. So is the heart that, denying pity, does a cruel thing, and the heart that denied suffers it. But acts of kindness improve the *morale* both of him who gives, and of him who gets. Indeed, it is both a sad and a lightsome thing to visit the dwellings of the poor. It clears our sky of vapours. We return more contented and happy; much stouter to endure the petty troubles of our own lot—seeing how comfortable our circumstances are compared with those of others, and how many would be glad to exchange condition and cup with us.

Next to peace with God, through our Lord Jesus Christ, there is no higher happiness on earth than lies in making others happy; nor is man ever so gracious and God-like as when shedding brightness and blessings around him. There is no flower in gay parterre so beautiful as the roses that grow on an orphan's cheek; no sunshine like the smile of a happy face; no sound of woman's voice, or lute or harp of sweetest strings, so full of music as the singing of a widow's heart; no jewel on queenly brows so brilliant as the tear in eyes we have lighted with gratitude and joy. Yes— it is more blessed to give than to receive; and these beautiful lines apply as well to charity as to mercy—

> "It droppeth as the gentle rain from heaven
> Upon the place beneath. It is twice bless'd.
> It blesseth him that gives, and him that takes."

Charity brings its reward in another world.

Some of the greatest masters have given us pictures of the Last Judgment; placing Him whom they had often painted dying on His cross amid a crowd of enemies, high above another crowd—crowned and seated on a great white throne. Around Him are the host of heaven, and stretching away into distant space are the hosts of heaven, His angel train. Before Him is the world; a vast assembly where, all on one level, stand kings and beggars, priests and people, the master and his slave, men and women, childhood and old age. Their attire, or some other expedient of the painter's, reveals what had been their condition; their place, and the passions on their faces, what it is. Here, on the right hand, some are on their knees, adoring—some forms stretch upward with eager arms — some strike golden harps—some are waving palms of victory; but all, with their eyes fixed on Jesus, look as if they had never sinned nor sorrowed. God has wiped away all tears from all eyes; and their beautiful faces, so serene, so pure, so radiant with heavenly joy, inspire the wish, as we gaze on the picture, Their place be mine! may I die the death of the righteous; and may my last end be like His!

Between these and those on the left, what a contrast! how great a gulf! Despair, horror, agony, are depicted in their looks; driven downward by armed angels, they fall headlong into the hell that opens its fiery mouth to receive them; while above their wail we seem to hear the words of Jesus, as, waving them away, He says, with a touch of sadness in His voice, "Depart from me, ye cursed, into everlasting fire, prepared for the devil and his angels!" These pictures, though often studied as mere works of art, are great sermons. Like Jonah on the streets of Nineveh, they might arrest the feet of busy crowds, as they cry from the walls where they hung, Remember that thou must die, and after death the judgment.

The picture on which I would fix your eyes is one of Christ's own painting. It sets before us not so much the scene as the ground of the last judgment. The multitude are parted into two great classes—at the close of the day to be for ever parted. "These"—I quote our Lord's own words; the *everlasting* is not mine, but His—"these," proving that no stern prophet ever spake such awful truths as the Saviour's own gentle lips, —"these go away into everlasting punishment, but the righteous into life eternal." Momentous verdicts! changeless destinies! On what pivot do they turn? on this, feeding the hungry, clothing the naked, visits to the sick and to the prisoner in his lonely cell. The tree is known by its fruit. Unhappy trees on which Christ, coming to seek such fruit, finds none! I am not saying that we are not to contend earnestly for the faith once delivered to the saints; or that there is no importance in creeds, or difference between churches; or that if people are sincere, it is of no consequence what they believe; or that there is any other name given under heaven whereby we can be saved but the name of Jesus. I have no hope but His cross. I may give all my goods to feed the poor, and my body to be burned; yet if I have not love, it profiteth me nothing. Still our Lord exalts charity to the poor into a test of piety — of living, saving faith. Identifying Himself with them, He says, "Inasmuch as ye did or did it not unto one of the least of these, ye did or did it not to me!" David returned to Saul, bringing the giant's head; the spies came back to Moses, loaded with grapes from Eshcol; Jesus ascended to His Father, bearing in His hand the soul of the thief, blood-won trophy of His victory; one has said that Wilberforce went up to God, taking with him the broken fetters of eight hundred thousand slaves. What proofs of true piety shall we carry to heaven? What works will follow us? Shall widows and orphans, the wretched and the ragged, coming from homes which our bounty has blessed, and our prayers have sanctified, though not our saviours—"for there is one God, and one Mediator between God and men, the man Christ Jesus"—be our witnesses? May their testimony, that the same mind was in us that was in Christ, call down on us this gracious approving sentence, "Well done, good and faithful servant; enter thou into the joy of thy Lord."

THE SHINING LIGHT.

"The path of the just is as the shining light, that shineth more and more unto the perfect day."—Prov. iv. 18.

EVERY man's life is a path. Long in some cases, it is in others so short that many—that all those, indeed, of whom our Lord says the kingdom of heaven is—leave no impression on the sands of time other than the prints of little feet and a few brief steps. With all varieties of length, this path presents also an endless variety of scenes and circumstances. Like travellers whose road, passing over a mountainous district, now climbs to the summits of the hills, and now plunges into their gloomy gorges—some meet many "ups and downs" in life; they come out of one difficulty to encounter another; their home is saddened by successive bereavements ; misfortune follows on misfortune, as do the billows on each other that come swelling in with foaming crests to break, and thunder on the beach. On the other hand, some who enjoy the peace of God and a good conscience, have so little in their outward circumstances to give them trouble, that their life, like a river flowing by wooded banks and through fertile fields, glides smoothly on ; and they are in considerable danger of loving the world too well, of forgetting a better one, amid so much in this to gratify their desires. But, long or short, bordered with flowers or beset with thorns, life is but a pathway which has, for all the crowd that travel it, in the cradle a common beginning, and in the coffin a common end.

The grave is the end of all men. Here all things earthly—the grandest schemes, ambition's ladder, love's torch, the marriage altar, the conqueror's sword, the poet's laurels, the rich man's gold, the poor man's sorrows, woman's beauty, and manly strength—find their tomb. "One dieth," says Job, "in his full strength, being wholly at ease and in quiet ; his breasts are full of milk, and his bones are moistened with marrow. Another dieth in the bitterness of his soul, and never eateth with pleasure. They shall lie down alike in the dust; the worms shall cover them."

But life is a path in another, and still more important, sense. We shift the scene. Now, in place of many roads that start from a common cradle to meet again, after diverging far apart, in a common grave, we see but two; and they proceed in entirely opposite directions. They open differently—a wide gate admits to this, a narrow one to that. They end differently—these the inscriptions above their respective portals: on this, "Wide is the gate and broad is the way that leadeth to destruction; and many there be that go in thereat;" on that, "Strait is the gate and narrow is the way that leadeth to life; and few there be that find it." Solemn words, which it were well all had grace to lay to heart! On the one path or the other our feet are planted; and since every step is one upward to heaven or downward to perdition, it is sufficient to cast a solemn aspect over the glories of each setting sun, to think that it leaves us a day nearer hell, or nearer heaven. Different in character

—that broad and this narrow; different in access—that wide and this strait; different in their ends—this terminating in heaven and that in hell: these roads, on which a motley crowd, kings and beggars both, may be met, differ no less in the character of those who travel them; and we are thereby furnished with tests for determining, each for himself, this grave and most important question—On which am I travelling? To which of the parties do I belong?

One of these lies in the progressive advancement of God's people in virtue, in holiness, and in all manner of heavenly graces—a distinctive feature of their character which it may be interesting and profitable to study, as set forth in this beautiful image, "The path of the just is as *the shining light*, which shineth more and more unto the perfect day."

But, before looking at the figure, let us, in the first instance, consider *Why God's people are called just.*

Of all who have lived in the world since Adam's fall, our Lord Jesus Christ alone was, in the strict and proper sense of the word, entitled to that high character—to an appellation which He obtained from an unlooked-for quarter in the darkest crisis of His history. The fulness of time has come. The hour of redemption strikes. All things are now ready—the altar and the victim both. There is the wood and the fire, and the Lamb also for a burnt-offering. Heaven and hell look on in high expectancy. The representative and substitute of an elect world, the Son of Mary and of God, stands before Pilate to be condemned to death; and pour out His sinless soul an offering for sin. At this moment, to human eyes, the fate of Jesus hangs in the balance: for though the Jews demand His execution, the Roman governor refuses His assent. Strange rumours about this same Jesus of Nazareth, how He cured the most inveterate diseases, calmed storms on the deep, cast out devils, opened the eyes of the blind, the ears of the deaf, and even the graves of the dead, have reached Pilate's ear; stirred, astonished, and awed the palace. The Roman hesitates to strike; not so much probably out of regard to justice, as because he is afraid to challenge and provoke the power of this unknown; and rouse perhaps a lion in this gentle Lamb. Besides, there is a strange calm, lofty, mysterious dignity in the bearing of the prisoner that strikes terror into the heart of his time-serving, guilty judge; making him shrink back like one who is about to take a leap in the dark—he knows not where. Indeed, once and again, he attempts to save the accused. He pleads his cause, but in vain. And now, as no way of escape seems left, either for the prisoner or himself, submitting like a heathen to the Fates, he resumes his place on the seat of judgment, and, though reluctant, is about to pronounce the fatal sentence. At this critical moment there is a stir among the crowd, through which one, wearing Pilate's livery, is seen elbowing his way. He comes in hot haste, a messenger from Pilate's wife; and ascending the steps, whispers this warning in his master's ear, "Have thou nothing to do with that just man, for I have suffered many things this day in a dream because of Him." Strange, of all the thousands whom Jesus had blessed and cured, there was not so much as one to cry, Crucify Him not! Strange, as the only confession of Him came from the lips of a dying thief, the only voice raised in His behalf came from the lips of a dreaming woman! Yet though He was despised and rejected of men, though He came unto His own and His own received Him not, well spoke that dreamer. Let the guards unbind His arms, let Him break the strange silence that seals His lips, and He holds up His hands high above that raging multitude, before them, before the priests, before Pilate, before heaven as well as earth, before God himself, to say, These hands are clean! He, and He alone, of all that ever lived, since sin entered our world, was without sin—guile, there was none in His mouth; guilt, there was none in His heart. In Him a clean thing came out of an unclean. Though entering the world by Mary's womb, He was by birth the Just One. Though called the friend of publicans and sinners, He—holy, harmless, and undefiled, separate from sinners, as oil from the water amid which it floats—was in life the Just One. Though condemned as a malefactor, and crucified between two thieves, He was in death the Just One. He died, as Scripture says, "the just for the unjust, that we might be saved"—that His righteousness, the merits of His holy life and of His atoning death, being imputed to us, we might appear righteous; in other words, be reckoned just in the judgment, and therefore acquitted at the bar, of a holy God. Thus the apostle says, "justified by faith"—in other words, made just through the righteousness which grace on God's part imputes, and faith on ours receives—" we have peace with God through our Lord Jesus Christ." So I remark—

It is through the *righteousness of Jesus Christ* that any, in the strict and proper sense of the term, are *just* in the sight of God.

Society divides itself into a variety of classes —an arrangement that to some extent seems as much a law of Providence as the division of the hand into fingers, or of a tree into boughs, and of its boughs into branches. So we speak of the higher and lower classes, of nobles and commoners, of sovereigns and subjects, of the rich and the poor, of the learned and the unlearned. Like the differences of stature among the individuals of a crowd, between even giants and pigmies, to one who surveys them from a lofty bartizan, the ordinary distinctions of society vanish in the sight of heaven; and in the eyes of Him who looks down on the world from the heights of divinity, there remains but one, only one distinction. It is that which divides the whole human family, princes and peasants both, into two great classes—the good and evil, the just and unjust—and so, for example, it is said, "God maketh his sun to shine upon the evil and the good; and his rain to fall on the just and unjust." At any rate, no other distinction but that survives the stroke of death; descending with us into the grave and making it our peaceful bed, or a doleful prison. You cannot tell the skull of a king from that of a beggar; and in the grave, beauty the most charming and deformity the most revolting moulder into indistinguishable dust. Yet Jesus knows them that are His. It is as the just they sleep in Him; and as the just they shall rise from their graves on that day when the trumpet sounds the resurrection, and it shall be said "to the north, Give up, and to the south, Keep not back; bring my sons from far, and my daughters from the ends of the earth!"

But how do any become just with God? It cannot be because they are sinless. There is not a just man on earth that doeth good and sinneth not; and the inspired author of that statement also remarks of those who may in a sense be called just, "a just man falleth seven times and riseth up again." And since the best do fall, and that not seven times, nor seventy times seven, but times and ways innumerable, notwithstanding that they do rise again, and, through the grace of God sanctifying the humbling lesson, may rise, like the fabled giant, stronger than before, then in the words of the patriarch, "How can man be just with God? If he will contend with him, he cannot answer him one of a thousand." Such being the case, the apostle argues with unanswerable logic, that by the deeds of a law which requires perfect obedience, in other words, by man's own righteousness, " no flesh can be justified in the sight of God."

The Shuhite asked, as you will find written in the Book of Job, "How can man be justified with God? how can he be clean that is born of a woman? Behold even to the moon, and it shineth not; yea, the stars are not pure in His sight. How much less man, that is a worm; and the son of man, which is a worm?" Bildad's question finds its answer, the grand difficulty of all heathen nations and ages its complete solution, in the gospel. Let this poor "worm" but creep through the dust to the foot of the Cross, and bathe itself in the blood of Calvary: and how it is changed! What a change on that which, once a creeping caterpillar, crawling on the ground and devouring garbage, now spreads its painted wings, and springs into the air to live in sunbeams and to feed on flowers! What a change on the leper, when, bending his way from the prophet's house to the banks of Jordan, he goes down into the sacred stream; and dips, and dips again, and, taking the seventh plunge, rises from the parting waters with a skin like a little child's! But a greater change is here. At the foot of the Cross, sprinkled with the blood of Christ, the sinner changes into a saint; the unjust into the just; the condemned into the acquitted; the child of hell into an heir of heaven. Putting off self-righteousness to put on Christ, he exchanges a beggar's rags for a kingly robe; once covered with iniquity as with a garment, he now stands apparelled in one finer, fairer, costlier than ever angel wore; and in the eyes of his Sovereign Judge, the believer, happy man! is without spot, or stain, or any such thing. "There is no condemnation for those who are in Jesus Christ, who walk not after the flesh, but after the Spirit."

As appears from this figure, the spiritual life of the just, the justified, the believer in Jesus, is one of *progress*.

A connoisseur in works of art, so soon as the dust of years has been wiped from an old picture, can name the master who painted the glowing canvas. So also, though time has left no record of their history, and no date stands carved on the crumbling ruins, an antiquarian can tell from its form when that arch was sprung; from their capitals, by what hands, long mouldering in the dust, these grand, impressive, silent pillars were reared on their massive pedestals. The works of all great men, and those of all great ages, are marked by properties peculiar to themselves. And features entirely their own are eminently characteristic of all the works of God; so characteristic of these that the untutored Arab when challenged to prove in God the existence of a being whom he had never touched, nor heard, nor seen, regarded the scoffer with amazement! nor deigned to return any answer to his gibes but one borrowed from the scenes of his native desert: "Just as I know," he replied, in terms worth a volume of divinity—"Just as I know," pointing to a footprint on the sand, "whether it was a man or a camel that passed my tent last night."

So distinguished by a divine wisdom, power, and goodness are God's works of creation and providence that all Nature, by the gentle voices of her skies and streams, of her fields and forests, as well as by the roar of breakers, the crash of thunder, the rumbling earthquake, the fiery volcano, the destroying hurricane, echoes the closing sentence of this angel hymn, "Holy, holy, holy is the Lord God Almighty, the whole earth is full of his glory!" But the works of God are not less marked by their progressive character than by the attributes of wisdom, power, and goodness. A work of time, the world was built story by story; and course by course the pyramid of animated nature rose from its base, till man, his Maker's image, and creation's crowning work, was placed on its lofty summit. Brief as is the history of creation compared to the large portion of the Bible which is devoted to the story of redemption, the opening chapter of Genesis, though leaving much unexplained and wrapt in impenetrable obscurity, shows us God working onward to His Sabbath rest by a series of successive creations; and when we close the pages of revelation to examine those of nature, they who are skilled to read that older record, see progress inscribed on all its stony leaves.

Then, the Providence that governs the world is equally characterised by progress. It is to be seen every morning in the approach of day—not flashing like an explosion to startle the world from sleep, but advancing, by silent though steady steps, from the first faint streak in the east through all the glories and changing hues of sunrise, of amber and saffron and gold and purple, to the blaze of the perfect day; we see it in the growth of plants, from the pale, tender shoot which lifts a tiny head above the soil to its maturity in the tree that, with its stately form rifted in the rock, throws out its giant arms, and, battling with the elements, defies the rage of storms; we see it in the change a few days make on the flowers of the garden, or a few months on our corn fields or a few swift years in our families where girls grow into women, and boys into stalwart men. Like God's works of creation, and His works also of providence, redemption, while displaying all His attributes in their brightest lustre, and forming His greatest work, is also marked by this never-failing feature of progress. The temple of salvation was not built in a day, or in a century, or even in a thousand years. Its foundation was laid in Eden, and at a time remote as the Fall—laid in that promise of a Saviour which God embosomed in the curse He pronounced on the cunning serpent, "I will put enmity between thee and the woman, and between thy seed and her seed: it shall bruise thy head, and thou shalt bruise his heel." Yet not till four thousand long years had come and gone did the Redeemer crown His work; and, in the dying but triumphant accents of His expiring breath, pronounce it "finished."

And it is with the work of our sanctification, the work of renewing grace in the soul, as with all God's works in all places of His dominion; "Hear, O Israel, the Lord thy God is one Lord." In this, as in all things else, progress is God's plan, and man's pathway to perfection. Let this yield comfort to some in whom grace seems but a little spark—a feeble, flickering flame, easily quenched and often ready to expire. Let them not be cast down; but pray God, with His Spirit and the breath of His mouth, to blow the smoking flax into a bright, burning, heaven-kindled, and ascending flame. The day of small things in grace is no more to be despised than the day of small things in sin; for it is commonly with Christ formed within us as it was with Christ on Mary's bosom, in the carpenter's house of Nazareth. He grew in wisdom as in stature; at first a feeble babe, hanging on a mother's breast, clinging to a mother's side, He grew betimes into a man whose voice hushed the tempest, whose foot trode the rolling billows, from whose presence devils fled, and whose behests even the dead obeyed.

T

Imitating Him whom faith receives both as our propitiation and our pattern, we are by pains and prayer to grow in holiness and humility; in sweetness of temper and heavenliness of mind; in active obedience and patient suffering; in conformity to the will and delight in the ways of God. Why should we be cast down, dispirited, disheartened, and ready to abandon all efforts in an unwarrantable despair? No doubt, whether our aim be high or humble, we always come short of the mark? Yet let us be thankful, though we have not reached, if we are nearing perfection; if, like the harbour lights, we see it ahead of us, not vanishing on the stern, but growing on the bow; if our course shows marks of progress; if our spiritual life is lighting up like the morning; and we can express our experience in the words of the apostle, "We all, with open face beholding as in a glass the glory of the Lord, are changed into the same image from glory to glory, even as by the Spirit of the Lord."

As does not appear in this figure, the progress of God's people in a life of grace may be *helped and hastened.*

The progress of those celestial luminaries that raise the tides of ocean and rule the seasons of the year, and make night and day, morning's growing dawn and evening's deepening twilight, is independent of us; both of our works and our wishes. Those heavenly bodies that roll through the fields of space, move in orbits beyond our reach; nor did man ever interfere with their machinery but on that occasion, when, for a special purpose and by miraculous power, Joshua laid his hands on their wheels—" So the sun stood still in the midst of heaven and hasted not to go down about a whole day; and there was no day like that before or after it, that the Lord hearkened unto the voice of a man: for the Lord fought for Israel." All experience confirms that observation of the inspired historian. Ah, time moves no slower for the wishes of the miserable wretch, in whose eyes, as he waits the day of execution, its sands never ran, and in whose ears its lessening hours never struck, so quickly—and the long night passes and the dawn comes no sooner for the wishes of the crew that, wrecked on the thundering reef, with a straining ship breaking up beneath and every moment threatening to ingulf them, scan the east with anxious eyes; and watching for the first streak of light, weary, and pray for the coming of the morn. The natural light which shines over our heads and brightens into the perfect day, obeys the unalterable decrees of heaven—our wishes cannot hasten its progress, nor can our indifference by one moment delay or hinder it.

It is otherwise with grace in the soul; in the life, habits, and hearts of God's chosen people. No doubt sanctification, like redemption, is the peculiar work of God—the life of grace in His people being as much His work as the light that breaks and brightens on the eastern sky when, with almighty hand, He throws open the gates of day. Yet, while God by His Spirit works in sanctification, we also are to work. In this field, as in that of the conversion of the world, Christians are honoured and are called to be fellow-workers with God—the injunction of the apostle being laid on them all: "Work out your own salvation with fear and trembling; for it is God which worketh in you both to will and to do of his good pleasure." Hence we are exhorted to grow in grace; to grow in the knowledge and love of our Lord Jesus Christ; to labour for the bread that never perisheth; to forget the things that are behind, and press forward, onward, upward—the path we move on, progress; the end we aim at, perfection. No effort of ours can either hasten or hinder the dawn of day; but by watchfulness and prayer, by the devout use of our Bibles and the hallowed observance of God's holy day, by waiting on Him in all the ordinances of His house and holding fellowship with our heavenly Head, and Lord, and elder Brother, we can do much to promote our growth in grace, and mature our meetness for the kingdom of heaven. Let us labour for such lofty ends. Anything beneath them is to mistake the grand purpose of life, and to peril the salvation of our souls. He who imagines that the grace of God, once received into his heart, will grow in that soil without either effort, or care, or prayer of his, as without these the dawn breaks and the day brightens above his head, is grievously, fatally mistaken. Alas! his case is described by another figure, though also borrowed from the break of morn:—

unlike the shining light which shineth more and more unto the perfect day, his goodness, a delusion, shall be "as a morning cloud and the early dew" that vanish away; and, dissolving into empty air, leave neither on earth nor sky so much as a trace behind them.

RISEN WITH CHRIST.—PART I.

> "*If ye then* [or, *since ye then*] *be risen with Christ, seek those things which are above.*"—COL. iii. 1.

THERE are tracts of country in some regions of the world where the soil feels hot to the touch, the ground rings hollow to the foot, and groaning mountains belch forth flames, clouds of vapour, and streams of molten rock. There, where the "solid earth" seems an inappropriate expression, earthquakes occasionally occur, to bury, not houses only, but whole cities, in their yawning chasms. Unlike these, which are connected with ordinary volcanic agencies, was the earthquake that, with strange signs in the heavens, distinguished our Lord's from all other deaths. It opened graves, not to bury the living, but set the dead free; and, wrenching the bars of death asunder, exposed to the eye of day the grim and silent tenants of the tomb.

So happened it when Jesus, God manifest in the flesh, gave up the ghost. Our earth was struck with terror. Seized with an extraordinary trembling, the rocks, in whose bowels the Jews hollowed out their tombs, were rent asunder; and such as had the curiosity and courage to look in, saw the dead—each lying in his stony chamber. They were waiting the hour of resurrection; nor could they rise till Christ had risen. A king goes foremost—not before, but after him his subjects; nor is it the feet but the head that rises first to the surface when a man, falling overboard, is buried in the sea. Such was the order of events on the morning of the third day. The angel, seated on the stone that he had rolled from the door, is silently waiting the issue with eyes fixed upon the tomb, when Jesus, untouched, unsummoned, awakes; and rising to put off shroud and face-cloth, passes forth into the morning air with the step of a conqueror. For this hour, for the joy set before Him, to redeem our souls from hell and our bodies from the grave, He had endured the cross and despised the shame; and He now lives to die no more. And as, so soon as the heart in a case of suspended animation resumes its functions, the blood begins to flow and pulses throb through all the body, even so they revive with Christ, who were to show forth the connexion between His resurrection and that of His saints at the final judgment. Prefiguring that great event, and leaving the graves the earthquake had opened, many saints arose. The evangelist St Matthew thus describes the scene :—" Jesus, when he had cried again with a loud voice, yielded up the ghost. And, behold, the veil of the temple was rent in twain from the top to the bottom ; and the earth did quake, and the rocks rent ; and the graves were opened ; and many bodies of the saints which slept arose, and came out of the graves after his resurrection, and went into the holy city, and appeared unto many." Our Lord's ascent from the grave was a fit counterpart to His descent from the skies ; both events being characterised by manifestations of the divinity that touched with resplendent glory the darkest mysteries of His life. He left heaven attended by a train of angels, and left the tomb with one hardly less, if not more remarkable—a band whom he had restored to life, and brought out of their graves. They, the strangest assembly ever met on earth, had "risen with Christ;" and so, in the plainest sense of the terms, St Paul might have addressed them, saying, "If ye then," or since ye then, "are risen with Christ, seek those things which are above."

Had the apostle addressed these words to that company, they could have had little interest, and no application to us. But the words occur in a letter he wrote to the church at Colosse; and were addressed to such as, far removed from the scene of this stupendous miracle, had no more share in it than we have. We shall therefore consider them as bearing on the whole Church of Christ, in every age as well as in every country of the world. Happily combining doctrine and practice, they present two distinct points for consideration; they delineate a character and enjoin a duty. Taking these in their order, let us consider—

Who are those that may be said *to have risen with Christ.*

There is a churchyard where the passenger who reads the inscriptions on the tombs, that stand up amid the long rank grass beneath the shadow of waving elms and an old gray steeple, will find one to surprise him; which, though quaint in form, I doubt not is true in substance. Here, no angel flying through the heavens sounds a trumpet; no figure of old Time, with bald head, shoulders a scythe or shakes an hour-glass; no cross-bones rudely carved, nor sexton's spade, nor grinning skull, give point to the trite " Memento Mori." Stranger still, the monument which is raised to the memory and virtues of one person bears the date of more than one birth: with long years between, it says, speaking in name of the dead, I was born the first time on such a day, and born the second time on such another day of another year. Strange, indeed! Yet, had John Baptist's disciples erected a monument to the memory of their murdered master, it might have recorded a more astounding fact; and, to those ignorant of the work of God's Spirit, a more inexplicable riddle.

For, contradiction in terms though it seems, the second birth in John's as in Jeremiah's case, went before the first—the Baptist being sanctified from his mother's womb. There, a babe yet unborn, he rejoiced in God his Saviour; " Lo," said Elizabeth to Mary, when the two cousins, both by and by to become mothers, met—" Lo, as soon as the voice of thy salutation sounded in mine ears, the babe leaped in my womb for joy."

The history of every saint on being completed, which it shall not be till the final judgment, and heads mouldering in the dust are crowned with immortality, will contain a record of two births, of two deaths, and of two resurrections—the first visible, the second invisible; the subject of the one change, the body; the subject of the other, which is a matter of faith and not of sight, the soul of the believer. This second birth and first death, or resurrection, are one and the same event. Here let me pause to say, How important an event! and to ask, Have we any experience of it? This change of heart is the door to heaven, the hinge on which turns our eternal destiny; without it Jesus declares that no man, however virtuous or honest, can see the kingdom of God; promising to bestow it, God says, "O my people, I will open your graves, and cause you to come up out of your graves—a new heart also will I give you, and a new spirit will I put within you;" and what God has promised in these, and many other no less gracious words, Ezekiel was privileged to see in vision—there, where the bones of a valley, once a battlefield, orderly arrange themselves into skeletons, and the naked skeletons get clothed with flesh, and no sooner does a wind from heaven come, sweeping along to stir their hair and kiss their lips, than every dead man, inspired anew with life, springs to his feet, and the valley, before so silent, echoes to the blare of trumpets, and is filled with "an exceeding great army,"—God's host, bannered and marshalled, and eager for battle.

The words "risen with Christ," which express the condition of such as are born of God's Spirit and have passed through the first resurrection, are in complete harmony with all that Scripture and conscience reveal of our lost state by nature. The Word of God pronounces all men dead, "dead in trespasses and sins;" and the most cursory examination of the subject teaches us that more is meant by that expression than the fact, alarming as the fact is, that, until justified by faith in the righteousness of Jesus Christ, we all lie under condemnation. What does he think of, for example, who lies in a condemned cell, sentenced within so many days to be taken to the place of public execution, and hanged by the neck till he is dead?—of what he shall eat, or drink, or wherewithal he shall be clothed—of comforts with which to surround himself—of the pastimes and pleasures in which he may spend his numbered hours? No. By his grated window the wretched man sits, inditing petitions for pardon: when the world sleeps, and all but his beating heart is still, he creeps softly from his pallet to try the strength of the iron bars; unlike those who neither pray nor solicit the prayers of others, he engages every possible interest to intercede with the Crown on his behalf, nor leaves any means untried to make his pardon sure. But, till awakened and converted by divine grace, do men show any such anxiety for salvation: or put forth one earnest effort corresponding to his? If they did, who should be lost?

None. With pardon freely offered—to be got for the asking; with liberty proclaimed and prison doors flung open; with God not willing that any should perish, but that all should come to Him and live, it is not possible to account for sinners perishing otherwise than by the fact that men, while under the sentence are also under the insensibility of death. Think you that unless the body stretched on the funeral pile by the banks of the Ganges were dead, it would lie passive there, to be wrapped in flames and reduced to ashes? Alive, how the man would watch the torch's fiery glare, and, perceiving it touch the pile, burst his bonds, spring from his bed, and fly for life! Much more, were men not "dead in trespasses and sins," would they work out their salvation with fear and trembling—give all diligence to " make their calling and election sure."

Besides being marked by insensibility, death is followed by corruption. It, not the glassy eye, nor marble brow, nor rigid form, nor heart that neither beats nor flutters, is the surest, saddest proof that life has fled: and so with the grand and bold imagery of inspiration, the prophet represents the dead as talking in their graves, saying "to corruption, Thou art my father; and to the worm, Thou art my mother and my sister." And turning from the physical to the moral aspects of man's case, alas! how much corruption is in his heart to prove him "dead in trespasses and sins." Let the Holy Spirit, before he begins to cleanse it, open a sinner's eyes to its depravity, show the man himself in the mirror of God's Word, and he starts back from the glass, aghast at his own image; shocked to see that there is no grave so foul as man's heart. "Ye shall loathe yourselves," says God to His people, "ye shall loathe yourselves in your own sight for all the evils that ye have committed." Need we wonder at such strong expressions? Why? Even saintly Ezra blushed to lift up his head: and Job, eminent above all the men of his time for uprightness, cried, "I abhor myself:" and St Paul, as if this greatest of apostles had been the greatest of sinners, feeling through the corruptions that clung to him like a living captive in a most horrible predicament — chained to one whom death had turned into a festering corpse, exclaims, "Who shall deliver me from the body of this death?" If it is so with renewed men, what must it be with those who are entire strangers to the grace of God—if such is the state of the green tree, how must it be with the dry?

I am far from asserting, though sin, like a poison carried along in the blood, has affected in a sense our entire nature, that the unconverted are without amiable, excellent, and valuable properties. I have seen flowers of lovely hue and fragrant odour clinging to the walls of a crumbling ruin, and I have seen such beauty lingering on the face of the dead as went far to deprive death of its repulsive aspect, and make it difficult to believe that life had fled. Such are the graces that belong to fallen humanity. They adorn, but cannot redeem it—pleasing man, but not propitiating God. If our Lord's body in the grave, to borrow an illustration from it, might be regarded as the type of a soul "dead in trespasses and sins," these natural virtues are but the fine linen in which Joseph wrapped the sacred form, the bed of spices on which with tender hand he composed the mangled limbs. What availed the snowy fabric of the loom, and fragrance that filled the sepulchre? Death was there—the dear form was cold; the eyes were fixed and filmy; silent the voice that hushed the tempest and cheered the weeping penitent; powerless the hand at whose touch blind eyes opened and old sores were closed; and, with its features muffled in a napkin, low on the cold ground lay the head that had lain in the bosom of God. Thus Jesus was under the insensibility as well as the sentence of death; and so remained till, after three days and nights, as the Jews expressed it, life returned to the lifeless body, and His heart with all other organs resumed its functions. Then He rose; declared by His resurrection to be the Son of God with power. And they who are risen with Him, undergoing a greater change than the saints who had their graves opened at His death, and their life restored at His resurrection, are those whose souls once dead in sin have become alive through grace. Your way to spiritual life opened up, perhaps, by convictions that have rent the rocky heart and shaken soul and body too, as earthquakes shake a trembling world, have you risen to newness of life? Then cast off, like grave-clothes, the habits of sin. In the strength of heavenly grace, burst its bonds, and go forth to enjoy the light and walk in the liberty of the sons of God.

For on those who have thus risen with Christ is

The duty enjoined—*seek those things which are above*, or as St Paul more fully expresses it in words we shall by and by consider, Set your affections on things in heaven, and not on things on earth.

When the doctrine of a resurrection was first revealed, it dazzled all eyes and blinded some. Reason started at the strange announcement; and treating its great preacher with undisguised contempt, the Athenians sneered—asking, as they curled the lip and pointed to St Paul, "What doth this babbler say?" To throw some light on that mystery, he employed the similitude of such familiar objects as corn-seed, which is cast on the soil, and, though when buried in the furrow a dry, sapless, lifeless-looking thing, rises to push aside the clods, and clothe the fields with verdure, and fill the barns of the husbandman with golden sheaves. In other realms of nature, science finds a still more remarkable similitude in the insects that, sporting in sunbeams and flitting from flower to flower, give life to the air and beauty to the scene. Once creeping worms, after a while they wove a shroud and wrapped it round them, and, dropping from bush or tree, sought a grave in the earth, where they lay entombed till spring winds thawed and summer beams warmed the soil, and at the appointed time shuffled off their shroud, and rose into the sunny air on silken wings—in form, in food, in tastes, in habits so different, that it might be said, "Old things have passed away, and all things are become new."

An image of the change on our bodies when this poor dust shall hear the trumpet, and mortality put on immortality, this is not less, but perhaps more, an image of the change wrought in our souls when the Spirit renews them at the second birth and first resurrection. Then, at least, in their dominant power, old things have passed away; and, in their bud and germ at least, all things have become new. The Bible, for example, so soon as a man is converted, reads like a new book; the Sabbath bell rings out new sounds;

Jesus, once despised, but now invested with new and attractive graces, is prized as the chiefest among ten thousand and altogether lovely—every feeling and affection leaving its old channel, flows in a new and opposite direction; and loving what once he hated and hating what once he loved, shunning what once he sought and seeking what once he shunned, the years the renewed man spent in sin seem to him like a strange, and guilty, and frightful, and horrid dream. Yet, though perfect in nature, this holy change is imperfect in degree—many being the hostile influences to which believers are exposed here; many the temptations that assail their virtue; many the difficulties that impede their course; many the conflicts they have to maintain against the love of the world and the remaining corruption of their hearts. Therefore St Paul urges them to withdraw their affections from things on earth, and, as those that have risen from sin to the enjoyment of a new life, to set them on things above.

Thus to rise and soar, though by no means easy, is a duty to which God's people will give earnest heed if they consult only their present happiness. The ivy which throws its arms around a hollow and rotten tree dooms itself to be crushed; and they are laying up suffering for a future day who allow affections which should be trained to the skies to be entangled with perishing earthly objects. God will not permit His redeemed ones to perish; but to save their souls He will sink their treasures—cast away the cargo to keep the ship afloat. If they choose Sodom, He will burn them out of it; to deliver them from idolatry, He will destroy their idols; and when precepts fail to teach it, He will teach them by bitter experience that "he builds too low, who builds beneath the skies." Startled by the whirring of a scared bird, the fall of a leaf, even their own shadow which the moon, shining through a glade of the forest, projects on the path, they may fear robbers who carry their fortune on their persons; but he who has his wealth in the banker's safe, walks light-hearted through the gloom of night, and whistles as he goes—careless though thieves be thick as forest leaves. Even so, the man who has his treasure in heaven is, in a sense and measure at least, prepared for the worst that can befall; nor, when misfortune comes to take away his wealth, or disease to take away his health, or calumny to take away his reputation, or death to pluck wife or child from his loving arms, has he to raise the old, bitter cry, "Ye have taken away my gods, and what have I more?" He who has his affections set on things above is like one who hangs on by the skies; and, having a secure hold of these, could say though he saw the world roll away from beneath his feet, "My heart is fixed, my heart is fixed, O Lord, I will sing and give praise!"

I do not say, notwithstanding all its sins and sorrows, but that there is much good in God's world. It is a good servant, though, like fire and water, a bad master; useful as a staff, though in the heart a tyrant's rod; good beneath a man's feet, though on his back a burden to make a saint groan, like Atlas. Be careful, therefore, by setting your affections on things above, to keep the world in its own place. Allow it to thrust itself in between you and God, and Christ, and holiness, and heaven, and it shall be with your souls as with our planet when the moon rolls in between us and the sun; though vastly inferior to that glorious luminary, yet blotting out all beauty, hushing the voice of song, turning day into sudden night, and striking terror into all nature, it wraps the world in the darkness of a cold eclipse. It matters little how much of the world is in our hands, if it is kept out of our hearts, and care be taken that neither business nor pleasures make us forget that heaven, not earth, is our home. Would that heaven had such a place in our thoughts as home has in the hearts of boys about holiday time, of soldiers when the weary war draws to a close, of exiles looking to see the ship sail round the headland which is to convey them and their fortunes from a foreign shore. As I have seen the twittering swallows, when their time of migration drew near, sit on house-tops pruning their pinions, and wheel in mazy circles through the air to try and to strengthen their powers of flight, so, living above and looking beyond this world, let us prepare for our departure—daily, prayerfully, assiduously cultivating that holiness which is the unfailing characteristic of believers, and which, perfected on their arrival at the gates of heaven, shall be their highest happiness and brightest crown.

But if we are to live separate from the world like oil among water—though in it, not of it—how, it may be asked, since men only do well what they do with a will, are we, with affections fixed on things above, to perform aright the secular, ordinary duties of life? If our hearts are engrossed with heavenly things, how are we to obey this other, and equally divine, commandment, "Whatsoever"—be it to sweep a floor or reform a state, hold the helm of a ship or of a nation—"whatsoever thy hand findeth to do, do it with thy might"—a way of doing ordinary work, let me observe, not more conducive to our temporal advantage than creditable to our religious profession. "With might" implies that the heart is engaged along with the head and hand; and having, though two hands, but one heart which, like the living child for whom the mothers wrangled, to divide were to destroy, how can we do things apparently so incompatible as to set our affections on the things of heaven and yet engage with "might" in the secularities of earth?

The two are perfectly consistent. Man standing between the celestial and terrestrial worlds is related to both; and resembling neither a flower which, springing from the dust and returning to it, belongs altogether to the earth, nor a star which, shining far remote from this lower sphere, belongs altogether to the heavens, our hearts may be fitly likened to the rainbow that, rising into heaven but resting on earth, is connected both with the clods of the valley and the clouds of the sky.

Let this familiar example show how Christians may have their affections set on things above, and yet give diligent attention to the duties of their earthly calling. With the salt tear standing in his eye, with a mother's precious counsels and a father's pious prayers, a youth leaves home for a distant colony. At the foot of the ladder he looks to its topmost round; resolved to climb, step by step, up to wealth and honour. For this end he saves with an economy that allows no waste; works with an energy that never wearies; submits without shrinking to trials and hardships; and throws himself into his duties with a zeal that merits fortune and commands success. People, and especially his fellows whom he leaves lagging far behind, fancy that his affections, like its trees, have taken root in that foreign soil, and that his heart is wholly engrossed with the cares and business of his post. They know no better. His heart is not there. It is at home—its affections, like an elastic chain, stretching unbroken over all the lands that lie and broad seas that roll between. Visions of his father's house float around his couch; the forms of loved ones move in his nightly dreams: where palm-trees wave, he longs to see the hills of dusky pines, and thinks, when the nightingale sings from orange groves, of the larks that carol, soaring over his native fields. Fond memory dwells on the past; fancy stretches away into the future; and he sets store on honours and wealth, chiefly for the pleasures they will yield to loved ones at home. Home is the centre around which his hidden life keeps turning; the dear word stands engraven on his heart: his settled purpose, his daily thought is one day to go home. And yet, whether his office in that distant land be to sit at the head of a council, or march at the head of an army, to manage a business, to hold a pen or guide a plough, whatever his hand findeth to do he does it with all his might.

Even so should it be with us in our earthly pilgrimage. So far from doing our earthly duties worse, we do them better by having our affections set on things above—the hope of rest strengthening us for labour: the example of Christ inspiring us with ardour; and no fears of ultimate disappointment clouding our prospects and weakening us by the way. One, long an exile, returns to his native land; but not to home. Ah! he finds no home. The voices are silent he hoped to hear; the cold grave holds those he hoped to see; his old friends are in the dust, nor live but in his dreams: and turning away from a generation that stare coldly on his gray hairs, he repairs to the churchyard, and, sitting down on a father's or mother's grave, weeps over the ruins of fondly cherished hopes—this the verdict on all his toil, and exile, and wealth, and honours, Vanity and vexation of spirit! But where Christ sitteth at the right hand of God, we shall find more than hope ever anticipated, imagination fancied, or love desired. Who after long years of exile goes up to the door of his old home, approaches it with a beating heart; knocks with a trembling hand. He knows not what has happened in his absence: an empty chair may meet his eye, and to the questions that tremble on his lips the only answer may be, Dead—all dead! How different his fortune who knocks at heaven's happy gate! It opens on scenes of surpassing glory. Arrayed in robes of light, long missed and long mourned ones hasten to meet him at the door; and lead him up through lines of shining angels to the throne where Jesus, his Saviour, seated in glory at the right hand of God, bends on him looks of ineffable affection, and bids him Welcome to the bliss of Paradise.

RISEN WITH CHRIST.—Part II.

> "*If ye then* [or, *since ye then*] *be risen with Christ, seek those things which are above.*"—Col. iii. 1.

THE world once boasted of possessing seven wonders; but a greater than any or all of them is, a true Christian. His feelings, enjoyments, aims, and objects are such, that he is more than a wonder; he is a mystery which none but those initiated, like himself, in the mysteries of the faith, are able to comprehend. Dying, yea, by nature "dead in trespasses and sins," he lives; sorrowing, he rejoices; having nothing, he possesses all things; poor, he makes many rich; reversing the common proverb, that "seeing is believing," he believes more firmly in what he does not see than in what he sees; contrary to the ordinary laws of nature, he is more powerfully attracted by distant objects than by near ones; his well, like Israel's of old, is a flinty rock; his bread grows on barren sands; his homeward path is at the beginning through a tumultuous sea, and at the end through a dark, roaring flood. He is confident of wanting nothing, yet depends on the bounty of One who depended for His own bread on others, and had not a place where to lay His head; for his joys, he looks to One who was a Man of Sorrows; and expects a crown of glory from Him who wore no crown on earth but a wreath of thorns.

If the world is right in its judgment of what constitutes true greatness, the humblest believer is a great man. What discoveries in science so important or sublime as those he makes—in the study of the Bible and of his own heart? Neither David with his sling, nor Abishai with his sword, slew such giants as he conquers and slays—in his sins. What victories does history record, or triumphal arches celebrate, so grand in their nature and enduring in their effects as those He wins—over "principalities, and powers, and spiritual wickedness?" No laurels crown his humble brow; his name is unknown to fame. Yet, mortifying his affections, controlling his passions, keeping his body in subjection, and subordinating his will to God's, this is what the wise man says of him: "He that is slow to anger, is better than the mighty; and he that ruleth his spirit than he that taketh a city."

No true greatness, there is no true faith, like a believer's. One of the grandest characters in history is Christopher Columbus; but what the bold Italian did, when, leaving the shores of Spain, he sailed west, and still farther west, over an unknown and a boundless sea, seeking a world none had discovered, and hardly any but himself believed in, the Christian does. "He seeks a country"—and with stronger faith; since from that world in whose existence he firmly believes, and on whose happy shore he hopes one day to land, not one of the thousands that have gone to seek it have returned. Columbus appeared again in Europe, loaded with the strange fruits and golden spoils of his brilliant discovery: but, like barks that, foundering at sea, have never been heard of after they left the port, none have come back from the other world—to say, " Arise, we have seen the land, and, behold, it is very good!"

Of boundless faith, whose aims and aspirations soar like the believer's? The world which the Macedonian subdued by his arms has wondered less at his achievements than at his ambition; nor has it ever ceased to regard as one of its strangest spectacles that man of universal empire sitting down to weep, because he could find no other world to conquer. And yet there burns a loftier ambition in that lowly cottage, where a sun-browned peasant sits reading his Bible, with a roof of thatch above his head, a rough clay floor beneath his feet, and no more of the earth to call his own than the graves where his fathers sleep. He is thankful for bread to eat, and raiment to put on; he is content to possess as much as will serve for staff and sandals to the end of the pilgrimage; yet he has a heart not one, nor a thousand worlds could fill. Nothing below, however it may gratify, can satisfy his longing soul. He sets his affections on things above, and turning from all created enjoyments to God, his language is the Psalmist's—"Thou art my inheritance and the portion of my cup. Whom have I in heaven but thee? there is none in all the earth whom I desire besides thee."

Nevertheless, naturally drawn like a falling stone to the earth, the best of God's people often feel constrained, amid the attractions and distractions of this world, to cry with David, "Quicken me, O Lord, according to thy word, for my soul cleaveth to the dust;" and to help such as have risen with Christ to rise to things above, let me point out some earthly objects from which they should be careful to withhold, and withdraw their affections. Pope, the poet and moralist, has remarked, that to attack vice in the abstract, and not in persons, is safe fighting, but is fighting with shadows; and, instead of indulging in such general observations against the love of earthly things as would furnish an unhappy illustration of his remark, let us come to close quarters; and select some of those objects on which we should not, and yet on which we are prone to, set our affections.

One of these is *the adornment of the body.*

I have seen a child in ignorance of its great loss totter across the floor to its mother's coffin, and, caught by their glitter, seize the handles, to look round and smile as it rattled them on the hollow sides. I have seen a boy, forgetting his sorrow in his dress, survey himself with evident satisfaction as he followed the bier that bore his father to the grave. And however painful such spectacles, as jarring our feelings, and out of all harmony with such sad and sombre scenes, they excite no surprise nor indignation. We only pity those who, through ignorance of their loss or inability to appreciate it, find pleasure in what should move their grief. When one is a child, as St Paul says, they speak as a child, and think as a child. Nor is it difficult also to understand how families which have lost their social position, either through injustice or misfortune, should retain, and take a pride in showing, the relics and memorials of their better days. These may secure the respect usually paid to fallen greatness; and if they do not exalt them in the eyes of others, they minister to self-esteem, and exalt them in their own.

The pride of dress, however, though excusable in those savage tribes who walk their forests daubed with paint and decked with feathers, is a passion in all other cases as strange as in some it is strong. Can a maid, says God, forget her ornaments, or a bride her attire? Yet, though this be an example of what is improbable, or indeed impossible, we might wonder that woman's attire, though sparkling with costly gems, does not cover her cheeks rather with the blush of shame than the glow of pride. The history of dress is humbling; not flattering to our vanity. I do not refer to special cases,—the hardships they endure who thread their needles with the threads of life, and die early victims to the demands of fashion; nor to those who, more vain than honest, purchase what they cannot pay for, and assume an appearance as false as the flowers they wear—nor to those who are more proud of being gaily attired than ashamed of casting their parents on public charity; nor even to those who buy their wretched fineries with the wages of iniquity, and abandon the paths of virtue for the sake of gaudy attire. Associations belong to dress, when most honestly obtained and modestly worn, and altogether suitable to the rank and condition of the wearer, sufficient to prevent it becoming an idol. No doubt robes of snowy white may raise our minds by reminding us of the fine linen of the saints, the spotless garments of Jesus' righteousness; and the spectacle of a queen at court or coronation, arrayed in jewelled crown and regal splendour, may recall the psalm where the graces of His Church are set forth under the imagery of a maiden's beauty, raiment of needlework, and cloth woven with threads of gold and blazing with costly gems. Still the oldest associations connected with dress are those of sin and shame. Sin was its beginning, as it is often still its end. It dates from the fall of our first parents, and has led to that of many of their children: and surely there is nothing, either in its root or in its fruits, to justify us setting our affections on it, or giving it any measure of attention beyond what propriety demands, or comfort and health require.

Apart from these considerations, vanity of dress is, more than anything else, "vanity of vanities." Man's soul is a spark struck from divinity; and with its expressive features and graceful symmetry, even his body presents a form of beauty worthy of the hand that moulded it; but in the matter of attire, man is as inferior to many other creatures as he is inferior in brute strength to an ox, or to a frog in the art of swimming. Let looms and needles do their utmost, the worm yield its silk, the rocks their gold, the mine its diamonds, the deep her pearls, and Nature all her treasures, to adorn the person and inflate the pride of a haughty beauty. The bird whose plume she wears, when it flashed a winged and living gem through tropic groves, was more gorgeously apparelled than she—the difference between her and it, that which lies between the Almighty's hand and ours. Here the proudest beauty bends to the flower that bends its head to the wind, and is crushed by a passing hoof. How miserable the vanity that feeds on dress! How wicked, in practically regarding the question, Wherewithal shall I be clothed? as greater than this, What shall I do to be saved? How utterly contemptible, since, with taste as true as divine, our Lord, pointing to a bed of lilies whose graceful forms and glowing colours bedecked the meadow, said, "Solomon in all his glory was not like one of these!"

A story is told of one whose bosom swelled and heaved with pride as, standing before a mirror, she decked herself out for triumphs. Suddenly, though none had entered the chamber, another figure appeared in the glass. An awful form, it was wrapped in a winding-sheet, and dressed out in grave-clothes, and stared at her with pallid face and glassy eyes. And if, on recognising herself in that hideous vision, she started back, and horror seized her, and her pride was humbled in the dust, how should it wean our affections from these vanities, and secure much of our daily and all our Sabbath time for the study of ourselves in the mirror of God's holy Word, to reflect that the fairest form which draws admiring eyes shall be wrapped in a shroud, and put away in a coffin, and thrust into the grave—for worms to hold riot on its damask cheek, and nestle their loathsome brood where the lights of life and love are flashing!

I have often wondered at the amount of precious time, at the eager attention, and at the vast sums of money lavished on vain attire, as on extravagant feasts. Where many have hardly rags to cover them, and shoeless children shiver on the winter streets, and cold and hunger banish sleep from the eyes of houseless wretches, and by the tongues of hundreds, Jesus, making their cause His own, being naked, beseeches us to clothe Him, one may wonder more to see Christians gay as butterflies—fluttering about in the very pride, and height, and extravagance of fashion. How unworthy such pride and pleasures of those who have in Jesus' blood-bought righteousness a robe beside which silks lose their lustre, diamonds their brilliancy, the very snow its whiteness; and royal apparel seems filthy rags! It is enough to sadden one to think of the time, and thought, and conversation, and keen and lively interest that are wasted even by God's people on the changes, and often absurd forms, of fashion. It almost makes one wish that our fashions were as fixed as the laws of the Medes and Persians; or the customs of the Arabs; or the colours of the flowers that are not ashamed to come out in the same robes year by year.

"Let our adorning," as St Peter says, "be the hidden man of the heart, in that which is not corruptible—a meek and quiet spirit, which is in the sight of God of great price:" ours be the treasure which moth and rust cannot corrupt, and thieves break not through to steal. Having in salvation "the pearl of great price," we possess a gem worth more than the costliest that ever topped kingly crown, or was fished from the dark depths of ocean. If we have put on Christ, what matters how homespun or humble our attire? What though no rings flash on fingers that shall ere long be mouldering bones, if the Father, accepting us in Jesus Christ, and regarding us as beloved for the Beloved's sake, has kissed the tear of sorrow from our eyes, and, calling for music and the dance, given forth the glad command, Put a ring on his finger, and shoes on his feet, and bring forth the fairest robe and put it on him; and let us rejoice and be merry, for this my son that was dead is alive again, that was lost is found.

Another is *money*.

When swimming a river where the current runs strong, who, however powerful his strokes, does not find himself borne a long way down, ere he reaches the other bank? It is even difficult to make one's way across a street along which a vast, eager, excited crowd is rushing, without being lifted off our feet and swept along—like a straw on the stream. Such are the contrary influences which impede, if they do not prevent, the heavenward progress of God's people. God's people are not the majority. The multitude goes the other way. And, since there is moral as well as material weight in masses, devout men and women in old times, to escape being carried away by the ungodly influences of those around them, fled to cloistered retreats; or, withdrawing altogether from the society of men, passed their days as hermits amid the silent solitudes of forest or desert. Let two musical instruments be placed on the same floor, within the walls of the same apartment, if a player sit down before one of these and strike its keys, the other instrument, as if some spirit's finger had lightly touched its chords, unapproached and untouched by mortal hands, sounds out the self-same note. And such, but still more remarkable, is the influence which, by the laws of sympathy, men have in forming the opinions and moulding the manners of each other—on the side at least of worldliness and sin. Recognising the existence of this law, and the danger to which it exposes the godly in an ungodly world, the Bible says, "Evil communications corrupt good manners;" David resolves, "Mine eyes shall be upon the faithful of the land, that they may dwell with me;" Solomon declares, "He that walketh with wise men shall be wise, but a companion of fools shall be destroyed;" and the Book of Psalms opens its divine melodies with this grand beatitude, "Blessed is the man that walketh not in the counsel of the ungodly, nor standeth in the way of sinners." It is not easy to walk on muddy streets and keep our garments clean; it is still more difficult to live in an infirmary, breathing its pestilential airs, and escape plague or fever; but it is most difficult of all to resist the immoral influences that surround us,—to live pure amid corruption,—to be in the world, and yet not of it,—while making and spending money, while enjoying the pleasures of possessing or suffering the serious inconvenience of wanting it, to walk the earth as they the Celestial city, who, walking on streets paved with gold, tread it beneath their feet.

We are neither to despise, nor refuse money. Honourably come by, or the reward of honest industry, this, like other gifts of God, is without repentance. Well employed, it affords much enjoyment; and, when applied to dry the widow's tears, to fill the orphan's cup, to help the deserving poor, yields one of life's sweetest pleasures to its fortunate possessor—saving him from the pangs they suffer, who, with the inclination, but without the ability, to assist suffering and do the kind office of a good Samaritan, have, though neither priest nor Levite, to "pass by on the other side."

Nor, however applicable to cases where wealth is found dissociated from worth, to scenes where, as in the parable, sin sits robed in purple and fares sumptuously every day, while saintship is clad in rags and fed on crumbs, is the remark one made so just as it is smart: "You may see how little God thinks of money by observing on what unworthy characters He often bestows it." It is the law of a wise and holy Providence that the hand of the diligent maketh rich; God promises that riches and honour shall be in the good man's house; and many are the instances in which He has bestowed great wealth on such as were persons of great worth. We have one in Abraham; and in his history a remarkable proof of that grand man's superiority to the love of money. Entitled by the laws of war to the whole spoil of battle, he might have swept all into his own hand—enriching himself like those who, taking advantage of the laws of commerce, make fortunes out of speculations that involve others in ruin. But he refuses the gains which law puts within his reach; and out of regard to the honour of his God, the wants and the welfare of his fellow creatures, he abandons his legal claims, and, declining to grow rich on other men's losses, leaves the spoil to its proper owners—saying, "I will not take from a thread to a shoe latchet, lest thou shouldst say, I have made Abraham rich." We have a second instance in David, who did not forget on the throne Him who had taken him from the sheepfold, nor, when riches increased, set his heart on them. David was dead and buried before the temple was begun. It rose from its foundations to look on his tomb; but the house that bore Solomon's name was a monument of his father's piety. It was built with David's money; and unlike such as never part with theirs for the best objects till death parts them from it, this good king, grieved that Jehovah should dwell in curtains while he dwelt in a house of cedar, would, but that God forbade him, have raised it with his own hands—in the fruits of peace and spoils of war, lavishing his treasures on the house of God. We have a third instance in Job. No man of his day was so perfect, and few men of any day so rich. Some there are who resemble the pestilential swamp that, poisoning the air and spreading disease around it, retains in its spongy bosom all the bounties of the skies. Not so the man of Uz. He resembled rather what imparts blessings and beauty to a landscape—the lake that with flowery verdure on its winding shores, life in its waters, and heaven reflected on its unruffled bosom, discharges at its outlet the full flood of streams that enter it; making glens and plains to smile. Their recollections of prosperity abused must exasperate, rather than alleviate, the misfortunes of many; but Job draws a picture of his days of prosperity which we look on with admiration, and he, amid changed and adverse fortunes, must have looked on with comfort:—"When the ear heard me, then it blessed me; and when the eye saw me, it gave witness of me; because I delivered the poor that cried, and the fatherless, and him that had none to help him. The blessing of him that was ready to perish came upon me: and I caused the widow's heart to sing for joy."

But though, as these cases prove, money may be found in the hand where the love of it is not eating, like a cancer, into the heart, there is danger of gold stealing our affections from God —as was strikingly put by Richard Cecil to one of his congregation. This person had suddenly and unexpectedly succeeded to an enormous fortune. Cecil met him sometime afterwards, and inquired anxiously about his welfare. The other having expressed surprise, Cecil said, "I heard that you had been in great danger." "In great danger," replied his friend; "I never was better in my life." "Have not you succeeded to a large fortune?" said Cecil, adding, as the other nodded assent, "Well, sir, I consider any man in your circumstances to be in circumstances of very great danger,"—there sounded the echo of Agur's words, "nor riches, lest I be full, and deny thee." The larger and more sudden the accession of wealth, the greater the danger — it being with riches as with rain. When showers fall slow and soft, they penetrate the soil, and refresh the ground without disturbing it; but, falling in waterspouts, descending in a deluge from the loaded air, they fill the river to the brim, and, bursting its banks, carry havoc and destruction along their tumultuous course.

But there are no circumstances under which we do not need to be on our guard against wealth. Its attractions are great to all, and seem to exert over some a resistless power. See what sad illustrations this sinful and suffering world presents of these words: "The love of money is the root of all evil." How are woman's virtue, and man's honesty, the liberties of the slave, the dignity of rank, the purity of justice, the sacredness of the pulpit, the claims of Christ's cause and of humanity, the love of God and of man, all sucked in and swallowed up by this roaring, devouring whirlpool! No doubt, this is the basest of passions; and one with which, amid all the faults recorded against them in the Bible, the saints are almost never charged. Still let none feel secure. Let him that thinketh he standeth, take heed lest he fall, and his fate resemble that of the almost invulnerable Greek, who, fearing neither the thrust of lance nor crash of battleaxe, fell by a wound in his least mortal and meanest part. Achilles was slain by an arrow that hit him on the heel.

To the love of money we trace the melancholy apostasy of Demas, the awful perfidy of Judas, the fatal lie of Ananias and Sapphira—all, and some of them distinguished, professors of religion. Be on your guard. Watch and pray. Their history is written for our instruction. Nor need any of His people who allow the love of money to entwine itself around their hearts, expect that in saving them God will do otherwise than the woodman who, seeking to save a tree, applies his knife to the canker that eats into its heart, or the ivy that has climbed its trunk and is choking it in its close embraces. He is a jealous God.

He will not give His glory to another. While then we have, and shall have so long as we are here, in some form or other to do with money, let us beware of setting our affections on it. There are better riches—those that take not to themselves wings and flee away—those that neither moth nor rust corrupt, and thief breaks not through to steal. In these, the riches of redeeming grace, seek the things that are above; saying with Bunyan, in these rude but expressive lines,

> " Our drossy dust we change for gold,
> From death to life we flee,
> We let go shadows, and lay hold
> Of immortality."

Another is *our living, or rather dying, fellow-creatures.*

The gospel does not forbid us to give them a place in our hearts who have one in our houses. On the contrary, it teaches us by the voice of Christ to love even our enemies. "Ye have heard that it hath been said," says Jesus, "an eye for an eye, a tooth for a tooth; but I say unto you, that ye resist not evil; and whosoever shall smite thee on the right cheek, turn to him the other also.

Ye have heard that it hath been said, Thou shalt love thy neighbour and hate thine enemy; but I say unto you, Love your enemies, bless them that curse you, and pray for them that despitefully use you; that ye may be the children of your Father who is in heaven, who maketh his sun to rise on the evil and the good, and his rain to fall on the just and unjust." And what is thus written with sunbeams, and sounds audibly in every falling shower, is, more affecting still, seen in the blood and heard in the groans of Calvary; all forgiveness extended, love-felt kindness shown to enemies, being but a faint echo of Christ's answer to the blows that sent the nails through his quivering flesh, "Father, forgive them, they know not what they do!" Well, it stands alike consonant to reason and religion, that if it is right to love our enemies, much more should we love our friends; still more our families. God is not a God of confusion, but of order; and the language of the Bible is always in perfect unison with the best feelings of nature.

Duty to Christ may require a man to leave father and mother, wife and children, and to act—

to use our Lord's strong figure—sometimes as if he *hated* them; but the gospel is not calculated, as it certainly was not intended, to cool, to freeze, to blight our natural affections; and, like the influences of winter on smiling, singing streams, to lock them in chains of ice. They were not saints, but sinners, of whom the apostle said, "They are without natural affection;" and elsewhere than in those streets where you see mothers buying drink to debauch themselves with the money that should feed and clothe the skeleton infants they carry in their arms, the ragged, shivering, hungry children at their side,—everywhere, indeed, sin is found blighting the affections that cling like sweet wallflower to the ruins of humanity. Religion makes better, but sin worse, husbands, wives, parents, children, brothers, sisters — producing such an effect on the heart as a cancer on the bosom it attacks. It hardens it; and next destroys what it has hardened; and at length turns an object of love and beauty into foul and hateful loathsomeness. But piety, ever favourable to humanity, intensifies, while it purifies, the best affections of our nature. And so, did I wish to illustrate, and by examples enforce, generous friendships and domestic love, I would seek them in the Bible—there where the old man clings to Benjamin, saying, with a voice choked by emotion, "Joseph is not, and Simeon is not, and ye will take Benjamin away;" or there where their brother, within whose bosom the tide of affection had been rising till his heart is ready to burst, no longer able to restrain his emotions, cries, "I am Joseph:" or there where David pours forth in tears and touching numbers his sorrow over the fate of Jonathan, or melts all who hear him as he goes up to his house, wringing his hands at the death of Absalom, and crying, "O my son Absalom, my son, my son Absalom! would God I had died for thee, O Absalom, my son, my son!" The natural affections found then, as they find still, their most congenial soil in pure and pious hearts.

But while we are encouraged, rather than forbidden, to hold them dear who are near to us, we are not to allow them to usurp the place of Him who says, "Thou shalt have no other gods before me." Beware of turning household delights into household deities, household goods into household gods. The danger against which we are to guard is not such attachment to loved ones as that, when death lops off a branch, the poor tree, shaken by the blow, is left wounded and bleeding; but such as makes gods of them, and murmuring, not merely mourning, at their loss, feels as if with them all joy, and peace, and hope, and life were for ever buried. Pliny the younger tells us that when the eruption of Vesuvius, which buried Pompeii, had covered with a pall of blackness the whole heavens, and the earth, rocking beneath successive and tremendous earthquakes, had no other light at broad noonday than the blaze of the burning mountain and broad flashes of lightning that occasionally penetrated but added to the effect of the gloom, — Pliny the younger tells us that people thought not only that nature was dissolving, but that the very gods were dying. And if a god had died, the terror and grief could hardly have exceeded that I once saw in the case of a mother who had set her affections too exclusively on the child we had met to carry to the grave. Seated at the head of the coffin, she seemed a statue; the grand work of some master hand, to represent the deepest, blackest grief. No tears were on her bloodless cheek. Fixed on the coffin, her eyes never left it. She neither moved nor spake, as on her face one could read these words, "My heart is withered like grass." Absorbed in sorrow, it mattered as little to her as to the dead who went out, or who came in. At length the moment came to remove the body. Then, as when the heavens that have been gathering blackness break out into a blaze of flame and roar of thunder, burst the storm. The form that had looked more like lifeless marble than one animate with life, now sprung up, threw itself on the coffin, clung to it with wails to pierce a heart of stone; and, when gentle force was employed to unloose her arms, she walked to the door—patting the poor coffin; and saw it borne out of her sight with an expression of agony, which, as she fell back fainting into the arms of kind neighbours, seemed to cry, Ye have taken away my god, and what have I more!

It is not so we are to love our loved ones. We

are to love our children, for instance, as they are to obey their parents, "in the Lord;" never forgetting that He who lends may resume His gifts whensoever it pleases Him; never forgetting that the fairest flowers of the family may soon wither and die; ever striving as we keep our children in their own place in the house, nor allow them to usurp ours, to keep them in their own place in our hearts, nor allow them to usurp God's: ever seeking in our nurseries to rear plants for heaven, and so train up our children in the faith, in the saving knowledge of Christ and the devout love of God, that we shall have the consolation of knowing, if death enters our house and plucks them from our arms, that our loss is their gain; that if a chair in the circle by our fireside is empty, a blood-bought throne is filled in heaven; that if there is one voice less in the psalm when we are assembled for worship, there is one more ringing sweet and clear in glory, praising Him through whose dying love and in whose blissful presence we shall join our lost and loved—to weep and to part no more.

To live thus, walking by faith and not by

sight, touching the impalpable, seeing the invisible, living for eternity in time, and for heaven on earth, with our affections not where we are but where we hope to be—where Jesus is, is no easy work. But prayer, drawing down strength from the skies, makes difficult things easy, and impossible things possible. Through Christ strengthening me, said the apostle, I can do all things. So may we. Turn to that source of superhuman power. Trust to it; nor doubt but that, as those risen with Christ, you shall walk with Him, living realisations of this old, quaint, but beautiful picture:—

> " Man of lofty nature looks up
> To heaven so calm, and pure, and beautiful.
> He looks below, but not contemptuously:
> For there he sees reflections of himself,
> As a poor child of nature: and he feels
> A touch of kindred brotherhood: and pants
> To lead the weak and erring into heights
> Which he so joyous treads; nay, more, descends
> Into the smoky turmoil and the roar
> Of the rude world: his hands at work on earth,
> His soul beyond the clouds, dwelling with God,
> And drinking of His Spirit."

EARLY PIETY.—PART I.

> "*From a child thou hast known the holy scriptures, which are able to make thee wise unto salvation through faith which is in Christ Jesus.*"—2 TIM. iii. 15.

THERE is no person, perhaps, who makes a profession of religion but has come to some decision or other on that all-important subject. People either believe on good or bad grounds that they are already religious, or they resolve to become so at a future time. True, many Sabbaths may have been spent, and many sermons heard, and many funerals attended which have awakened no serious thoughts, nor led to such questions as these: Am I saved?—What shall I do to be saved? In the case of many, more or less in the case of all, who are mere hearers of the Word, familiarity with divine things breeds indifference; if not contempt. Under its influence they become as insensible to the most solemn threatenings of the law as the inhabitants of the Indies to the thunderstorms that, though terrific, are common there. The mercy of God, and the bleeding love of Jesus are set forth in the sermons of every Sabbath and the symbols of every sacrament, but they are as little impressed by these as by the nightly glories of the starry sky. Death is such a common event, an obituary so certainly finds a place in every newspaper, and they are so accustomed, on inquiring, to hear that this old acquaintance is dying, and that one is dead— they are invited to so many funerals, and meet so many hearses in the street with their nodding plumes and sable array—and, till more decent customs were adopted, they so often saw the mouldering relics of the dead " scattered at the grave's mouth, as when one cutteth and cleaveth wood on the earth," that they grow familiar with death; and can hear him knocking at a neighbour's door without once thinking that, whether they are ready or unready, his hand shall soon knock at theirs.

True; and pity 'tis 'tis true! Yet there are occasions which awaken serious thoughts in the most careless—however they may endeavour to suppress and banish them. Some event occurs, like a clap of thunder, to rouse the sleeping conscience; and, calling up terrible visions of death, of judgment, and of hell, she insists on men thinking of the subjects that belong to their peace; and one of two things happens: either they conclude, on insufficient grounds, that they are saved, or, as is much more common, they resolve to be so at some future time.

In the first case, without altogether ignoring Jesus Christ and His salvation, they trust to something meritorious in their works, or in themselves. One builds much on his honesty,—his motto the adage, "An honest man's the noblest work of God;" another on his integrity—his boast this, that "his word is as good as his bond;" another on his charity—seeking no better inscription for his tombstone than one I have read in an old churchyard, "He was kind to the poor!" They have, or fancy they have, amid many sins, some virtues. These be thy gods, O Israel! Alas! that we should forget that sinners cannot get to heaven on the fragments of a broken law, as in St Paul's shipwreck some got ashore on the planks of the broken ship. St Paul himself has made that plain. Speaking of the works of the flesh—adultery, fornication, uncleanness, lasciviousness, idolatry, witchcraft, hatred, variance, emulations, wrath, strife, seditions, heresies, envyings, murders, drunkenness, revellings, and such like—they, he says, who do such things shall not inherit the kingdom of God. And what does it matter, though men are not guilty of all, if they are guilty of one of these sins? "Cursed," says the God with whom we have to do, "is *every* one who continueth not in *all* things written in the book of the law to do them." Other hope therefore man has none but what lies in accepting the righteousness which, wrought out by Christ and imputed to believers, is not of works, but of faith. And how sad it is to see men leave this solid rock, and having to build a house, against whose rocking walls fierce winds shall rave, and angry waters roar, build it on a sand-bank that the last flood cast up, and the next shall sweep away.

But those I have now to do with, belong to a different class. They are convinced that they have no righteousness of their own; yet they put off embracing Christ's—they fear, were they to die this night or drop down dead this moment, that they would be lost; yet they delay to seek a Saviour till the evil days come, and the years draw nigh when they shall say they have no pleasure in them. A dangerous delay; a very desperate venture!—yet not one for which a "heart, deceitful above all things and desperately wicked," cannot urge some specious pleas. All who put off salvation have reasons, of a kind, to plead for the step they take. So had those who, with the forms of polite respect, declined an invitation to the "great supper:"—I have bought a piece of ground, says one, and I must needs go and see it, I pray thee have me excused—I have bought five yoke of oxen, says a second, and I go to prove them, I pray thee have me excused—and, with less manners but more appearance of reason, I have married a wife, says a third, and therefore I cannot come. Even so procrastinators have reasons, though not so plausible, for declining, meanwhile, Jesus' gracious invitations. But whether it is that they are so engaged in the world's business that they have no time, or are so bewitched with its pleasures that they have no inclination to turn religious, one idea is common to them all — this, namely, that not childhood, nor youth, nor manhood, but old age is the most suitable period for becoming devout. They argue thus: In old age we shall have less to do with the business of this world, and have consequently more leisure for that of the next; then this world will afford us little enjoyment — our passions, like fierce fires, will have burned themselves out; our bodies, withered and bent beneath a load of infirmities, will be incapable of debauchery or excess — and, with more time, we shall thus have more inclination to turn to religion. The vessel that, racked by storms, is falling to pieces and gaping at every seam, makes all haste to port: so will we. Unfitted by age for active pursuits, and compelled to withdraw from the giddy circle that goes its round of pleasures, we shall be left to quiet scenes and twilight hours favourable to meditation. Brought in the course of threescore years and ten to the borders of another world, it cannot fail to occupy much of our thoughts; nor when the head has turned gray, and the hands are palsied, and the limbs shrunk and tottering, and ears are deaf and eyes are dim, can we miss to recognise these as the heralds of the grim king, and hear the voice that says, Be ready, the Judge is at the door!

Is this our hope? Hope tells a flattering tale. It is a wild fancy—a mockery and baseless delusion. See how God, with one blow of His hand, one sentence of His Word, dashes the fabric to pieces! Talk of old age, gray hairs, passion quenched, life's quiet evening, and sands running to the threescore years and ten!—what if He should say, Thou fool, *this night* thy soul shall be required of thee?

To uproot an idea which stands in the way of all attempts at, and hopes of, early piety, I observe that conversion is more *difficult* in old age than at any other period.

At whatever age it takes place, this change is

properly the work of God—"not by might nor by power, but by my Spirit, saith the Lord of hosts;" or, as our Saviour said to Nicodemus, "Except a man be born of water and of the Spirit, he cannot enter into the kingdom of God." Be he Jew or Gentile, old or young, learned or ignorant, with many or few religious advantages, no man can become a partaker of the present or future blessings of grace unless he is born again; is changed into the divine nature; is renewed in spirit; has Christ formed within him: is, in short, so far as his motives and affections, principles and practice are concerned, made a new creature in Jesus Christ. Regarded as a work of God, this change, I admit, cannot be more difficult at one age than another. With equal ease the great ocean bears ships and seaweed on its bosom, the earth carries mountains and molehills on its back; and still more are all things equally easy to God—to preserve, for instance, an angel or an insect in life, to kindle a sun or a glow-worm's fire, to create a world or a grain of sand. And as it had been as easy for divine power to raise

Adam, who had been dead four thousand years, as Lazarus, who had been dead only four days, or to raise Lazarus after four years as after four days in the tomb, it is not more difficult for God to convert an old than a young sinner. The dying thief was saved in the jaws and very throat of death—he stept into heaven from the edge of hell: John Baptist, again, was born the second time before being born the first, being sanctified from his mother's womb—and both these events were equally within the compass of His power, to whom nothing is impossible—who has in either, or in any case, but to say and it is done: to command, and it standeth fast. Therefore let none despair.

Nevertheless, since we are fellow-workers with God, there is a sense in which the difficulties of conversion increase with years—every year adding strength to our sinful habits; deepening, as by the constant flow of water, the channels in which they run.

Take a sapling, for example. It bends to your hand, turning this or that way as you will. When seventy springs have clothed it with leaves, and the sun of seventy summers, ripening its juices, has added to its height and breadth, who is strongest? Now, it scorns not your, but a giant's strength. Once an infant's arm could bend it; but, with head raised proudly to heaven, and roots that have struck deep in the soil and cling to the rocks below, now it braves winter's wildest tempests. They may break its trunk, they cannot bend it; nor is it but in death that it lays its head on the ground. Every year of the seventy, adding fibres to its body and firmness to the fibres, has increased the difficulty of bending it. That was less easy the second year than the first, and the third than the second; till, as time went on, what was once easy grew difficult, and what was once but difficult became impossible. Who, wishing to give it a peculiar bent, would wait till the nursling had become a full-grown tree, or stood in its decay, stiff and gnarled, hollow in heart and hoar with age? None but a fool. Yet, with folly greater still, we defer what concerns our conversion, a saving change, and our everlasting welfare, till long years have added to the power, and strengthened the roots, of every wicked, worldly habit. Oh, that men were wise, that they understood this!

Human life, to borrow an example from it, furnishes many, and some very melancholy, illustrations of this growth and power of evil habits. Take the case of the poor drunkard, for instance. The rust of years eats into other chains, making it easier to snap them asunder; but the links of his grow stronger with time. Other cups may quench thirst, his but increases it: till the love of drink becomes, not a passion, but a madness; and, deaf to all arguments, and less blind than careless to all consequences, he holds out the goblet in palsied hand to cry, "Give! give!" The day was when that wreck of honesty and manly strength — that sad ruin of grace and womanly beauty, was filled with sorrow and remorse; but these feelings became more and more enfeebled, while drinking habits, fed by every new indulgence, increased in strength — making reformation less hopeful by every day's delay. And now, like a boat swept on in a foaming rapid, which neither oar nor arm can stem, with all the dread consequences full in sight—a ruined character, a beggared family, his body descending into an untimely grave, his soul to the doom of these awful words, "no drunkard shall inherit the kingdom of heaven"—he yields to a torrent that sweeps means, character, wife, children, body and soul, into one common ruin.

With such touching and terrible illustrations before their eyes, men talk of delaying to turn to God for ten, twenty, or forty years! Is it painful now to tear the world from our hearts?—when the love of it has grown with our growth, and strengthened with our strength, when it has spread its roots wider, and struck them deeper, to tear it up will demand a mightier effort, and inflict a greater pain. If sin has already so seared the conscience, that we can hear another St Paul reason of "righteousness, temperance, and judgment," nor tremble in our seats as the Roman trembled on his throne, in what state shall our conscience be when the sins of future years have passed over it like a hot iron — searing, till, all sensibility destroyed, it becomes as hard as horn; like callous flesh, which the knife finds it difficult to penetrate, and impossible to pain? This is no exaggeration. Of all tasks, we know none so difficult as to touch the feelings, and rouse the conscience of godless old age.

Besides, will conversion be more likely and easy when age has dimmed our eyes, and the Bible is become "as the words of a book that is sealed"—when the church-bell rings for others, but not for us; and, unable to creep beyond the door, our Sabbaths are lonely and silent? Which is the better time—when, in the enjoyment of health, we can give undistracted attention to the things that concern our peace, or, when sinking under the infirmities of years, or racked with the pains of disease, we are reduced to such weakness, or suffer such torture, that we can neither pray, nor join in prayer?

Besides, second childhood, to a greater or less extent, comes with age—the faculties of the mind failing with, sometimes even before, those of the body. Like the leaves of the ash-tree, these which were the last to appear, are occasionally the first to depart; leaving the mind a more melancholy wreck than its shattered, crazy tabernacle. And where the soul, asserting its immortality, seems to grow larger, like a setting sun at the close of day, and its faculties survive amid the decays of age, it is by no means rare to see life's last hours passed in a disordered day-dream; their realities offering a striking contrast to the phantoms and fancies of the dying chamber—fancies which restore the preacher to his pulpit; the weaver to his loom; the merchant to 'change; the sailor to the slippery deck; the soldier, who has no enemy now to fight but death, to the battle-field, where, deliriously shouting out the word of command, he mixes in the *mêlée*, or heads the desperate charge. What man in his right mind would select such times and scenes for working out his salvation? Which is better—to remember your Creator now, or delay till conversion is a thousand times more difficult; sinful habits have struck a deeper root; age has dulled the mind, deadened the feelings, and seared the conscience—till you are but the wreck and shadow of what you were; and all your pitiful attempts to turn to God only recall the warning, "Can the

Ethiopian change his skin, or the leopard his spots? then may ye also do good, that are accustomed to do evil."

Conversion in old age is a very *doubtful* matter.

It is doubtful whether we shall ever reach old age. Few do; and the probability is that we never shall. It is still more doubtful whether, suppose we do, we shall be more serious than in earlier years. The probability is all the other way—it being true of other sinners besides seducers, that they, as Scripture says, "wax worse and worse." But suppose that we are spared to old age, and, by the devout attention we give to the Bible, to prayer and the house of God, appear to have undergone a gracious change, it lies open to the gravest suspicion. The possibility of conversion at the eleventh hour I do not deny; still, its reality is exceedingly doubtful.

Take the case, for instance, of a convicted thief. You find him where silver plate, gold, and jewels glitter temptations on his eye. Alarmed, you reckon up your money, examine your treasures—to be agreeably disappointed. They are safe;

and you naturally conclude that he has turned over a new leaf, and become an honest man. But, however willing to judge charitably, how would your confidence in him vanish on discovering that his hands were shackled, and that, though it was in his heart, it was not in his power to rob you? So far as many gross vices are concerned, such is exactly the position of hoary-headed sinners. Age has frozen their passions, and unfitted them for pleasures after which they once "ran greedily;" and so many infirmities have come with years, that a regard to health, and to life itself, forcing them to refrain from debauchery, produces an apparent reformation. A boat rotten in every plank, and gaping at every seam, has to avoid the seas and swell that others brave; and it were death to old men to venture on debaucheries in which others indulge. Thus the decorum which in some cases marks the closing years of such as had been notorious for vice, may be due to other causes than an inward, saving, and gracious change. The lion has not become a lamb when he has lost his teeth.

But here is a hoary penitent. Poor old man,

he trembles to hear of death and judgment; his aged limbs carry him to what he once neglected—the house of God; the glasses through which he scans his Bible are bedewed and dimmed with tears; bitterly lamenting his sins, he warns others; and on knees unused to bend, pours forth prayers for pardon in tones of deepest earnestness. It seems cruel to entertain doubts of such a case. But what is it we doubt? Not that he is sorry for his sins, after a fashion; not but that he would give a world, which he must any way soon part from, to be saved. In this case we may cling to the hope that He who can save at the uttermost has called him at the eleventh hour; still, this sorrow may only correspond to what the felon feels for crimes which have brought him to the gallows—cut short a mad and guilty career. Sorrow for sin, and wishes to be saved? What death-condemned man does not feel these? does not bitterly lament the hour he embrued his hands in blood? does not petition the Crown to spare his life? would not give the world for a file to cut his chain—for a key to unlock his prison? Repentance for crimes at the foot of a gallows is not more open to suspicion than repentance for sins on the brink of a burning hell.

Solemn warnings have come from scaffolds; but no one standing on the brink of time, with the white cap on his head, and his feet trembling on the drop, as he made his last speech to the awe-struck crowd, ever uttered voice so full of warning as the recorded experience of the chaplain of a large jail in England. With the death-bell slowly tolling, he had accompanied many to the scaffold, and also prepared not a few for execution who were unexpectedly reprieved. Of these a large number seemed to be converted. Their repentance appeared sincere; and had they suffered the penalty of their crimes, he and others would have believed that, whom earth rejected, Heaven in its mercy had received—for the sake of Christ's righteousness acquitting at its bar those whom man had condemned at his. But they were spared—to lead a new life? Alas, no! Thrown back into the world, the reality of their conversion was put to the test. The glittering coin was tested, exposed to a fiery trial; and what deceived others, deceived perhaps themselves, proved counterfeit. With hardly an exception, all who seemed to be converted within the prison, under the shadow of the gallows—in circumstances to the condemned corresponding with old age and the closing days of life—returned to their former courses; went back like the dog to his vomit, and the sow that is washed to her wallowing in the mire. A melancholy fact! What a dark suspicion does it cast on late conversions? In these cases the sun that sets on this world may rise to shine in a better; but dark clouds obscure such a close of life; and so long as men will risk their souls on these desperate ventures, however trite the remark, it cannot be too often, or too loudly, or too solemnly repeated, that the Bible, which ranges over a period of four thousand years, records but *one* instance of a death-bed conversion—one that none may despair, and but one that none may presume.

EARLY PIETY.—PART II.

> "*From a child thou hast known the holy scriptures, which are able to make thee wise unto salvation through faith which is in Christ Jesus.*"—2 TIM. iii. 15.

TO everything, says Solomon, in the Book of Ecclesiastes, there is a season, and a time to every purpose under the heaven: a proposition which, like a flower full blown, he spreads out into such particulars as these—"a time to be born, and a time to die; a time to plant, and a time to pluck up; a time to kill, and a time to heal; a time to weep, and a time to laugh; a time to mourn, and a time to dance; a time to get, and a time to lose; a time to rend, and a time to sew; a time to love, and a time to hate; a time of peace, and a time of war." Religion, it may be observed, has no place in this remarkable catalogue; and, paradoxical as the assertion seems, its absence only makes it the more conspicuous. It has no place among births or deaths, saving or slaughter, feasts or funerals, the calm of peace or the tempests of war, because, unlike these, it belongs to no season, but to all seasons, to every period and time of life. Its functions are like those of breathing, which, distinguished from eating, resting, or working, are carried on throughout all the years of our existence, nor cease even when reason sleeps and the bodily senses are all steeped in slumber.

Notwithstanding, there is a sense in which religion also has its season. As there is a time to be born, there is a time to be born again: to turn to God; to die to sin, and live to righteousness. And which of all the periods of human life will prove most favourable to that great change, is a question we can neither too soon nor too carefully determine. Interests are involved here more important far than those which belong to any, or to all those other times; to the loves or hatreds, the wars or peace, the births or burials of a life, whose joys and sorrows in a few more years will be nothing to us—no more than the suns that shine, or the storms that beat upon our grave. The great English dramatist, accepting the threescore years and ten of Scripture as the ordinary span of life, divides it into seven decades; and, borrowing imagery from the stage and shifting scenes of his own profession, represents each as an act played out on the boards of a theatre—beginning and closing his famous description thus:

> "All the world's a stage,
> And all the men and women merely players:
> They have their exits and their entrances,
> And one man in his time plays many parts,
> His acts being seven ages. At first the infant,
>   .   .   .   .   .   .
>   Last scene of all,
> That ends this strange, eventful history,
> Is second childishness, and mere oblivion."

Without following the French, to regard all children under fourteen years as being, to use their term, *sans discernement*, and not properly amenable to punishment, let us here exclude infancy and mere childhood from consideration; periods, these, when many, hardly able to act for themselves, are plastic as a piece of clay

—taking shape and form from the hands into which they fall. And of the three remaining periods,—youth, manhood, and old age,—which is the most fitted for working out our salvation, for giving all diligence to make our calling and election sure, for fighting the good fight, for running the Christian race? The very terms of the question supply the answer. Solomon says the first. Well, if he is right, if in this judgment he sustains his fame as the wisest of the sons of men, if he spake thus in the noontide of that wisdom which dawned in his early choice and rose like a sun on the eyes of a dazzled world,— I need not ask, if he is right, how many are wrong? Not but that they intend some day or other to become religious; only not now, when their blood is hot, and the reins lie loose on the neck of passion, and the cup of pleasure is foaming to the brim. Were the plans and wishes of many expressed in words, they would take the very shape of the striking but shocking prayer of Augustine, Lord, convert me! but not now— not now!

They have no wish to die as they are. On the

contrary, knowing, at least fearing, that they have never been converted, and are not at peace with God, they recoil from such a thought;—their type, one in whose company we once happened to be placed in alarming circumstances. The carriages flew along the iron rails; they flashed by stations, post, and pillar; and began so to sway from side to side, that my fellow-traveller, by profession a minister of the gospel, got much alarmed, and asked, "Do you think there is danger?" "Think there is danger!" I gravely replied; "we may be in eternity in another moment." Struck to the heart as by a knife, his full and florid countenance turned pale as death, while, with an emphasis no acting could imitate, and a look of horror never to be forgotten, he raised his hands to exclaim, "God forbid!" Equally dreading a present and sudden death, how many live and sin on in the hope that, after spending their days as lovers of pleasure, they shall end them as lovers of God; that they will turn over a new leaf when they are old; and that, to use a common expression, it will be all right in the end? Bubbles, fair to look on, but fragile as those the touch of a finger breaks! and the breath that blows up such vain expectations is the belief that of all the periods of human life none is so favourable to religion as old age. A great, yet not a wonderful, mistake!— one into which, on the contrary, it is very natural for unreflecting and inexperienced youth to fall. Young people fancy that when the days are come when they shall say they have no pleasure in them,—when, in other words, there are no pleasures to enjoy,—it will be easy to cease being lovers of pleasure, and become lovers of God; they fancy that when they have fallen "into the sere and yellow leaf," fading sight and health and hearing cannot fail to warn them of the approach of death, and prepare them for his coming; they fancy that religion, like ivy, which gets no hold of a close and firm wall, grows best on what is old; and that as the weathered stones, the cracks and gaping rents of the shattered ruin, by offering a hold to its arms, helps it to climb till it crowns the summit and clothes the grim old tower in a green, graceful mantle, so the infirmities and decays of age will prove helpful to piety—giving it a hold on our hearts it had not obtained, but that they have been shattered by the disappointments, and trials, and shocks of life.

Alas for those who embark their salvation on such bad bottoms, such ventures, and worthless speculations! Experience is the true test here. Youth speaks from fancy, but old men from facts; and all experience—whether that of Solomon, or of others much less wise than he—pronounces these hopes to be utterly false, mere delusions. Old fruit, still hanging on the tree, comes away to the touch; but it is seldom without a wrench that old people part with life. Have not I seen, and wondered to see, how some aged saints would cling tenaciously to life, and be almost as happy on recovering as one in the green spring, or flower and summer of their days? Earthly joys are like the sun, which never looks so big as at his setting; and be it life, or children, or pleasure, or money, it is natural to love that which we are soon to lose, not less, but more.

> "I loved him much, but now I love him more.
> Like birds whose beauties languish, half-conceal'd,
> Till, mounted on the wing, their glossy plumes
> Expanded shine with azure, green, and gold:
> How blessings brighten as they take their flight!"

Then as to the effect on man of the near approach of death, youth has to learn what experience teaches age, that death resembles the horizon. Within the lessening circle of advancing years, death may seem much nearer than once it did, and the expression, "If God spares me," may be oftener in the thoughts and on the lips; still it presents this remarkable feature of the visible horizon that, whether it seem near in a misty, or distant in a clear, fair, open day, as we advance, it recedes—ever flies before us. Youths count on forty or twenty years; and where is the old man who does not, even from his stand-point by the grave, see one or two years, at least some days or months, before him?

Suppose it otherwise; suppose also that the powers of the mind do not fail with those of the body; suppose that no aged Christian ever had to complain of the evil days when he could not pray, nor meditate, nor fix his thoughts, nor rise, as on eagle's wings, in heavenly meditations, as once he did; suppose that none ever blessed God on their death-bed that they had not left their peace to seek amid the weakness and infirmities of age; suppose that sin may be safely yielded to till it becomes habitual; suppose, so to speak, it were found as easy to bend an old tree as a young one, to turn a swollen river as a tiny stream; suppose it is not true that

> "Ill habits gather by unseen degrees,
> As brooks run rivers, rivers run to seas;"

suppose that for once Solomon is wrong, and that of all the periods of life old age is best for getting a change of heart, an interest in Christ, peace with God, a title and a meetness for the kingdom of heaven,—yet, I say, it were well and wise not to delay, because *we may not live to be old.*

The oak lives a thousand years. The yew reaches a much greater age: a churchyard among our Scottish mountains boasting one, specially mentioned by Humboldt, under whose green canopy we have sat, which flourished in the days of Solomon, and stood, white with snows or hoar frost, a mighty tree that Christmas eve on which our Lord was born. In contrast with the giant forms and stubborn lives of trees that, yielding slowly to their doom, look down on the graves of many generations, are their leaves. Fragile and fading, these are often nipped in the bud; they are easily crushed; their life does not extend beyond a few months; the cold of autumn is their death, and the snows of winter are their shroud. For these reasons a leaf has been a favourite emblem with poets, both sacred and profane, of man, of his feebleness, of his mortality. So, when stripped of all his property, his children suddenly whelmed into a common grave, these his dead griefs and his wife a living one, his few friends the "miserable comforters" whose unskilful hands widened the wounds they sought to close, so spake Job: turning to God, he plaintively expostulates with Him, crying, "Wilt thou break a leaf driven to and fro?" Thus also spake the prophet who saw a picture of man, his sins and sorrows, where the wind at the close of autumn, tearing through the tinted woods, swept off their leaves in showers, and scattered them swirling and eddying along the ground—"We all," he exclaimed, "do fade as a leaf, and our iniquities, like the wind, have carried us away!"

We fade as a leaf! In one sense we do, and in another we do not. Most leaves live out all their days, but not many men—few men the half of them. Of all our race, nearly the half die in infancy, and are torn from mothers' bosoms to lie in the cold arms of death. Another large proportion drop into the grave ere the summer of life is past. The woods retain their foliage till days grow short, and fruits grow mellow, and fields fall to the reaper's sickle; but how small the number of men who survive, in gray hairs and stooping form, slow step and shuffling gait, to wear the marks of age ere they follow their companions to the tomb? Ask that hoar old man where are the playmates of his childhood, where the boys who sat by him at the desk in school, where the youths, flushed with health and full of hope, with whom he started in the race of life, where the guests of his board, his competitors or his partners in business? In the grave!—all mouldering in the grave: save one and another who, amid new faces, now find themselves to be strangers on this earth, and remain the last vestiges of their generation,—clinging to life just as I have seen a few brown leaves hanging on the tree, and whirling in the winter wind when skies were dark with storms, and fields were white with snow.

To the eye of faith this survey, these bills of mortality, present nothing melancholy. An early death to those who are in Christ is but another expression for an early deliverance; and if, in place of being long becalmed, or tossed about by storms, and perhaps driven out once and again to sea when their ship was in sight of land, those voyagers who make a short passage count themselves happy, fortunate, are not they rather to be envied than pitied who, by an early death, escape much of the sins and sorrows of this world?—like birds of passage, they just light on it, rest for a little while, and then, as if they found nothing tempting them to prolong their stay, take wing and soar up to heaven. Viewed in this aspect, but for the cold, the cruelties, the hunger, the wants and sufferings which, springing to a large extent from parental vices, account for the circumstance, there is nothing melancholy in the shortness of many lives, and that nearly the half of all born die under five years of age; leaving but a small fraction to see the threescore years and ten. But what more melancholy, more marvellous, than to see thousands setting at nought these well-established facts; delaying their salvation, and, where interests of the highest moment are concerned, counting on years which not one in a hundred of them shall ever reach? No wise man acts with such infatuation in other, and far less important matters.

For example. Prudent men insure their lives; and why? Because, they answer, life is uncertain; because there is nothing more uncertain; because the chances are that they shall not live to be old. And if I should be cut off suddenly, early, what, says a man, is to become of my family? The children of this world are indeed wise in their generation. Oh that men would reason as soundly, and act as wisely, where higher interests are at stake! If you should be cut off suddenly and early, what is to become of your family? Well, let me change but a little the terms of the question, and ask him who, reckoning on years, is putting off the things that concern his peace, If you should die suddenly and early, what is to become of your soul—your precious soul?

Prudent men, again, make their wills when their bones are full of marrow, and there is not a gray hair in their head. The deed shows their name written with a strong and firm hand; nor is it by their death-bed that, hastily summoned to the scene, the lawyer, the physician, and the minister of the gospel meet. In many respects it would prove much more convenient, saving the trouble and expense of codicils, to delay the settlement of their affairs to future years—to old age, should they ever reach it—when they shall have retired from business and realised their fortune. Should they ever reach it! But they know that few reach it, and that they may never do so; and therefore, with health bounding in every artery, and blooming on their cheeks, they sign their last will and testament. In matters where the interests and peace of families are concerned, wise men repudiate delay, nor venture anything on the chance of living to be old. Is the peace of our souls less worthy of our care? "Set thine house in order, for thou shalt die," said the prophet to the king; but how much more need, with a higher foresight, that we should set our hearts than our houses in order? We may die to-morrow—"Thou fool, this night thy soul shall be required of thee."

Prudent men, again, by the practice of economy and self-denial, make provision for dying in their prime. Young, they seem to have reasonable ground for expecting that many years are before them; and that they may live to see their children standing on their own feet—fighting their own battle, altogether independent of a parent's help. Why should not they then, launching on the tide of prosperity, take their enjoyment of the world? —in place of being haunted by fears of a widow and children left with a scanty provision, why should not they anticipate a venerable, green old age, a long day and a quiet evening, with their children's children climbing their knee and playing at their feet? Why? Because, they answer, though many fancy such a picture, there are few that sit for it. Few live to be old; nor on such an unlikely chance will they venture the happiness and well-being of their children—not they. Would to God we were all as wise in what involves the happiness and well-being of our souls! and that every sinner without an hour's delay turned to Jesus, to embrace Him as his Saviour, to cry, in his great extremity, Save, Lord, I perish!

Old age is a most *unsuitable* period.

The work to which we are called, which must be done by all in this world, and by some this day, or never done, is well described in the words of Nehemiah, "I have a great work to do, therefore I cannot come down." It requires our utmost energies. You have seen a man who had thrown himself into the crowd that blocked up a narrow door, battling his way through, with broad shoulder throwing the living mass aside, as the vessel does the water that breaks and foams and flashes from her brow—so we are to strive to enter in at the strait gate. You have seen the smith swinging his heavy hammer at the glowing forge, with the veins standing out on his brawny arms, and the sweat on his swarthy brow—so we are to labour for the bread that never perisheth. You have seen the sinewy frame of a lithe and young competitor in the race go by like the wind, as with flowing hair, expanded nostrils, eager eye, heaving breast, and flying feet, he bends to the course—so we are to run the race set before us; so, forgetting the things which are behind, and looking to those which are before, we are to press toward the mark of the prize of the high calling of God in Christ Jesus.

Whoever sat to Solomon for this graphic picture—the keepers tremble, the strong men bow themselves, the grinders cease, the windows be darkened, the almond tree flourishes, and the grasshopper is a burden—it is plain that neither the old man he painted, nor any at his age, is fit for tasks like these. The Scriptures, whatever figures they employ, everywhere represent the work of salvation as one demanding the highest energy, powers untouched by time and unimpaired by decay. Look at the subject in the light of that figure, where the kingdom of heaven is represented as a city taken by assault. Defenders man, and assailants swarm round the beleaguered wall. It is breached; the breach is pronounced practicable; the forlorn hope lie in the trenches, ready when the bugle sounds to spring to their feet, and with a run and a dash to throw themselves headlong into the yawning chasm; but this must be bravely, quickly, vigorously done, for the breach is bristling with bayonets, and men within stand by their guns to sweep it with showers of death. Now when the stormers are waiting a leader whom they expect to come with elastic step, and bold carriage, and manly form, and eagle glance, and sword flashing in the sun, and a voice that, crying, Follow me, rings through the ranks, and starts all to their feet, let an old man advance, tottering on a staff, with panting breath and piping voice, to bid them follow,—who would follow? Amid all the solemnities of an hour that should be the last to many, they would laugh his gray hairs to scorn. Let these and like feeble steps keep the garrisons at home; but the assault of cities, and storming of the deadly breach, require the pith of manhood, the fire and flower of youth. So does the work of salvation. It is inconsistent with the feebleness and decay of age; for "the kingdom of heaven suffereth violence, and the violent," says our Lord, "take it by force."

True, salvation is not of works. "By grace," as St Paul says, "are ye saved, through faith; and that not of yourselves; it is the gift of God: not of works, lest any man should boast; for we are His workmanship, created in Christ Jesus unto good works, which God hath before ordained that we should walk in them." And since God occasionally magnifies and illustrates the exceeding riches of His grace by calling one, and another, at the eleventh hour, making them, after being grafted into Christ, bring forth fruit even in old age, making, so to speak, "the barren woman to keep house and be a joyful mother of children," there is no age, and no case hopeless. The words, "Is anything too hard for the Lord?" are as applicable to the new birth of an old man as to the birth of Isaac by an old woman. So fast as their tottering steps can carry them, in the last lingering lights of day, let hoary-headed sinners hasten to Jesus. He will not reject them. He might, but He will not say, When I spake ye would not hear, and when I called ye would not answer; now when ye speak I will not hear, and when ye call I will not answer; I will laugh at your calamity, and mock when your fear cometh. Fear not that—

> "As long as life its term extends,
> Hope's blest dominion never ends;
> For while the lamp holds on to burn,
> The greatest sinner may return."

Notwithstanding this, and that the Word of God assures us that whosoever cometh unto Him He will in nowise cast out; the homage we owe to truth, and the duty we owe to souls, require us to say, that, judging by results, old age is, of all the ages of life, the least fitted for the work of salvation. No doubt we have read of hoary sinners becoming as little children, and turning to God; but in the experience of more than thirty years we have never met with one such case.

At the close of a dark and stormy day we have seen the sun break forth at his setting, to bathe the whole landscape in a flood of glory, and having painted a rainbow on the storm-cloud, to sink to rest amid the odours of flowers, and the joyful songs of groves and skies. But whatever others may have done, we have met nothing corresponding to this in the realm of spirits; not one old man who lived the life of the wicked, and died the death of the righteous. I am not speaking of those who, in circumstances that were more their misfortune than their fault, had no opportunity of knowing the truth till they were old—who, like the penitent thief, perhaps, received their first as well as last offer of a Saviour at death; never had Christ in their offer, as Simeon never had Him in his arms, till their eyes were dim, and their heads were gray with age;—I speak of those who have gone Sabbath after Sabbath to the house of God, whenever Christ was brought forward, to reject Him, and cry, like the Jews of old, "We will not have this man to rule over us;" who have put Him off, again and again, with the most miserable excuses; who have resisted the influences of the Holy Spirit of God; who have wilfully shut their eyes to the truth; who have obstinately refused to be saved; who have spent long years in fighting neither with the devil, nor the world, nor the flesh, but with their own conscience; and wounding it to the death, have at length won the victory. Now they have no qualms in sinning; and they may have no bands in their death. They have triumphed; but their victory reminds us of the saying of the king who, holding the ground after a hard fought day, but seeing it covered with the bodies of his bravest knights and stoutest men-at-arms, exclaimed, Another such victory and we are ruined! So fatal are victories obtained over conscience! Delay till your head is hoary, and your conscience seared, and you are, as they say, "gospel-hardened," and there is none to whom these words of hope are less applicable and appropriate, "Thou art not far from the kingdom of heaven."

Still God does not shut the door in an old man's face. The blood of Christ cleanseth from all sin—even from his—and the door of mercy stands open to the chief of sinners. Only, none can come too soon. Our position resembles his who, sole survivor of the wreck, was seized by a mountain wave, and, borne upon its crest onward to the cliff, was flung into a cave midway between the top where anxious spectators had gathered and the sea that raged and foamed below. Over a precipice no foot could scale, dangling above a sea where no boat could live, friendly hands lower a rope—but, alas! the beetling rock overhung his place of shelter; and though he stood poised on its utmost ledge with outstretched arms, the rope hung beyond his reach, mocking his misery. Quick to devise and prompt to act, like all seafaring men, his brave friends above haul in the life-line, and, now loading its end, they toss it once more over the crag, but seaward this time. It has got the motion of a pendulum, and now swinging back, it comes in beneath the beetling cliff. With eager eye watching its coming, he makes a grasp; but alas! his hand closes on the empty air, and the rope swings out again to sea. Ere long it returns, but to be as far, or farther, from his reach; and he now observes with horror that each time it swings it comes less near him. A few more oscillations, and the line dangles in the air—a life-line could he reach it, but beyond his utmost reach. If, balancing himself on the utmost ledge, he leap to catch it at its next approach, he may still be saved—not otherwise—nor shall this long be possible. Once more, again, it comes; and a voice seems to ring in his ear, Now, or Never! With a prayer on his lips, and his eye on the rope, he bends to the spring, and, rising into the air, makes one desperate bound out from the cliff. The line is caught; he is saved; and cheers from above that go up to heaven greet him, when, swinging out from below the overhanging crag, a living burden hangs on that rope with the grasp of death. So are we to understand the words, "Lay hold on eternal life." Such is the diligence we are to give to make our calling and election sure. For here, as there, Soon and Saved, or Late and Lost, are very near the truth. For anything, indeed, we can tell, it may be Now, or Never.

EARLY PIETY.—PART III.

> *" From a child thou hast known the holy scriptures, which are able to make thee wise unto salvation through faith which is in Christ Jesus."*—2 TIM. iii. 15.

DREADFUL is the havoc which intemperance works among us, on the finest virtues of man and woman, on the peace of families and the membership of Christ's Church. The sad miseries it produces, the fair characters it ruins, the kind hearts it breaks, the innocent children it murders by want, cold, cruelty, and neglect, the gray hairs it brings with sorrow to the grave, should make us seek to protect the young from its dangerous influences. Our hope for society lies, not in adults, but in them, in the rising generation — the position of social reformers resembling that of the priests who went down into the Jordan bearing the ark of God, and, leaving the waters that had already passed to pursue their course and find a grave in the Dead Sea, arrested the descending current. We have tried to accomplish something like this. And when for that purpose advising parents, as they valued their own peace, the safety of their children, and the reformation of society, to rear their households in the entire disuse of all dangerous, because intoxicating, stimulants, we have found them excuse themselves on the ground that children brought up in this, or in any other strict way, are afterwards much more likely than others, by the very law of recoil, to carry innocent indulgence to excess.

There is no more vulgar or pernicious error than this. It is a groundless fear—the old cry of "a lion in the way!" wherewith many excuse themselves for not doing what in truth they have no inclination to do. We appeal from them to history; to the character as well as happy fortunes, for example, of a family whose stout adherence for successive generations to the simple and sober manners of their father is recorded with the highest approbation in the Word of God. Commissioned to try them, Jeremiah says, "I set before the sons of the house of the Rechabites pots full of wine and cups, and I said unto them, Drink ye wine. But they said, We will drink no wine: for Jonadab the son of Rechab our father commanded us, saying, Ye shall drink no wine, neither ye, nor your sons for ever. . . . Thus have we obeyed the voice of Jonadab the son of Rechab our father in all that he charged us, to drink no wine all our days, we, our wives, our sons, nor our daughters." Three hundred years had passed since Jonadab was laid in his grave; but these, which had seen other families rise and fall, wax and wane, win and lose their character, had wrought no change on Jonadab's. Teaching us how men live after they are dead for good or evil in their manners and morals, the character which their sire had impressed on his family remained through the lapse of centuries—like features cut in granite. How many families which vice has reduced to abject poverty, sweeping some of them even from the face of the earth, would have inherited, had they been trained to virtuous practices, the happy fortunes of the sons of Rechab; and that through the ordinary operation of the laws of Providence? "Thus saith the Lord of hosts, the God of Israel: Because ye have obeyed the commandment of Jonadab your father, and kept all his precepts . . . . Jonadab the son of Rechab shall not want a man to stand before me for ever."

The case of these Rechabites demonstrates that strict training is not, as some believe, or at least allege, likely to be followed by loose living. The idea that children carefully instructed in the principles and strictly reared in the practices of piety, in a severe sobriety and holy observance of the Sabbath, are more prone than others to run into vice, cannot stand with the opinion of Solomon, "It is good for a man to bear the yoke in his youth." This notion, which is no less pernicious than absurd, sounds as different from Solomon's judgment as the ring of good money from bad. Nor can it bear the test of experience and Scripture more than a counterfeit coin the drop of acid that bites through the silver and lays bare the brass.

But as this notion, were it allowed to stand, would stand in the way of the cultivation of early piety, let us look at one proof of it very commonly adduced. This is the fact, as they call it, that the children of the strictly religious, especially those of the manse, of ministers of the gospel, have been often observed to be more vicious than others. Cases of that kind have certainly occurred. But it is not difficult to account for such a melancholy result. It often happens that men discharging the functions of the sacred ministry, or those who devote themselves to redress the wrongs and promote the welfare of society, have found their time and talents so taxed, so occupied, so engrossed by the public interest, that they have neglected their own. They have bestowed the care which belonged to their children on the affairs of others. As they contemplated the misconduct of this son, and the misfortunes of that, and were reminded, by the wreck which vice had wrought on their family, of the sad old plaint, " The boar out of the wood doth waste it, and the wild beast of the field doth devour it," how might they add, "They made me the keeper of the vineyards, but mine own vineyard have I not kept!" But the bad result in such cases is not due to the children being reared too strictly, too carefully, too piously. Suffering, on the contrary, from neglect, they have been sacrificed, unintended but unhappy victims, on the altar of the public good.

Nor when the children of pious people turn vicious is it wonderful that they become worse than others. The sweetest wine turns into the sourest vinegar; the blackest shadows are cast by the brightest light; the angel that falls becomes a devil—and so, sinning against light and conscience, the prayers, counsels, warnings, and tears of godly parents, the children of the good, on becoming wicked, become more remarkable than others for their wickedness. Like Jeremiah's figs, "the evil are very evil, so evil that they cannot be eaten." And being also from their birth and position as a city set on a hill, their case attracts more attention than that of others. While others escape notice, these are observed and talked of; and thus people fall into the vulgar, pernicious mistake that a strict and virtuous training is apt to result in a loose and vicious life.

Such is the complete and satisfactory explanation which we give of those cases that impart any semblance of truth to so gross an error. At the same time we can adduce facts to prove that it is an entire mistake. I have in my eye a district of my country sufficiently large, and containing a sufficient number of families, to form the basis of a wide and sure conclusion; and, on looking to the history of the children who went forth from its manses to make their way in the world and fight the battle of life—poor, but well, strictly, and virtuously educated—I can aver that, take them overhead, they have not done worse, but better, than others. Doing credit to their homes and virtuous training, the sons of clergymen stand above the common average, both in point of character and of the position they have won. Unhappily, some good people, by their sour tempers and severe, forbidding manners, have made their children recoil from a pious life. By rough and injudicious treatment they have broken the twig which more skilful and gentle handling, with God's blessing, had trained upward to the skies. Accustom the young to associate the Sabbath, and the Bible, and piety, not with gladness, but with gloom; train them so that their affections are not won over to the side of religion; and no wonder that, after being held in, like a horse, only by bit and bridle, when they go forth on the world with the reins loose on their own necks, that they plunge into a career of vice—as the war horse rushes into the battle. But let justice be done to religion; let gentleness temper severity; let there be as much pains taken to win the heart as to instruct the head of youth; let mothers, as of old, employ their loving, tender hands to give it a Christian shape and form; and the results will prove the soundness of the advice, "Remember thy Creator in the days of thy youth."

The importance of this will appear if we consider that youth is the *critical period* of man's life.

An infant is a bud unblown, with green impervious sheath hiding the flower within; nor, though hope may paint fair visions of the future, can any tell whether the cradle in their house holds a Cain or Abel, a Jacob or an Esau. Childhood corresponds to the next stage—the bud has now blown out into a fragrant, lovely flower; but whether, as the bud has changed into a flower, the flower shall change into fruit, the child shall fulfil the wishes and reward the care of parents, who can tell? I have seen the blast strew the ground with the hopes of the garden, and trees stand barren in autumn that had been white with blossoms, as with a shower of snow. However genial the spring, or cloudless and warm the skies of summer, there is a critical period when the two seasons shade into each other. This, which holds the fruits and future of the orchard in its hand, fulfilling or disappointing the hopes of the gardener, lies in those few days and nights when, to use a common expression, the fruit is setting. Wrapped up in its warm sheath, the flower sleeps through the winter, nor feels nor fears the frost; when, waking to the voice of spring, it throws aside its coverings, and, disclosing its beautiful form, opens its bosom to the sun and its treasures to the bees, it is full of life; and, once changed into fruit, though its sweetness may depend on the character of summer, it battles bravely with adverse circumstances, and lives and ripens in spite of cold and rain. But there is a critical time, on which its whole future depends; and that lies in the few days and nights when, in its progress from one stage to another, the flower is changing into fruit. To use a fine Scotch expression, this is *the tyning* (losing) *or the winning time.*

Such a period is youth in human life. Then impressions are received which remain for ever; then the character, like the colour fixed by the mordant in cloth, is fixed; then the die is struck; then a life of virtue or of vice is begun; then the turn is taken either for God or the world; then the road is entered on which leads to heaven or to hell. The period is one which corresponds to a knoll I know, where you stand on the watershed of the country, midway between the two seas which wash our shores; and there, standing on the doorstep of a shepherd's cottage, as you turn your wrist to this side or to that, depends the course of the water you fling from your hand!

whether, after long travels and many windings, it reach the east coast or the west, to mingle with the waves of the German or Atlantic Ocean. It is the youth, not the boy, as is commonly said, who is father of the man. What importance, then, belongs to this over any other period of life—what care does it call for on the part of the young, and on the part of those also who are charged with their up-bringing! Childhood receives impressions easily; but, like the sea that bears no traces of the birds that skim, or the keels that plough its waves, it does not retain them. Manhood, again, like the solid rock, retains impressions once made, but does not easily receive them. Now, it is in youth that our minds, like the wax to which the seal, or the clay to which the mould is applied, possess both the power of receiving impressions, and the power of retaining them. This, therefore, is the crisis of life—the time to be most careful of our company, our pleasures, and our pursuits. Then the slightest thing may fix our character, and determine our future destiny—the wax is cooling, the clay is hardening into stone, the soul is receiving its form and shape, and, as if time to some extent anticipated the irrevocable decrees of eternity, it may be said in many instances of our youth, what shall be afterwards and absolutely and universally said of our departed spirits—" He that is filthy let him be filthy still, and he that is righteous let him be righteous still."

Youth is the most *dangerous* period of life.

There is no age which may not put principle and piety to trial. Old men who shock the world by their crimes, the occurrence ever and anon of cases where vice, like a long pent-up power, overcoming at length all restraint, breaks forth like the volcano that pours its burning lava on the woods, cornfields, and vineyards that clothe its slopes—these, and many things else, warn us that we are never safe till we are in heaven, and have laid off with our bodies the infirmities that belong to them. Here, like travellers on those Alpine slopes where a coating of snow hides the treacherous ice, and one false step may prove their ruin, we walk in slippery places, and have ever need to lean on an arm stronger than our own, praying— " Hold up my goings that my footsteps slip not." In no circumstances, and at no age, can any of us afford to forget the caution—Let him that thinketh he standeth take heed lest he fall.

Still youth is of all ages the most dangerous. With its ardent temper, its inexperience, its credulousness, its impetuosity, its impatience of restraint, its unbroken passions, and feeble hands to control and guide them, it requires the utmost care and vigilance. "Lead us not into temptation," should be its daily, constant, earnest, anxious prayer.

The most interesting and picturesque scenes, it has been remarked, are found in those half-highland, half-lowland districts, where the wild and shaggy and savage grandeur of the mountains mingles with the rich and softer beauties of the plain; and so the most interesting period of life is that where in youth the lightness and buoyancy of childhood blends with the gravity and wisdom of age. But as it is among scenes intermediate between the mountains and the plain that the river, which winds like a silver stream through the glen, and after pursuing its calm and widening course through the plains loses itself in the sea, takes its wildest leaps, and, tearing its way through rocky gorges, now eddies in black pools, and anon rushes roaring and foaming on its way; so it is in youth, when man, subject to the turmoil and disturbances of impetuous passions, leaves the home of his birth to enter on the world, that virtue has to sustain her severest trials, and not seldom to suffer her sorest falls.

How critical, how dangerous, I will say how dreadful, the position of many launched, without father or friend to counsel or control them, on the temptations of a large city! In what a multitude of cases are large cities large graveyards of virtue, honour, and honesty; large shambles, if I may say so, to which youths fresh from the country and yet uncontaminated by vice, come up like sheep to the slaughter? Read the list of wrecks that happen yearly on our winter nights and stormy shores. And even when fancy fills our ear with the shrieks of the drowning, or shows us their imploring faces and dying struggles, the corpses that strew the beach, the wild grief of widows, the desolate home where the fatherless boy weeps at a mother's knee, and the infant, unconscious of its loss, smiles or sleeps upon her breast—what is that list of wrecks to that which were written, had we such a record, of the men and women who are year by year wrecked in their youth on the dangers and vices of our towns! Let the places of business, where employers show no regard to the welfare, but only to the work, of those in their service,—let the houses where no friendly interest is taken in their domestics, in the way they pass the Sabbath, in their company and associates,—let the scenes of public amusement, the haunts of drunkards, and the hells of vice, give up their secrets, as the sea does the drowned it casts on its beach, and we should have a roll like the prophet's, "written without and within with lamentation, mourning, and woe" — something more shocking than the shores which the tempest strews with wrecks, than fields which war covers with its horrid carnage, the writhing forms of the wounded and the mangled bodies of the dead.

We have always considered it a hard crook in the lot of many, that they require to send their children away from the virtuous influences of home at the very period of life which forms the character, and requires, more than any other, a parent's kind and Christian care. A dangerous transition, they pass at once from the shelter and genial air of a conservatory to the blast of rude tempests, to the cold night and its biting frosts. Yet such is the trial to which many a youth is exposed. His boyhood past, the day arrives when he must leave the safe and happy home where, ever since she first clasped her boy to her bosom, a mother's eye has watched over him, and a father's steps have guided his to the house of God, and his voice has mingled in the evening psalm, and his knee bent in the prayers which hallowed that home. It is a dark morning in the house. Every face grave and sad, they meet to pray and then to part; and for the last time a father's voice, amid a mother's sobs, tremblingly commends the boy to God. But the trial is past; and, the quiet harbour left far behind, with no other than his own inexperienced hand on the helm, the youth finds himself among the snares and sins of the city—breakers a-head; roaring breakers on this bow and on that. He is beset with temptations; and has now means and opportunities of indulging in sin with which his principles and virtue have never yet been tried.

At first shocked with what he hears and sees, the raillery and ridicule of the wicked fail to shake his virtuous resolutions. For a while he finds guardian angels in those memories of home that are still fresh and fragrant in his heart; in the recollection of a mother's last look and a father's last touching, tender prayers; in the knowledge that it would wring their loving hearts should he consent when sinners entice him. But time wears on; and familiarity with vice softens its harsher features. It looks less shocking every day. He begins to doubt whether he is not too puritanical and precise. And now comes the struggle. The Philistines are on thee, Samson! The hour of fate is arrived. He has put his foot on a slide, down which, unless God interpose and help, he goes to destruction with growing, flying speed. Not altogether approving, but quieting conscience by promises not to repeat it, he consents for once to desert the house of God for some Sunday pleasure-party; to venture for once, but only once, into scenes where virtue breathes the air, and dies. That first act wherein he yielded to the enticement of sinners, and whereby he did violence to conscience, is, so to speak, the first parallel of the siege. The ground is not lost without many a sore struggle; yet step by step, from trench to trench, the besiegers push on the attack; at length the last wall shakes, totters, falls, and a wide breach is made. Now, unless Christ hold it, unless, as the enemy comes in like a flood, the Spirit of God lift up a standard against him, unless God save at the uttermost, vain all further struggle, vain the efforts of expiring virtue. Exhausted after some feeble strokes and show of resistance, she yields, and vice conquers; and after a while parents who, forgetting and forgiving all, open their doors to a child returning to die beneath their roof, find nothing left to mourn over but a miserable wreck—their only consolation, perhaps, as they stand weeping by his grave, that the turf lies light on the breast of a penitent prodigal.

As the French proverb says, "It is not only the *first* step that costs." Against that fatal step—the beginning of evil—let me warn the young; for if Satan, to use a homely proverb, gets an inch, depend on it, he will take an ell. The beginning of sin, as well as that of strife, is like the letting out of waters—at first a drop like a diamond lies in a fissure, or hangs sparkling from a grassy tuft of the embankment; by and by, a succession of drops like pearls falling from a broken string; by and by, a thin crystal stream; then a gush; then a torrent; and then, hurling down the dike, a wide, thundering, resistless flood, carrying havoc and death before it. Watch and pray, therefore; for safety lies in avoiding the approach as well as abstaining from the appearance of evil—all toying, all tampering, with temptation; in a prompt obedience to the apostle's advice, Flee youthful lusts. Fight not, but flee; or if fight you must, copy the old Parthians, who, seated on fleet coursers and armed with bow and arrows, shot from the saddle, flying as they fought. If you cannot flee, then in Christ's name and strength face round on the foe, and make a bold stand for God; and the virtues of youth shall rebuke the vices of age, and hoary sin shall go down before you armed with God's word, as did the Philistine before the young shepherd and his sling. Giving yourselves and the dew of your youth to Christ, so far as sin is concerned, be those maxims your rule—Touch not, taste not, handle not. When sinners entice thee, consent thou not; but, recalling tender memories of home, a father's authority, and a mother's love, follow the advice of Solomon, "My son, keep thy father's commandment, and forsake not the law of thy mother; bind them continually about thine heart, and tie them about thy neck. When thou goest, it shall lead thee; when thou sleepest, it shall keep thee; when thou awakest, it shall talk with thee. For the commandment is a lamp; and the law is light, and reproofs of instruction are the way of life."

EARLY PIETY.—PART IV.

> *"From a child thou hast known the holy scriptures, which are able to make thee wise unto salvation through faith which is in Christ Jesus."*—2 TIM. iii. 15.

SOME live fast; and growing old in constitution while yet young in years, die before their time—their "sun is gone down while it is yet day." Others work fast. Animated by ambition, and sustained by untiring energy, they win for brows not yet touched by its silver the fortunes and honours of age. Alexander the Great, for example, ere he was two-and-thirty years old, had conquered Greece, Palestine, Egypt, Persia; fought I know not how many battles, and gained I know not how many victories. Ere he had numbered half the years of human life, this remarkable man had earned the proud title of the conqueror of the world; bestriding it like a colossus, he covered it with his shadow, and at death shook it by his fall. Leaving old to come down to modern times, some half century ago, he who guided the helm of this great empire had just entered on manhood; yet amid a hurricane of revolution that shook ancient kingdoms and hurled monarchs from their thrones, he was hailed as the " pilot that weathered the storm." Nor is the history of the two greatest generals of our, or of almost any other, days, less remarkable; seeing that ere the sun of either had reached its meridian, or there was a gray hair in their heads, both had shaken Europe with their battles, and filled the whole world with their fame. It is in the early part of the season that trees make those shoots which the last months ripen : it is youth that lengthens the bones which future years mature and strengthen. Though they do not reach their vigour, most men and women reach their height before they are twenty; and so, as history shows, with some few and famous exceptions, the greatness of all distinguished statesmen, warriors, orators, philosophers, poets, though age was required to bring their talents to perfection, has been blocked out in the season of their youth.

The history of most pious men presents the same features. Few people are converted when they are old; some are in manhood: but in most, the seeds of the new life, though they lie dormant for months, perhaps for years, are sown in the spring-time of life. When his persecutors set before the aged martyr a heathen altar and a stake, bidding him decide to sacrifice to the gods or burn in the fire, he boldly chose death, saying, I have served my Master too long, and loved Him too well, to forsake Him now! And as, on the one hand, no man who, like him, remembered his Creator in the days of his youth, forgets, or is forgotten by Him when his head is hoary; on the other hand, few have remembered their Creator in manhood, or old age, but those who were brought to Christ before mid-life. A pious old age following a youth of vice, and a manhood of worldliness and indifference to religion, is not the rule, but the exception — and a rare exception. There is a close analogy here between the phenomena of the material and the spiritual world; conversions in old age, or advanced manhood, being as uncommon as a fine afternoon with cloudless skies and a glowing sunset, unless the rain ceases, and the weather clear before twelve o'clock.

Look, for example, at the brightest names, the greatest saints in Scripture history. Almost all were examples of early piety. Look at David! Called by Samuel in his boyhood to be a king, but ere that anointed with oil more precious than flowed from the prophet's horn, how young his years, yet how mature his piety; and how wonderful the faith which accepted the giant's challenge, and entering the lists against a son of Anak, proved itself the strongest of the two! Look at Josiah wearing the crown when eight years old; the youngest king who ever sat on a throne, yet swaying the helm of state with a firmness that astonished his oldest and ablest statesmen. It was a sight to see that child seated on David's throne; robed priests and gray-haired councillors bowing before him; and the boy, with a hand that hardly grasps the round of the sceptre, guiding it with a wisdom that would have saved the kingdom from shipwreck had that been possible. But the palace presented a still more illustrious spectacle; this boy, belonging to a class that has few kings in it, walking with God when his years were only twelve, and his feet were surrounded by the snares and temptations of a court. More than that, he was working for God—with the energy of a Luther attacking abuses, bringing out God's own Word to the light of day, and pursuing the work of public reformation with a zeal which has never been surpassed in the best periods of the Church's history. Look also at Daniel and his three companions—the captive youths who maintained their purity amid the seductions of a heathen court, and, though borne away into distant exile, unlike many of our youths, remembered in Babylon the house of their God and the land of their fathers. With prayer, they sustained their faith, and sanctified their chamber; and many a time the sentinels, as they walked their nightly rounds, heard them singing—strange sounds within palace walls—the songs of Sion and of Jerusalem, their chiefest joy. Unless piety had struck its roots deep when their hearts were soft, yet young and tender, and had grown with their growth, and strengthened with their strength, it had never endured their fiery trial; nor stood erect against a power that bowed the heads of the multitude before the royal image like reeds or corn before the wind. They grew up into the stoutest men, with frames of strongest bone and toughest muscle, who are not stinted, but well fed in youth; and to early piety those brave, ancient witnesses owed the faith that stood undaunted before the ravening lions, and the blaze of the fiery furnace.

In further recommending early piety, I observe that youth is the *best period for acquiring religious knowledge.*

This remark holds so true of all knowledge, secular as well as sacred, that in another country they use this striking saying, "What the boy does not learn, the man does not know." In powers of attention, if volatile, easily roused, in restless activity, an insatiable curiosity, enthusiasm, buoyant spirits, and a ready as well as tenacious memory, God has given to youth such an aptitude for acquiring knowledge that it may well be called the seed-time of life; and to this season let both parents and children, teachers and scholars, apply the wise man's advice, "In the morning sow thy seed." It is the young and tender root that penetrates the soil; it is when its fibres are delicate that, entering the fissures and following all their windings, it passes into the heart of the rock; and the earlier the mind, brought in contact with religion, is turned on its great and greatest subjects, the better hold it takes of them; and though at first feeling lost in a maze of mysteries, the more thoroughly in after life will it comprehend, and, like a root warped around the rock, the more firmly will it hold them.

Of the advantage of a thorough religious instruction in early life, where could I find a better illustration than in my own countrymen — their faults, which I would rather correct than conceal, notwithstanding? Germany, while boasting of them, has to a large extent abandoned the faith of Luther and her other great Reformers. Geneva prides herself on having been, if not the birthplace, for that honour belongs to France, the home of Calvin; yet his creed—not in any of its peculiar but in all of its broadest evangelical doctrines—is repudiated in most of her pulpits. Her pastors preach doctrines which his soul abhorred, and her people love to have it so. In other countries, what a diversity of religious opinions prevail, not among different churches only, but within the distracted bosom of the same church!—these lands, not merely in their ecclesiastical but in their doctrinal systems, wearing creeds of as many colours as Joseph's coat. Now why is it that, notwithstanding the divisions in Scotland, her people, to whatever section of the Presbyterian Church they attached themselves, have clung with proverbial tenacity to their fathers' faith; and in the contest with Popery or Infidelity, Antinomianism or Socinianism, have stood as firm as her sons in bloody battles and on other fields? When other churches have left their old anchorage, and, "driven with the wind and tossed," have made shipwreck of the faith, how is it that during the last three centuries the people of Scotland have stood by the old truth as "steadfast and immovable" as the mountains that guard her glens, or the rocks that girdle her storm-beaten shores? How is it that here, where we have our full share of ecclesiastical divisions, no minister of the gospel has lapsed into Popery, and hardly one of her people?—not more, certainly, than will be found in every age flying off, at a tangent, into some religious absurdity? How is it that Rome has made so few recruits here?—that the Scarlet Woman has seduced so few with her music, painting, dramatic spectacles, and meretricious ornaments? These are facts, and, though we say it in no spirit of boasting, very remarkable facts. Now, since there is no effect without a cause, there must be some way of accounting for this. Nor is it far to seek. The circumstances admit of an obvious and easy explanation.

When George Whitefield came to Edinburgh nothing struck or pleased him so much as the sound that rose in the church when he happened to quote a passage of Scripture—giving book, chapter, and verse. His hearers, as was their wont, had taken God's Word with them to God's house; and as they turned up the passage, the leaves of two thousand Bibles rustled, like the sound of the wind among trees, in his astonished ear. To their thorough Bible-knowledge instruction, illustrated by that anecdote, and given to her youth in the house and in all her schools, and to the complete drill and training which her children, young men and women, get in that Shorter Catechism which, the work chiefly of English divines, and a remarkable compend of theology, takes a hold of the mind singularly firm, Scotland owes it that though a hundred storms have blown, and blown their worst, she rides to-day over the very ground where the Reformers dropped their anchor three centuries ago. The tenacity with which, in spite of all their faults, and differences, and divisions, my countrymen have adhered to their ancient and common faith, illustrates the effect—for to nothing else can it be ascribed—of a thorough religious training in youth. Rich stores of divine knowledge are then most easily acquired. Deep and saving impressions are then most easily made. It is young recruits that become the best soldiers, and young apprentices the best mechanics; and the best Christians, in like manner, are those of whom, trained by a Lois or a Eunice, a saintly mother or mother's mother, we can say, in St Paul's words to Timothy, "From a child thou hast known the holy scriptures, which are able to make thee wise unto salvation, through faith which is in Christ Jesus."

In youth *the heart is most impressible.*

Children are emotional—as easily moved by anything calculated to make them weep or laugh, love or hate, be grave or gay, be sad or merry, as the surface of a lake by the breeze that sweeps over it. But the affections of childhood, having at that inexperienced and unripe age no sound judgment to direct them, resemble those pliant tendrils which are ready to attach themselves to any object whatever; to cling, to twine themselves as readily in close embrace around some broken branch that lies rotting on the earth, as around the tree on whose strong and stately stem they might climb to the skies. Besides being characterised by a want of sound judgment, childhood wants steadiness in its affections. They are easily transferred to new objects. The impressions made on its heart are lively, but not deep or abiding. How soon the infant forgets a dead mother; and with the arms it throws around her neck transfers its love to the nurse that fills a mother's place. Before the sod is green above his grave, the boys that wept a father's loss, and walked so pale and pitiful behind his coffin, have resumed their gaiety; and, but that memory sometimes casts a passing shadow on their enjoyments, are as bright and buoyant as the happiest of their playmates. Calamity passes through their hearts, not like a ploughshare through the soil, but a ship's keel through the sea; the furrow soon fills up, and in a short while childhood retains hardly any more trace of trials in its heart than of tears on its cheek.

In manhood, on the other hand, the judgment is or should be ripe; but what the intellect has gained in ripeness, the heart has lost in tenderness, in impressibility. Cooled by age as well as by contact with the world, it has lost the glow of early days; and since religion addresses itself both to the judgment and the affections, both to the understanding and the feelings, as well to the head as to the heart, youth, since, lying midway between childhood and manhood, it possesses the lively affections of the first, and the somewhat matured reason of the second, is, therefore, of all the ages of life, the most favourable for receiving saving impressions and turning to God. At the mouth of our great valleys, on the shores of those noble estuaries where our largest rivers join the arms of the sea, there lie alluvial lands, flat and fertile. There, in former ages, vast floods that filled the glens and swept their hill-sides, deposited the rich soil they carried in their muddy waters. There now the husbandman raises his richest crops ; not, however, unless in tilling the land, ploughing and sowing the fields, he seizes that auspicious time between the wet and the dry, when the clayey loam is neither hard nor soft, but between the two. Such a season youth offers for that higher cultivation, where the seed is the words of eternal life, the soul is the soil, preachers are the sowers, angels shall be the reapers, and heavenly, eternal blessings are the rewards of faith and patience, of love and labour. Once gone, this most auspicious period never returns. Once lost, it is never recovered.

The prayer, "Remember not against me the sins of my youth," no doubt holds out hope to such as have let slip this precious time. Thank God, they are not to despair. Still, though Almighty grace may work a saving change at a later, and even in the latest period of life, not only does the probability of that grow less with every year's, and indeed hour's delay, but the finest specimens of piety are found in those who were converted and called when, as in the case of the good King Josiah, their hearts were young and tender. The practice of sin, persevered in, and prolonged over a period of guilty years, so blunts the conscience that it never recovers the fineness of its edge; nor is the heart capable of receiving the most delicate and beautiful impressions of Christ's image, unless they are stamped on it while, like metals or melted wax, it is soft and tender—ere it has grown hard and cold.

And what so adapted to youth as religion; what offers so many, such suitable, and such noble objects to its affections? Youth is enthusiastic:

and what field for the loftiest enthusiasm like the salvation of a miserable and perishing world? Youth is brave: and more courage is often required of the Christian than of him who throws himself into the life-boat, and pulls through the breakers to the sinking wreck. Men have found it a harder thing to stand up for Christ before a battery of ridicule than, dashing through the smoke of battle, to charge a battery of cannon! Youth is generous: and where such scope for the purest generosity as in the call to take up our cross, deny ourselves daily, and follow Jesus in living and labouring for the good of others? Youth is earnest and impetuous: and this is the very temper religion urgently requires; it calls us to give all diligence to make our calling and election sure, since we know not what an hour may bring forth; this, not another, being the accepted time; to-day, not to-morrow, being the day of salvation. The door is closing, and the grave is opening: haste, for your life, it says; leap into the ark; another day, another hour, even another moment, may be a long eternity too late. Once more, youth is prone to love: and in all

God's universe what object so fair, so lovely, so worthy of our warmest affections, as He, the dear divine Redeemer, to whose bleeding brows belongs the wreath that David wove for Jonathan's, "Thy love to me was wonderful, passing the love of woman!"

It is well to give Jesus even blighted affections and a broken heart; it is well, when the world cannot fill our hearts, to turn our trembling steps from its broken cisterns to the fountain of living water; it is well, when experience has taught us that earth has no pillow without its thorns, to go and lay the aching, weary head on Jesus' bosom; it is well when the battered ship, with sails blown to ribbons and masts gone by the board, makes through the roaring sea for a harbour of rest and refuge; it is well when man turns from his shattered fortunes, and maids from their false lovers, and mothers from their sweet, pale, lifeless coffined idols, to throw themselves at the feet or into the arms of Jesus. But it is better still, seeking Him early, to give our youth to Christ; with its glistening dews to bathe the Rose of Sharon; to honour God with our first-fruits;

to assign the Saviour such a place in our hearts as His poor, mangled body found in Joseph's tomb— one where no man had been laid.

It is a grand testimony to religion to see a gray and bent old man standing by the door of mercy, and with voice and hand, with loud and urgent knocking, imploring God to open and let him in; but much nobler the testimony, and finer the spectacle, while he is muttering of the world, "Vanity, vanity, and vexation of spirit," to see a youth in the very flower and beauty of his age refuse her tempting cup; turn away his head from her alluring smiles; and, in happy ignorance of her forbidden pleasures, resolve to give himself to Christ and a life of high and holy virtues—saying, both of the fair tempter and her temptations, "My soul, come not thou into their secret; with them, mine honour, be not thou united!"

Youth, as securing him the best of our life, should be *consecrated to God.*

In old age, men offer Him but the dregs of the cup; and a wonder it is that any one is spared to have dregs to offer. When men employ their time and talents, their health, their strength, their genius, not to serve, but injure, the cause of God, and turning His gifts against the Giver, wound the very hand that blesses them,—one wonders at the long-suffering and patience of God; that He does not shake them off, as St Paul did the viper, into the fire. Who can think of the load of obligations under which daily mercies lay us,—on the care of that ceaseless Providence, without which we would expire any instant, our health would turn into sickness, our reason into madness, and our blessings into curses,—and especially on what, in the person of His beloved Son, God has done and given to save us,—who can reflect on these things and not be astonished at the base ingratitude which would put Him off with the wretched services of old age; the forced reformation and repentance of a dying bed? Ingratitude and insensibility this, against which God with a sublime majesty might appeal again to creation, saying, "Hear, O heavens, and give ear, O earth: I have nourished and brought up children, and they have rebelled against me. The ox knoweth his owner, and the ass his master's crib; but Israel doth not know, my people doth not consider. Ah sinful nation, a people laden with iniquity, a seed of evil doers, children that are corrupters; they have forsaken the Lord, they have provoked the Holy One of Israel."

There are many formidable and fatal heresies. Some deny the divinity of our blessed Lord, reducing the Son of God to the common level of humanity. Some strip the Holy Bible of its lofty claims to inspiration, reducing it to the common level of other books. Some repudiate the doctrines of the fall of man; of the corruption of our nature; of the atonement; of the imputation of our sin to Christ, and of His righteousness to us. But, with whatever horror we may regard such dangerous errors, there is no error more dangerous or fatal, more likely to sink a man into perdition, than the notion that it is sufficient to seek God at the close of a life devoted to sinful pleasures, and passed in worldly pursuits. Other heresies slay their thousands; this, I fear, its tens of thousands.

In His dear Son, God has given to us the best He had to bestow; and is He not entitled to the best of ours in return? Insult is harder to bear than injury; and what more insulting to the kindness, love, mercy, and majesty of our God than in effect to say, I will turn to Him when I can do no better; so long as I can sin safely, I will do it; so long as I can venture to despise Him, I will do it; so long as my portion lasts, careless of my Father's displeasure, I'll play the prodigal, nor seek His house till want sends me a beggar to His door—till the roar of the cataract warns me that to persevere will be to perish. I will sail down the stream of pleasure, nor heed the voice that entreats me to turn, crying, "Turn ye, turn ye, why will ye die!"

Suppose, then, it were as easy to bend a bough when its bark is hoar with age, as when it was green and young; suppose it as easy to stop the course of a stone when it is whirling, smoking, leaping, thundering down into the valley, as when, just loosened, it began to move from its bed; suppose it as easy to turn the river from its course, where it sweeps on to the sea, as the rill by its mossy fountain; suppose it as easy to mould the clay, when grown dry and hard, as when it will receive on its plastic surface the impression of a new-blown leaf; suppose you could expect to reap a crop from land neither ploughed nor sown till trees were bare and hills were white; suppose old age were a favourable time to be saved;—are the poor services that it can render such as this lost world needs—such as the interests of the Church of God require—such as the cross of Calvary deserves—such as He who gave His Son for us should receive at our hands? Let us reject the notion. How plainly is it rejected, how strongly condemned, in this touching expostulation: "A son honoureth his father, and a servant his master. If then I be a father, where is mine honour? and if I be a master, where is my fear? If ye offer the blind for sacrifice, is it not evil? and if ye offer the lame and sick, is it not evil? Offer it now unto thy governor; will he be pleased with thee, or accept thy person? saith the Lord of Hosts!" Rejecting a thought that equally insults the majesty of Heaven and the mercy of the Cross, let us offer the best, first-fruits of our life to God, and Remember our Creator in the days of our youth.

RETROSPECT AND PROSPECT.

> "*The harvest is past, the summer is ended, and we are not saved.*" — JER. viii. 20.

IT is in the form of one bending beneath the weight of years, and advancing with feeble steps, that Solomon paints man travelling to the grave; and, though done with a trembling hand, how graphic and true his touches? "The keepers of the house shall tremble"—the arms that held the plough, or plied the shuttle, or wielded the sword, shake with palsy; "the strong men shall bow themselves"—the limbs, those pillars of the frame, shrunk and shrivelled, totter beneath its weight; "the grinders cease"—the teeth decay, and drop from their sockets, warning man that he himself shall soon drop into his grave; "those that look out of the windows be darkened"—the eye, that window where the soul sits looking out on the world, grows dim with years, and man enters the shadow of the tomb before he enters itself; "he shall rise up at the voice of the bird" —the sleep of the cradle is calm, that of robust youth long and deep, but old age brings broken slumbers, and wakes with the birds that sing in the dawn; "the daughters of music shall be brought low"—deafness swells the train of infirmities, and amid the cheerful circle the old man, cut off while alive from communion with the living, sits with furrowed brow and snowy head in a solitude which only religion can cheer; "they shall be afraid of that which is high"—with heart enfeebled, he leaves others to breast heights and hills, and, staff in hand, creeps along the flat shore or the level sward; "the almond tree shall flourish"—his head is white as its blossoms, with the frost of age; "the grasshopper shall be a burden"—such his weakness, though as the tiny insect leaps from blade to blade, the grass hardly bends beneath its weight; and, last of all, "desire shall fail "—the very wish for pleasures dies with the power of enjoying them. A miserable existence, unless where holy desires survive the decay of nature, and the saint longs for the hour when the dissolution of his old, crazy, earthly tabernacle shall set him free for his flight to heaven!

So Solomon paints man, to use his own words, as going "to his long home." But instead of a gray, decrepit man creeping slowly along a shadowy vista, with a grave yawning to receive him, he might have introduced a beautiful, rosy, gleesome child, bounding on over the short course between its cradle and a tomb. The journey to the long home—one which we begin with life and are all engaged in—is long to some and short to others. The infant commences it before it has learned to walk; the old man continues it when his limbs are too feeble to bear him across the floor. It is one we carry on sleeping as well as waking—on Sabbath as on other days—on which we never halt, till we stumble into the grave which is dug at the end of the road. On this journey we go swiftly — flashing through the threads of life like a weaver's shuttle; we go incessantly—moving night and day, like the hands that circle round the hours; our heart beating on like a pendulum, till the clock, wound up to go a certain time, has run down, or accident stops its motion.

We all are on the way to the long home; and at this season of the year* our position is that of travellers who have reached the summit of a mountain range that parts two great valleys. Standing on one of Time's lofty watersheds, we have left one year behind, and the next, into which we are about to descend, lies stretched out before us. In such circumstances it is natural to do two things :—first, to look back, taking a retrospect: and, secondly, to look forward, and try to pierce the veil which, like a gray mist spread over the valley, conceals the future from our view.

The Retrospect.—One of the strangest things we meet with is to see consummate wisdom so far as the interests of this world are concerned, and consummate folly as to everything belonging to the next, in one and the same person—just as in

* This discourse was preached on the last Sabbath of the year.

the bed of the Rhone after it has received the turbulent Arve the spectator sees two volumes of water that for a while flow on side by side—the one foul, the other so beautifully blue and pure that it looks like a liquid sky. Once on a time a vessel, freighted with gold, was wrecked in circumstances which left her crew no chance of life but swimming to the distant shore. Some had committed themselves to the deep; others were stripping for the struggle; when one, turning an avaricious eye on the treasure, seized the fortune at his hand. Infatuated wretch! His fellows remonstrated, but in vain. Loaded with gold, he leaps from the ship, and strikes out bravely for the shore. But by and by his strokes grow feebler, quicker—then a short convulsive struggle—and then, borne down by the weight he carries, he sinks beneath the wave. What a fool he was! We had not been such fools!—so many say, and perhaps truly; and yet, guilty of greater folly, they allow themselves to be so engaged, and indeed engrossed with the pursuits of time, whether of business or pleasure, as to neglect their salvation, and lose their souls.

The children of this world are wise in their generation! If a man is building a house, he takes good care, in the first place, to get a sound foundation. Is it a lighthouse, to stand with its tall form and burning head a lonely pillar amid tempestuous seas?—beneath the sand and shells that storms have flung on the fatal reef he goes down to the solid rock, seeking a foundation which cannot be moved. And after having secured a good foundation, in laying one course on another, in raising story over story, the work of examination keeps pace with the work of building. By square and plummet he proves his work; teaching us, even when we are resting, in the righteousness of Christ, on the Rock of Ages—in view of events which shall try every man's work, how we should bring ours to the test of God's holy Word.

This retrospect should embrace the way in which we have discharged our duty to *God*.

It is much easier to say what God has done for us than what we have done for Him. That opens up a vast subject; His bounty presenting the aspect of a majestic river, which, never frozen by winter nor dried by summer, winds full and flowing through the past. To reckon up the blessings which we have received at His hand would prove, in fact, a task as impossible as to number the dew-drops on the glittering sward, the leaves of a forest, or the sands of ocean. No doubt, as life is at the best but a chequered scene, we may have been afflicted; yet how far have our mercies outnumbered our miseries? Besides, who has not been afflicted less than his iniquities deserved? Besides, does not faith in the assurance that all things shall work for good to them who love God, and are the called according to His purpose, fling a bright bow on life's blackest cloud?—work such change on our trials as the branch which Moses cast in on Marah's waters, turning bitter to sweet and evil to good?

When God has done so much for us, nothing can be more reasonable than to inquire what we have done for Him; and anticipate by a few years, or days perhaps, the hour when He shall address to each of us these solemn words, Thou shalt be no longer steward; give an account of thy stewardship.

Opportunities of serving, honouring, glorifying, speaking for Him have occurred every day of the past year; and have they been improved, or neglected? Of our whole time He claims a seventh part—fifty-two days in every year, and therefore no less than ten whole years in the threescore and ten of human life—all this for His special service; communion with Him; and preparation for a world of which this is but the vestibule. How much work for God might we have done in fifty-two busy days?—how much has been done? Required to do all for His glory—even in matters of eating and drinking, can we recall any one thing we have done for that end? —any one word we have spoken on behalf of His cause, to the praise of His honour?—any one effort we have put forth to be saved, or to save others? Alas! on reviewing the past, the holiest, the best and busiest of us have to acknowledge ourselves "unprofitable servants;" and as to others, with a whole year misspent, abused, utterly lost, they seem miracles of sparing mercy; nor does one know whether most to wonder at their ingratitude, or admire His long-suffering who even yet delays to strike, waiting to be gracious.

This retrospect should embrace the way in which we have discharged our duty to *our own souls.*

It were sad if, on reviewing the past year, with all its opportunities, we could come to no other conclusion than this—"The harvest is past, the summer is ended, and we are not saved!" We may have increased our store of earthly comforts, we may have clambered up some steps higher in society, we may have added broad acres to our estate—hundreds or thousands to our wealth; but, if we are not saved, we have only increased the difficulties of our salvation and the terrors of death. Nor, should we die now, have we any other sentence to pronounce on our works than Solomon pronounced on his—I looked on all the works which my hands had made, and on all the labour which I had laboured to do; and behold all was vanity and vexation of spirit; and there was no profit under the sun. We have spent our money for that which is not bread, and our labour for that which satisfieth not: and, with more toil and care and trouble than had been required to build a bower in Paradise, we have been training up a green, dying gourd in the vain hope of finding beneath its leaves the happiness found only in Him who is as an hiding-place from the wind, and a covert from the tempest; as the shadow of a great rock in a weary land.

Happy those who did not see the old year die with unforgiven sins on its gray head, nor dread meeting it again at God's bar of judgment. Happy those whom it found in a state of enmity, and left at peace with God. Happy those who, on taking stock and striking a balance, if I may so speak, find themselves poorer in spirit and richer in grace—who, on examining into their position, find that though nearer the grave they are riper for heaven, nearer to glory; and that a year which, making many wives widows and children orphans, turning some hopes into fruit and blasting others in the flower, has wrought many changes, has changed them to the better—chastened and sanctified them; so that they say, "we all, with open face beholding as in a glass the glory of the Lord, are changed into the same image from glory to glory, even as by the Spirit of the Lord."

This retrospect should embrace the way in which we have done our duty to *others*.

The Life of Jesus, the title of many good and some bad books, has filled volumes. So full was that life of gracious utterances, and so crowded with works of majesty and mercy, that the evangelist St John says, "If they should be written every one, I suppose that even the world itself could not contain the books that should be written." Yet the Life of Jesus may be summed up in this one short sentence, He went about doing good. This brought Him from heaven and nailed Him to the cross: for this object He lived, for it He died. Fancy our Lord on one of those mountain tops, where, with the world beneath and the heavens above Him, He courted solitude, taking a quiet survey of one of His years—looking back on all the works which His hands had wrought, and on all the labour that He had laboured to do. How crowded the year with miracles and mercies —sinners warned; mourners comforted; the dead rising at His word; the blind gazing on His blessed face; the deaf listening with rapture to His words; the dumb singing His praises and proclaiming His name and power; more good crowded into one short day of that life than is spread over long years of ours!

Unless the same mind be in us that was in Jesus Christ, we are none of His. So it behoves us to consider what testimony, in good attempted or done to others, the past year bears to the genuineness of our Christianity. Whom have we warned? In our family, or in the circle of our friends or neighbours, whom have we sought to bring to Jesus? What hungry ones have we fed, what naked clothed? Whose wrongs have we sought to redress, whose sorrows attempted to alleviate? Whose cup has been filled out of ours? What widow's heart have we made to sing for joy? Of the two, a river that fed of heaven and swelling beyond its banks spreads its waters on the thirsty fields, or a whirlpool that, moving around itself, and drawing all things to its centre, swallows them up into its own greedy and devouring vortex — which does our course most resemble? In the year that is gone has the world been the better or the worse of us?

It behoves us to consider these things, nor go recklessly on with such as, during the whole past year, and indeed their whole past life, have never given one hour of self-examination to a serious review of their life. What recklessness is this?—in our circumstances, what madness? Do we sail a sea where there is neither storm, nor cross tides, nor sunken rock, nor shifting sandbanks, that we go so merrily on with songs below, and dances on the deck; neither keeping watch, nor taking observations, nor heaving the lead for soundings? There were fewer souls, as well as ships lost, if men would use the means of safety. We shrink from examining ourselves; but if, when judging our own cause with a strong bias in our own favour, we cannot bear to examine ourselves, how shall we stand at the bar of divine judgment—how endure the searching eye of God? "If thou hast run with the footmen and they have wearied thee, then how canst thou contend with horses? and if in the land of peace wherein thou trustedst they wearied thee, then how wilt thou do in the swelling of Jordan?" Here, more than anywhere else, it is well to know the worst. None are beyond the reach of redemption, whom to awaken to a sense of their condition would only be to torment before their time. Men are going to ruin; but not like the boat that was seen shooting the rapid, and had reached a point above the cataract where no power could stem the raging current. To the horror of those who watched it shooting on to destruction, a man was seen on board, and asleep. The spectators ran along the banks. They cried; they shouted; and the sleeper awoke at length to take in all his danger at one fearful glance. To spring to his feet, to throw himself on the bench, to seize the oars, to strain every nerve in superhuman efforts to turn the boat's head to the shore, was the work of an instant. But in vain. Away went the bark to its doom, like an arrow from the bow. It hangs a moment on the edge of the gulf; and then, is gone for ever. Suppose a man to be as near hell!—if I could awaken him, I would. The dying thief was saved in the act of going over into perdition. Christ caught and saved him there. And He who is mighty to save, saving at the uttermost, can save, though all our life were wasted to its last breath, if that last breath is spent in gasping out St Peter's cry, "Save me, Lord, I perish!"

The Prospect.—Inspired of God, men have foretold coming events; and so have others who were neither prophets, nor prophets' sons. To Kirkcaldy of Grange, then holding out Edinburgh Castle against the Protestant Reforming party, with whom he was once associated, John Knox (as I remarked on another occasion) sent a remarkable message from his death-bed. "Warn him," said the dying man, "not to trust in yon craggy rock, from which he shall be shamefully dragged to be hanged up in the face of the sun." And, improbable as to many at the time it seemed, it fell out as Knox had predicted. He was dragged from his stronghold, like a ruffled eagle from her rocky nest, and ignominiously hanged in the face of day. The secret of the Lord, says the Bible, is with them that fear Him; and in regard to extraordinary communications of His will and mind, who shall limit the Holy One of Israel? But the great Reformer made no claim to the gift of prophecy; and whatever powers were attributed to him in a superstitious age, those who honour his memory regard Knox as having been nothing more than a man of more than ordinary sagacity. Penetrating through the mask of false pretences into men's real designs, and reasoning from causes to their legitimate effects, he owed his fame, as one inspired, to the seer-like certainty with which he foresaw and foretold the natural issue of affairs.

History, in a sense, is prophecy; since, according to the words of Solomon, "that which is to be hath already been." It is so to a large extent in the kingdom of Nature; her sequences and her seasons being fixed by unalterable laws, each running year just repeats the past. And thus, though groves are mute and fields are naked now, we can predict that spring shall come with opening buds and singing birds; and summer come, her green lap filled with flowers; and brown autumn come, armed with the reaper's sickle and crowned with ears of corn.

Taking men in the mass, so is it in regard to their fortunes and destiny—to vary the mode but not the sense of the wise man's adage, That which hath already been is that which is to be. This does not apply to individuals; since many who lived last year three hundred and sixty-five days, shall not live this year as many hours. Nor does it apply to individual homes and households —the cradle shall give place to the coffin; the marriage last year formed, this shall dissolve; and, on the other hand, a tide of good fortune coming with the turn of the year, many before its close, taking their harp from the willow-tree, shall sit singing with Hannah, "My heart rejoiceth in the Lord; mine horn is exalted in the Lord; for the Lord killeth and maketh alive; he bringeth down to the grave and bringeth up." But though the fortunes of individual persons, or single families, may vary much from year to year, it is otherwise with masses of men. In regard to these, the events of last year, whether they were good or evil, shall find their counterpart in this, and thus the retrospect becomes a prospect, and the past presents a magic mirror in which we can descry the future.

Thus some shall *continue to neglect salvation.*

A rope thrown to a drowning man, if well thrown once, does not need to be twice thrown. It needs no eloquent speaker on pier or bank to address the sinking wretch and persuade him not to "neglect so great salvation." Let it go spinning out within clutch of his eager hands, and how he grasps it; and holds it with the grim gripe of death! But it is not once, or twice, or twenty times that salvation in these last twelve months has been offered; and to this day many have obstinately, madly, refused to accept it. By preachers and His providences, even as a father pleadeth with his children, God has pled with them; His Son has implored them; though vexed and grieved by their obstinacy, His Spirit has continued to strive with them — the year has brought them a thousand opportunities of being saved; yet it is gone, and they are not saved. Alas! in the words of Scripture, "The harvest is past, and summer is ended, and we are not saved."

Give men an opportunity of escape—do literally what Christ is figuratively said to do, "proclaim liberty to the captive, and the opening of the prison to them that are bound," disarm the warders, throw open the cells — and what a rush for liberty! and, after a brief space of wild shouts and tread of hurrying feet, what a profound silence and perfect solitude! Yet how often has the door of mercy been thrown open? With kindness in His looks, and love in His heart, and His hand pointing to an open door, how often has Jesus appeared to us, saying, "Behold, I have set before you an open door!" and turning over to the other side for a little more sleep, how often have we dismissed Him with this reply, "Go thy way for this time; when I have a convenient season I will call for thee!" Is this to go on for ever?— each year repeating the risk, the sin, and folly of the past? The prospect looks even more melancholy than the retrospect. There is less hope for us each year and day we live in sin. Every hour we are drifting out to sea — the helpless, helmless barque is leaving the lessening shore farther and farther behind. Our disease becomes incurable. Like those stones which, though soft as clay on being raised from the quarry, grow hard as flint through exposure to the weather, our hearts are growing harder day by day. Let such as have been delaying, delay no longer; dare no more. The axe is raised, gleaming, against the tree; and though it should not fall before the year expires, before that God may be provoked to withdraw His Spirit, and leave us to our fate, saying, "They are joined to their idols, let them alone."

Some shall be *converted*.

Like the loftiest snow-crowned peaks that tower above the common Alps, there are periods and events in history which are peculiarly marked and memorable. Such a period in the history of the world was that of the Deluge, when all mankind were drowned but one family; and also that Christmas night when angels announced the advent and sung the birth of the new-born King. Such a period in the history of nations was that of the Hebrew exodus, when Israel burst his bonds, and left the land of Egypt; and that also when He who had delivered His people by the hand of Moses summoned a woman to the rescue, and saved them by the hand of Esther from the cruel wrath of Haman. Such also was the era of the Reformation in our Church, and of the Revolution in our country — events whose influence, growing with time, and extending with distance, and widening out on all sides like the watery circle that leaves the middle of the lake to break in wavelets on its strands, is felt this day on the shores of America and the plains of Hindostan.

In the history of individuals also there are memorable periods—events on which turns man's eternal, as well as his present, destiny. And of all his years and days that is worthiest of a Christian's remembrance on which, passing from a state of nature into one of grace, he was born again—he drew the first breath, and, in an earnest prayer, uttered the first cry of a new life. Many usher in each new year with revelry, and celebrate their birth-day as it comes round with feasts, and songs, and dances, and delights, who shall regret they were ever born—saying, " Let the day perish wherein I was born—why died I not from the womb ? " But the last year shall be one of everlasting and grateful remembrance to all whom it found the enemies, and left the friends of God; whom it found slaves, and left freemen; whom it found on the way to hell, but, converted, washed, and sanctified, it left on the road to heaven. That which is to be is that which hath already been. Only let us pray that if the past year has witnessed thousands, this may witness tens of thousands of souls converted, poor sinners saved; that if its fields yielded harvests of thirty, this, in a revenue of glory to God and good to men, may yield, not thirty, but sixty, even an hundred-fold. We cannot but hope that many shall be saved this year—plucked as brands from the burning. God is making up the roll of His elect; Christ is gathering the jewels of His crown; heaven is filling fast; and why should we see others enter in countless crowds, and be ourselves left out? The cry comes forth, "Yet there is room," room to spare! While the door stands open, rush in—for that matter strive to enter in; and while a mouldering tombstone shall bear the date of your first birth, of the year on which you were born for the grave, let this happier year be engraven on your grateful and enduring memory as that on which you were born for God and glory.

Death shall *summon many to judgment.*

Though, as he lies a-dying, every one feels as if he were alone in the valley, none but himself on that dark road, he is not a solitary traveller—a great throng crowd the way, passing in at the gates of the eternal world. Men die in such numbers, that for every breath we draw some one breathes his last; with every beat of our hearts some heart ceases to beat. Let a knell be rung for every departing spirit, and that bell would toll on without a pause till Time's own knell was rung, and Death itself should die.

That which hath been is that which is to be. Willing or unwilling, fit or unfit to die, converted or otherwise, voyagers to a land of bliss or bound to misery, many in this have entered on their last year. Like time and tide, death — regardless of his convenience and deaf to his prayers—will wait on no man. If in past years God has set a mark on our houses, and turned the angel of death from our door, as by the blood in Egypt, that immunity cannot last for ever. The more the years of our life, this one is the more likely to be that of our death — the farther the tide recedes, the higher at the flow it throws its foaming waves on the beach; the longer the cloud is gathering, and thickening, and darkening before it bursts, the brighter the lightning flashes, the louder the thunder peals.

Since death is gain to the Christian, and through faith in Christ may be so to all, we should familiarise our minds with that event: beginning every year, and indeed every day, as if it were to be—what it may be—our last. Joseph of Arimathea prepared himself a tomb, probably placing it among the flowers and delights of his garden, that the sight of the "long home" where he was to lie might keep him mindful of his latter end. One whom I knew, with the same object and from no contempt of death, had his coffin made, and studied the Bible with that memorial of our mortality standing up, tall and black, beside him. One of the greatest monarchs went further still. Having resigned the sceptre and retired to a monastery, he prepared a tomb for himself, and fixed a day for the ceremonies of his burial. The funeral procession is formed; and with the bell tolling for the dead, it takes its slow way to the tomb, the king himself bringing up the rear—a ghastly form attired in a long white shroud. He is laid in his coffin; round the body the priests go, sprinkling showers of holy water, and swinging incense out of golden censers. The service for the dead is chanted over him; the last prayer is offered; the last psalm has died away in solemn echoes; the candles, types of life's flame, are extinguished; and, closing the door, they leave the living man alone, stretched out in a coffin, enclosed within a tomb, to meditate amid its lonely and awful darkness on such subjects as this singular and terrible solemnity was calculated to suggest. Violent and revolting as such expedients seem, better thus to be kept mindful, than live habitually forgetful, of our latter end, and leave death to break in on our fatal slumbers with the suddenness and surprise of a thief. Watch, is the word of Christ—watch, for ye know neither the day nor the hour when the Son of man cometh. To be prepared for death—so prepared that it may be the happiest event that ever befell us, so prepared that we may show how calmly a Christian can die, so prepared that we may confront this king of terrors without the shadow of a doubt or any sense of fear, so prepared that, seeing the heavens opening above our heads and angels descending to carry us to glory, we shall be better pleased to go than to stay—let us make our calling and election sure. Let us work out our salvation with fear and trembling; looking to Jesus for pardon, and to God to work in us by His Holy Spirit both to will and to do of His good pleasure.

THE END.

content.com/pod-product-compliance
urce LLC
rg PA
32300426
00006B/156